P9-CRD-245

To Wendy
(from Ken Hom + Al)
Merry Christmas
Love
Bill

AN ILLUSTRATED GUIDE TO THE FUNDAMENTAL TECHNIQUES OF CHINESE COOKING

_____

PHOTOGRAPHS BY WILLIE KEE

Chinese

中
國
式
烹
飪

Technique

KEN HOM

WITH

HARVEY STEIMAN

SIMON AND SCHUSTER · NEW YORK

COPYRIGHT © 1981 BY KEN HOM AND HARVEY STEIMAN
ALL RIGHTS RESERVED
INCLUDING THE RIGHT OF REPRODUCTION
IN WHOLE OR IN PART IN ANY FORM
PUBLISHED BY SIMON AND SCHUSTER
A DIVISION OF GULF & WESTERN CORPORATION
SIMON & SCHUSTER BUILDING
ROCKEFELLER CENTER
1230 AVENUE OF THE AMERICAS
NEW YORK, NEW YORK 10020
SIMON AND SCHUSTER AND COLOPHON ARE TRADEMARKS OF SIMON & SCHUSTER.
DESIGNED BY EVE METZ

MANUFACTURED IN THE UNITED STATES OF AMERICA

10   9   8   7   6   5   4   3   2

LIBRARY OF CONGRESS CATALOGING IN PUBLICATION DATA

HOM, KEN.
   CHINESE TECHNIQUE.

   INCLUDES INDEX.
   1. COOKERY, CHINESE.   I. STEIMAN, HARVEY.
II. KEE, WILLIE.   III. TITLE.
TX724.5.C5H66   641.5951   81-5711
                                 AACR2

ISBN 0-671-25347-6

ACKNOWLEDGMENTS

I have always believed that no one can accomplish anything without the help of many friends, and that is certainly true for this project. I should begin with Jacques Pépin, whose pioneering work on French techniques inspired this one; I am grateful for his hard work and his invaluable support. I also wish to acknowledge the support of my mother, Mrs. Ying Fong Hom, and my friends, Ron Batori, Roberto Ceriani, Serena Chen, Rosy Chu, Rich Curley, Murray Jaffe, Ted Lyman, Susan Maurer, Norton Pearl, Jerry Peterson, Carol Pogash, Vernon Rollins, Carol Steele, Daniel Taurines, Tom Williams, Paula Wolfert, and Jim Wood. And special thanks to Harvey Steiman for his contribution to the book.

I owe special gratitude to Kathy Knopoff and Jeanne Kee for their work in the production of the book, and to Martha Sternberg for her invaluable contribution. I was lucky to have Ann Bramson for my editor—she asked questions I never even dreamed of.

Finally, thanks go to all my students for their constant support and for teaching me so much.

TO ALL THOSE WHO STRIVE TO MAKE
THE ART OF CUISINE
A SOURCE OF HAPPINESS FOR ALL MANKIND

CONTENTS

INTRODUCTION

My knowledge and love of Chinese cooking came from watching and imitating as a young apprentice in a restaurant. Later, as a teacher, I was struck by the fact that although many of my students had read of this or that technique described in one or more of the fine Chinese cookbooks that are available, it was only when they saw the techniques demonstrated that they finally understood. Only then would they attempt to duplicate what I had shown them. The step-by-step procedures that I presented and lectured about became the basis of my teaching for amateur and professional cooks alike. The cliché about pictures (or a demonstration) being worth a thousand words has validity indeed, as you shall soon see.

China has one of the world's oldest culinary histories and traditions. Its cuisine is unique because it developed independently of the West. A lack of ovens, a shortage of fuels, an ancient insular civilization and culture, a poor transportation network, and a lack of arable land forced Chinese chefs to accommodate their art to necessity. Later, as the Chinese moved abroad, they carried this heritage with them. If one wishes to understand the essence of Chinese cooking, therefore, it is important to make a cultural mental leap.

The Chinese chef is engaged in visual harmony—in the size and shape of the food, in fragrances, and in contrasting tastes and textures. Above all, he sets out to attain a balance among all these elements.

Often my students are surprised by the simplicity and logic of the principles and techniques of this ancient cuisine. The tools we use are remarkably few and simple, and experience has condensed and focused the techniques so that chefs of other cuisines now use many of the same methods.

You will find that Chinese technique is not really very complex—and you should try the techniques step by step, drawing from previous cooking experience. Be bold. Trust in your palate and sense of taste. Follow the techniques and principles outlined, but feel free to add your own touches. Adjust, invent, as Chinese chefs have always done. Incorporate ingredients you prefer in preparing other cuisines. Use the techniques you've learned from this book and build upon them.

It is my hope that the pleasure of cooking and the pleasure of eating will become as well balanced as the ingredients on your plate.

A Few Words about Recipe Yields

A Chinese meal always consists of several different dishes. As the number of persons to be served increases, another dish is added to the menu rather than increasing the recipe quantities to yield more servings. Therefore, portion sizes vary greatly—the more dishes there are, the less of each one each person gets to eat. As a general rule, unless otherwise indicated, each recipe in this book yields six servings in the context of a Chinese meal, or the number of servings indicated in each recipe.

A Note about the Wine Selections

The beverage recommendations that follow the recipes in this book are merely suggestions, not dogmatic pronouncements. Where varietal wines or wines from a specific European district are listed, it is because our experience has been that their flavors combine well with the food; you may very well like something else better. In each case where a dry white wine is suggested, any other dry white wine of the same general type (light, full-bodied, and so on) would be as effective.

NOTE: We have intentionally used English words and phrases throughout this book to identify the techniques and most of the recipes. The names used in China differ from region to region, and English transliterations and pronunciations of those names vary even more. We have used Chinese titles only in the few instances when a recipe—for example, Mu Shu Pork—is best known by that name.

Equipment

ONE OF THE BEAUTIES OF THE CHINESE KITCHEN is its simplicity. With very few implements, Chinese cooks can turn out elaborate multicourse banquets. All it takes is a few cleavers, a cutting board, a wok and its four utensils (long chopsticks, a ladle, a spatula, and a frying strainer), a bamboo steamer, and a source of heat.

None of these pieces of equipment is expensive. In fact, the three cleavers we recommend can be purchased for less than half the price of a good French chef's knife. The best wok costs less than a good skillet, and the equipment is built to last several lifetimes, if properly maintained. You will be surprised how quickly you feel comfortable with the wok, not only for stir-frying or deep-frying Chinese dishes, but also for such non-Chinese procedures as stir-frying spinach in olive oil and garlic, or making *pommes soufflés*.

THE CLEAVER

Carbon steel is the preferred material for the cleaver blade. It needs care, but holds a sharp edge and will last for years. Stainless-steel blades are easier to care for and keep clean, but don't hold an edge as well and are expensive. Metal-handled cleavers are better balanced than wooden-handled cleavers, but they are heavier and harder to handle if you are not especially strong.

Cleavers come in various weights and shapes. Each has its purpose. A lightweight (narrow-blade) cleaver is used for boning, chopping light foods, and delicate slicing. It is easily identified by a black band on the blade. Though often used in restaurants, it is too light to serve as an all-purpose cleaver.

A medium-weight (thick-blade) cleaver is the best all-purpose cleaver. It is used for all but the heaviest chopping tasks and is heavy enough to crush ginger, slice any vegetable, cut up chicken and duck, or do most chopping and mincing jobs.

A heavyweight (thickest-blade) cleaver is too heavy for delicate tasks. It is used to cut up whole crab, hack through bones, and cut through tough ingredients.

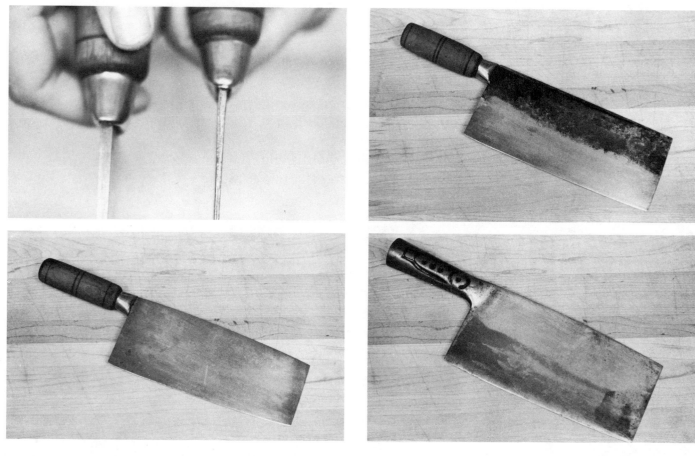

Seasoning a New Cleaver

A new cleaver has a coating of machine oil to keep it from rusting. This must be scrubbed off and the cleaver dried thoroughly.

Coat the new blade with a thin film of mineral oil (vegetable or other cooking oils will turn rancid), applied with a paper towel. From this point on, never let the cleaver stay wet. Make it a habit to rinse and dry it well as soon as a task is completed.

Sharpening the Cleaver

Have your cleavers sharpened by a professional knife sharpener once a year or so to hone the edge, then keep the edge sharp with the help of a standard steel or ceramic sharpener.

Holding the cleaver at a slight angle, run the edge across the steel or the ceramic, moving it down the sharpener as the edge moves across. Repeat on the opposite side.

THE WOK

The traditional cast-iron wok used in China is seldom seen here. Instead, most woks are made of carbon steel. Since the wok is not moved around on the stove, it can be heavy; but it should not be too thick, or it will take too long to heat. Usually, woks sold in Chinatown stores, gourmet cookware shops, the cookware sections of department stores, and even those from some mail-order houses are acceptable.

The best size of wok for Western stoves is 14 inches in diameter. A wok this size is big enough to hold a whole fish, chicken, or duck easily, but not so big as to be unwieldy. Never fill a wok completely; most of the heat is concentrated at the bottom, and most foods cook in the lower third of the wok. Don't buy a small wok. It is easier to cook a small quantity in a large wok than to try to accommodate a large quantity in a small wok.

We have found the wok with one or two wooden handles, one of them long like a saucepan handle, the easiest to use comfortably on Western stoves. Most woks come with a matching ring and cover.

The wok rests on the ring and is not moved during cooking. The wok ring sits on the stove burner, narrow side up on a gas stove, wide side up on an electric stove to get the bottom of the wok closer to the heat source. Electric stoves provide adequate heat for stir-frying, but they require more patience since they take longer to heat up.

Seasoning a New Wok

Wash the wok thoroughly to remove the coating put on at the factory to keep the surface from rusting. Use an abrasive cleanser to do a thorough job. *This is the only time you will use a cleanser on the wok.* With a paper towel, rub the entire inside surface of the wok with a vegetable oil. Put the wok on its ring over a low flame, and let it heat slowly for 15 minutes.

Wipe the oil from the inside of the wok with a clean paper towel. Repeat the process—add more oil, heat the wok, then wipe it—until the paper towel comes out clean. This may take five or six repeats.

The first time you use the wok it will start to turn black. It is supposed to. The more black crust that builds up, the more efficiently the wok cooks.

Wok Implements

Chopsticks: Long chopsticks are useful for picking out small pieces of food from the wok and for mixing and moving food around in the wok. Because they are made of wood, they don't conduct heat.

Frying strainer: The best strainer has a bamboo handle and flat, slightly concave wire mesh. The bamboo handle does not conduct heat, and the wire mesh is perfect for removing deep-fried food from hot oil. Larger sizes are preferable because they can accommodate a whole chicken or duck.

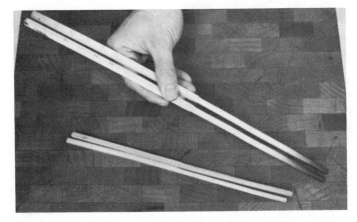

Spatula: The wide blade of the spatula scoops up food efficiently for stir-frying. The long handle keeps hands away from the heat.

Ladle or scoop: The ladle serves a dual purpose: it scoops cooked food from the wok, and it functions as a small bowl for mixing sauce right over the wok. (The latter is an advanced technique used by experienced cooks and restaurant chefs.)

Removing Food from the Wok

The most efficient way to transfer food from the wok to a serving plate is to use the ladle and spatula in combination. With the spatula, shovel as much food into the ladle as it will hold. Holding the food in the ladle with the spatula, lift it from the wok to a serving plate. Repeat this procedure until all the food is transferred from the wok to the plate.

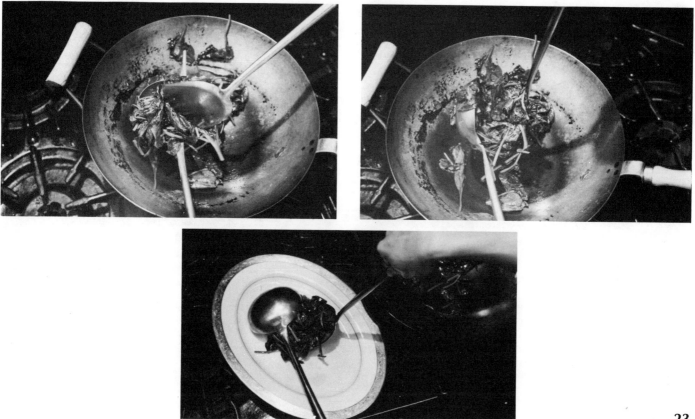

THE BAMBOO STEAMER

Bamboo steamers are designed to fit inside a wok and can be used one at a time or stacked one atop the other to make efficient use of the same heat source. Never wash the steamer with detergent; the bamboo absorbs the flavor of the detergent. To wash it, simply rinse it well with hot water.

The food to be steamed can be placed on a plate in the steamer, or the steamer can be lined with cheesecloth or muslin and the food placed on top of the cloth. The liner keeps food from sticking.

Cover the steamer with its bamboo lid and set it over boiling water in a wok. The water should be at least 1 inch below the bottom of the steamer. Have hot water on hand to replace evaporated water as needed.

Ingredients

EACH CUISINE BRINGS TO THE KITCHEN its special and distinctive tastes and seasonings. A typical Chinese cupboard includes bottles of thin and dark soy sauce, Chinese vinegar, Shaoxing rice wine (or dry sherry), oyster sauce, cans of hoisin sauce, chili sauce, and brown bean sauce. Many dried ingredients, such as dried red chili peppers, five-spice powder, and dried fungi, are also kept on hand. And add some fresh seasonings such as garlic, ginger root, scallion, Chinese parsley (also called coriander or cilantro), and Smithfield ham, a close equivalent of Chinese ham.

Different types of spices and seasonings characterize the various culinary regions of China. For example, from the Western part (including Sichuan and Hunan) come dried red chili peppers, chili sauce, and Sichuan peppercorns. Yet these spices are utilized throughout the country. China's long culinary history has tended to cross-pollinate the regional specialties of the country's kitchens and restaurants.

Because the Chinese traditionally preserve, using salt and the sun, or oil, brine, and wine, many ingredients are bottled, dried, or canned. Lack of refrigeration and poor transportation systems inspired ingenious ways of preserving foods so that they would retain some element of their taste and texture.

Many Chinese ingredients are now readily obtainable either in supermarkets or by mail order. If you live near a large Asian population, local markets probably carry all these ingredients and more. Nothing here is really indispensable, but if you wish to get an authentic taste of China, a few of these ingredients can make a dramatic difference, one your palate will soon demand.

One could gradually build a collection of ingredients by starting with Shaoxing rice wine, soy sauces, and sesame oil, all of which can also be used in your other cooking. For example, soy sauce is a good marinade for most types of meats and fowl to be barbecued. Or use some Shaoxing rice wine instead of Madeira to deglaze a pan or as a splash in a sauce.

Using the Chinese techniques in this book, prepare dried mushrooms and add them to Western dishes for texture. With more esoteric ingredients, such as preserved salted fish or preserved mustard greens, be more cautious with quantities when experimenting. You will soon be using ancient practices to add some unusual and tasteful touches to your expanding knowledge of cooking.

Almond Powder

Almond powder is available in sweetened and unsweetened forms. Use the sweetened kind in desserts

and the unsweetened for coatings in place of cornstarch or flour for a light and slightly nutty taste (see, for example, Sweet-and-Sour Pork, page 200).

Bamboo Shoots

On rare occasions fresh bamboo shoots can be found, but generally you'll have to buy the canned variety, packed in either water or brine. The fresh ones have a subtle, crisp taste; prepare them by removing the tough outer skin and cooking them in boiling water for about 15 minutes. The canned ones, once opened, should be used as soon as possible; rinse them first. Leftovers may be kept for a few days in a jar filled with water, but the water should be changed every day. Use

bamboo shoots in stir-fried vegetable dishes and in stuffings (see, for example, Eight-Jewel Duck, page 187). There are two kinds of shoots—winter and summer; the latter are younger and are more crisp and tender.

Bean Curd

Bean curd, known best by its Cantonese name, tofu, is made from soybeans in a simple process that is seldom attempted at home. Soaked soybeans are ground and cooked in water, then strained to make a soy milk. The curdling agent (such as vinegar, epsom salt, or gypsum) added to the milk forms a custardlike substance, which is drained and pressed into molds to form bean curd cakes. In Chinese communities, commercially made bean curd is available fresh, packed in water, and refrigerated. It is beginning to be available fresh in supermarkets around the country as well. Chinese

bean curd tends to be firmer than the Japanese variety, so look for packages marked "Chinese-style" or "firm."

Red bean curd (also known as red bean curd cheese and preserved bean curd—red) is made from fresh bean curd preserved with salt and spices. It has a pungent aroma that complements slowly braised dishes like Chinese Beef Stew (page 217). It comes in crocks, glass jars, and cans. It looks like a red cheese and has a shiny, smooth surface and a creamy, moist, soft consistency. It will keep indefinitely in a tightly closed jar in the refrigerator.

Two other types of preserved bean curd are wet bean curd and fermented bean cake.

Beans, Fermented Black

These small black beans are preserved by fermentation with salt and spices. They are never eaten by themselves, but are used as a flavoring ingredient, often coupled with garlic, adding a distinct "Chinese" flavor to foods. They are used with fish (see, for example, Steamed Fish with Black Beans, page 231), in sauces (Shrimp in Lobster Sauce, page 261), and with meats

(Braised Spareribs, page 206). Fermented black beans come in bottles, in plastic bags, and in cans; avoid the canned ones because they have a slightly tinny taste. Do not confuse them with dried black beans. Fermented black beans are soft and are speckled with salt. Rinse them slightly before using. The beans will keep indefinitely at room temperature.

Bean Sauce (Brown Bean Sauce, Brown Bean Paste)

Bean sauce comes in two forms—whole bean and ground bean; whole bean sauce is preferable. Both are very salty and are made from soybeans, flour, and

salt. Bean sauce adds a rich bean taste to sauces (see Braised Sichuan Fish, page 233) and internal marinades (see Salt-Roasted Chicken with Marinade, page 116, or Cantonese Roast Duck, page 171). It comes in cans and should be transferred, once opened, to a tightly covered jar and stored in the refrigerator, where it should keep almost indefinitely.

Bean Sprouts

These are the sprouts of small mung beans. Usually, there are two varieties at Chinese markets, one very young and a larger, more mature variety that has a bigger husk. In elegant dishes, bean sprouts are often trimmed on both ends to give them a clean, fresh look. They are now widely available in supermarkets throughout the United States. Avoid the canned ones, since one of the reasons for eating bean sprouts is their fresh, crisp taste. Look for white, plump, fresh-looking sprouts; avoid thin, brownish ones. They can be kept in the refrigerator in water for a few days.

When used in small amounts, bean sprouts can add a refreshing flavor to stir-fried dishes; or use them in salads.

BOK CHOY. See Chinese Cabbage

BROWN BEAN SAUCE. See Bean Sauce

Caul Fat

This is the thin covering of the lower part of the pig's intestine; it looks like a lacy sheet of marbled fat. It is found in Chinese, French, and Italian meat markets and is used to wrap and keep foods moist while they cook. The texture turns crisp when it is fried (see, for example, Fish Roll, page 251), but is moist and almost melts away when gently baked in a dish like Beggar's Chicken (page 124). Caul fat freezes very well and can be ordered from your butcher in advance. The French generally use it to wrap pâtés. It contributes a savory, rich taste to the food wrapped within and keeps stuffings and ground meat or fish intact.

The next time you make a roast loin of pork, wrap it in caul fat and you'll see how tender and juicy it keeps the meat.

Celery Cabbage (Napa Cabbage)

There are two varieties of celery cabbage: a short, thick, round white type with light green tops, and a long, light green type with broad green leaves. Both have the mild taste of cabbage and are a little sweet.

Celery cabbage can be used in soups, such as Peking Duck soup (page 177), stir-fried with beef or chicken, or pickled (see Pickled Chinese Mustard Greens, page 88). It keeps in the vegetable bin of the refrigerator for a few days.

CELLOPHANE NOODLES. See Transparent Noodles

Chestnuts

The Chinese use chestnuts in stuffings (for example, Eight-Jewel Duck, page 187) and in braised dishes (Chinese Beef Stew, page 217). Fresh chestnuts have to be peeled; the dried ones are already peeled and need only be soaked in hot water for a few hours or overnight. The fresh ones should be used within a few weeks; the dried ones keep indefinitely in jars at room temperature.

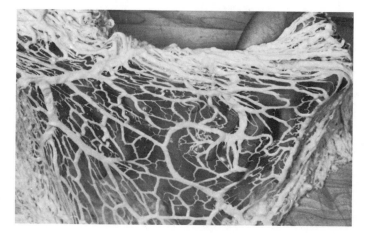

Chili Peppers (Hot Red Peppers, Red Dried Chili Peppers)

Use these spicy and hot, small, thin, dried red peppers to flavor hot and spicy sauces like the one for Spicy Chicken with Peanuts (page 145), or to flavor oil to be used in stir-fried dishes. You can make your own chili

oil by cooking a few dried peppers in 1 cup of oil at a moderate temperature (325 degrees) for about 5 minutes. Turn off the heat, let the oil cool, and strain it into a bottle. This is used at the table as a condiment. The number of peppers you use depends on how hot you would like it. You can make Sichuan peppercorns (see page 69) oil in the same way. Dried chili peppers keep indefinitely in a tightly covered jar at room temperature.

Chili Paste (Chili Sauce)

Chili paste is made from chili peppers and salt, often with garlic, and sometimes with black beans, soybeans, or other ingredients. There are several varieties; recipes specify which is called for. Chili paste

comes in jars or cans and keeps in the refrigerator indefinitely. Use it with care, as it is quite strong.

Chinese Cabbage (Bok Choy)

This popular Chinese vegetable, its white stalks topped with green leaves, looks somewhat like Swiss chard. The younger and tastier variety has yellow flowers that are edible (see page 76). Chinese cabbage is delicious alone or with meats.

Chinese Chives

Although related to common chives, the Chinese variety is quite different. The blossom—the flat-headed spray of star-shaped white flowers—is used as well as the blade. The blossoms have a very pungent smell and are more like garlic than onion in flavor. The blossoms appear only during certain times of the year, however; the rest of the time Chinese chives resemble more closely the common variety. Chinese chives are hard to find in other than Chinese markets, but are very easy to grow at home. Try them in place of common chives in salads and the like, but use them sparingly, as they are stronger. Rinse and dry them well,

and store them in a plastic bag in the vegetable bin of the refrigerator; try to use them as soon as possible. Regular round chives can be substituted if necessary.

Chinese Cinnamon

These barklike dried cinnamon pieces are larger than the curled cinnamon found in supermarkets, though they are similar in flavor and fragrance. They add a rich and nutty flavor to sauces and braised dishes and are

an important ingredient in five-spice powder. Chinese cinnamon is subtler in taste; if you substitute regular cinnamon for it, use less. Stored at room temperature in a tightly covered jar, it keeps indefinitely.

Chinese Edible Fungi (Wood or Tree Ears, and Cloud Ears or Mo-er Mushrooms)

These Chinese fungi grow on trees and are highly prized for their unique and unusual texture. Besides absorbing the flavors of other ingredients in a dish,

they contribute a slight earthy flavor of their own and a contrast in color. They need to be soaked and trimmed before using (see page 67). Rarely eaten by themselves, they are often stir-fried with other ingredients or added to sauces. Wood or tree ears are thicker than cloud ears, which have no stems and are smaller. Both come in packages and are sold dried. They are quite brittle prior to soaking.

Chinese Mustard Greens

Chinese mustard greens were brought from Asia to this country by Chinese workers and are now grown commercially on the West and East coasts for the Chinese market. They are not as pungent as native American mustard greens. The stem is often used by

itself. It can be pickled (see page 88), or simply stir-fried in ginger-flavored oil (see pages 77–78) for a delicious warm salad. The vegetable can also be treated like bok choy (see page 76) or used in soups.

Chinese Okra (Silk Squash, Silk Melon)

Chinese okra is similar in shape to American okra, but in taste it is like a cross between zucchini and cucumber, with a delicious, juicy bite. It can be stir-fried

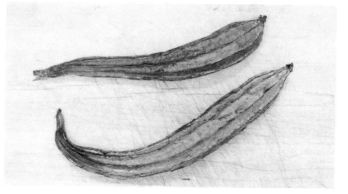

alone (see page 99) or with meats or fowl. It is available in Oriental markets from spring to summer and will keep in the refrigerator for about a week. The ribbed grooves must be pared before using.

Chinese Parsley (Cilantro, Coriander, Celantro)

Chinese parsley has a pungent, musky, citruslike flavor and is similar to Italian flat-leaf parsley in appearance, with leaves more deeply cut and feathery. The leaves are minced or cut into lengths, depending on their use. To store, wash the fresh leaves in cold water,

drain thoroughly, and wrap in paper towels. They will keep this way in the vegetable bin for several days. Chinese parsley is available in many ethnic markets and some supermarkets. Once you get used to its distinctive flavor, you'll find yourself using it in all the ways you use regular curly or Italian parsley.

Chinese Pickles (Preserved Sichuan Mustard Greens, Kohlrabi, Mustard Pickle)

There are many different types of Chinese vegetables that are pickled as a means of preservation. One of the

most popular is preserved Sichuan vegetable. These very spicy preserved mustard greens are packed in cans or plastic bags with salt, chili, and spices. They emerge green and knotty, with a thick mantle of chili around them that gives them a red hue. They need to be rinsed thoroughly before being used. They are crunchy in texture; sour-tasting, hot, and salty in flavor. They are diced and used in stuffings (see, for example, Beggar's Chicken, page 124), or sliced and stir-fried with vegetables, or chopped fine and sprinkled on soups. Use small amounts, and after opening, store the rest in a tightly closed jar in the refrigerator, where it should keep for many months.

Two other popular pickled greens are snow pickle (also called Red-in-Snow), which has a salty, mildly sour flavor, is greenish in color, and comes in cans; and salted cabbage (also known as winter pickle), which is sold in ceramic jars and is brownish green and mildly salty.

Chinese Radish (Icicle Radish, Chinese Turnip)

These long, white radishes are found fresh in Chinese or Oriental markets. Like most root vegetables, they should be peeled and then sliced. They are spicy and absorb the flavors of the sauce of the dish in which they are cooked, yet they keep their own radish bite.

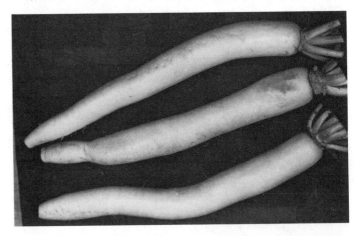

Look for hard, firm radishes. They keep well in the vegetable bin for about a week. They can be roll-cut (see page 98), sliced, or shredded and added to soups or simply stir-fried with meats. They can also be pickled (see pages 87–88).

Chinese Sausage

There are three varieties of Chinese sausage: pork, duck or pork liver, and beef. The sausages are usually

hung together in links and are rather small and hard. Although they have been cured, they need to be cooked quickly before they are eaten. Steamed with rice (see page 283), their juices flavor the rice. In stuffings (see Whole Stuffed Chicken Skin, page 120, and Eight-Jewel Duck, page 187) they are delicious. Unlike most sausages, these are sweet and mild. They are delicious just stir-fried with vegetables like bok choy. Although you can keep them for a week at room temperature, they should be refrigerated if kept longer. They last many months well wrapped in the freezer. You can find them in Chinese markets; they come loose but are sometimes found wrapped in cellophane.

Chinese Sugar

You can find Chinese sugar in several forms: in amber crystals like rock sugar, in small compressed cones, or in slabs. It is more subtle in taste and less cloyingly sweet than granulated sugar. It is used in braised dishes (see Five-Spice Braised Duck, page 168), to add richness and balance to sauces, and to make a nice glaze. It keeps indefinitely in a tightly covered jar at room temperature.

CHIVES. See Chinese Chives

CINNAMON. See Chinese Cinnamon

Citrus Peel (Dried Tangerine Peel, Tangerine Peel, Fruit Peel)

Citrus peel can be tangerine, grapefruit, or orange peel—or a combination—that has been dried in the sun until very hard. The pieces are generally used in braised and smoked dishes, but they are equally good chopped and added to stir-fried dishes, steamed fish, soups, or sauces. They have a sweet, spicy, tart taste. Before using, soak them in warm water for 10 to 15 minutes, until they are soft. They are sold by the ounce in cellophane bags and keep indefinitely in a jar at room temperature. To dry your own peel, remove the white, pithy part and lay the peel out in the sun to dry until it hardens.

Fennel Seed

This aromatic, anise-flavored seed from the fennel plant adds a rich flavor to braising liquids, such as the one used for Soy Sauce Chicken (page 112), and to

marinades. It is sold in packages, in dried form. Stored in a tightly closed jar, it lasts indefinitely. Use it in small amounts, as it is strong in flavor. Fennel seed is an excellent condiment and a fine complement to fish prepared in either a Western or an Eastern manner.

FERMENTED BLACK BEANS. See Beans, Fermented Black

Five-Spice Powder (Five Spices, Five-Fragrance Powder)

This is a blend of spices that includes star anise, Sichuan peppercorn, fennel or anise seed, clove, and Chinese cinnamon. Some blends also contain dried citrus peel or ginger or nutmeg. In some Chinese markets the spices can be bought whole, but they are

most commonly available in powdered form in plastic bags. Five-spice powder is fragrant, cocoa-colored, and strong—a little goes a long way. It shares an affinity with *épices Parisiennes (quatre épices)* and can be used in its place in pâtés. It is superb in dry marinades for any meat or fowl to be roasted, grilled, or smoked. It keeps indefinitely in a jar at room temperature.

Ginger

This fresh, knobby root of the ginger plant is irregular in shape and comes in various sizes. It is an essential ingredient in Chinese cooking and is used minced, shredded, in chunks, and sometimes just squeezed to extract its juice. Look for hard, smooth-skinned ginger, which indicates freshness and juiciness. Older ginger is used in braising and in herbal and medicinal brews. It is used like lemon with shellfish and fish. It is also used to flavor oil and to season many Sichuan dishes. It pairs well with mustard green stems, countering their bitterness with a sharp, spicy, slightly hot taste, and contributes heavily to marinades. If the ginger is very fresh, it really does not need to be peeled. Fresh ginger is becoming readily available in supermarkets and ethnic markets; it keeps for up to two weeks in the vegetable bin of the refrigerator, and somewhat longer placed in Shaoxing wine or sherry and kept refrigerated. You can also grow your own. Powdered or dried ginger is not an acceptable substitute.

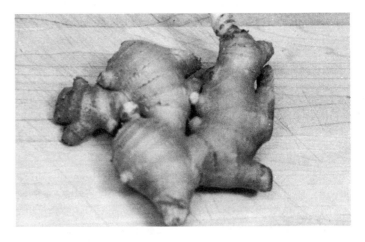

Gingko Nuts (White Nuts)

Gingko nuts, the round pits of the gingko fruit, are generally used in stuffings, such as for Eight-Jewel Duck (page 187). They are available fresh in Chinese markets or in cans in brine. When fresh they need to be cracked and peeled (see page 97). Fresh gingko nuts will keep, uncracked and unpeeled, in the bottom bin of the refrigerator for a couple of weeks. Once cracked and peeled, they should be used immediately. Canned ones, of course, will keep indefinitely, unopened. Gingko nuts have a moist, tender, yet slightly firm and fleshy consistency and are rich, mild, and nutty in taste. They pick up the flavor of other ingre-

dients and add a texture of their own. They can also be used in soups.

Ham

Ham is an important seasoning in Chinese cooking. It is used in small amounts—either sliced or minced—to add its distinctive smoky and salty flavor to foods. Smithfield ham is very similar in taste, texture, and color to Chinese ham and is actually sold in Chinese markets by the slice or the pound. Since it is cured, it will keep almost indefinitely in the refrigerator or in the freezer if well wrapped. Another good substitute is Westphalian ham or Italian prosciutto. Save ham

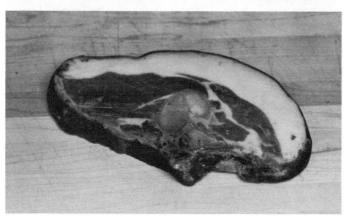

bones to use in braising liquids and soups. Though ham is generally used uncooked, it is also delicious braised and served in slices. Remove the rind before using.

Hoisin Sauce (Duck Sauce, Red Seasoning Sauce)

A thick, soy-based sauce made from soybean flour, red beans, chili, sugar, salt, garlic, and spices, hoisin sauce has a dark, brownish-red color and a slightly sweet, hot flavor. It is used as a seasoning in many preparations (see, for example, Twice-Cooked Pork, page 203), for marinating pork (see Barbecued Pork Strips, page 193), and as an important dip for Peking Duck (page 176) and Mu Shu Pork (page 196). It is sold in cans and should be transferred to jars once opened. Kept refrigerated, it should last indefinitely.

Lily Stems (Golden Needles, Tiger-Lily Buds)

Lily stems add a mild, flowery fragrance, a soft texture, a pretty golden color, and an interesting shape to stir-fried dishes and slowly simmered meats. They must be

soaked in hot water for 15 minutes (or until they are soft), and the tough tips of the stems must be trimmed away (see page 67). They are sold in packages and will keep indefinitely at room temperature if they are well wrapped.

Lotus Leaf

Dried lotus leaves are sold in packages in Chinese food stores and are used to enclose stuffings or wrap chicken (see Beggar's Chicken, page 124) to be baked or steamed. They should be soaked for an hour in warm water until they are soft, then drained and dried of excess moisture. Although the actual lotus leaf is not eaten, it imparts its delicate flavor to the food wrapped within. Bamboo leaves can be substituted but must be soaked overnight. Dried lotus leaves last indefinitely in a cool place.

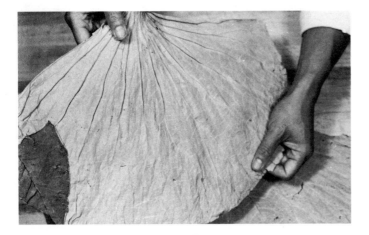

Malt Sugar (Genuine Maltose)

Heavy malt sugar comes in ceramic crocks and is used for coating meat and fowl in dishes like Peking Duck (page 176) or Barbecued Pork Strips (page 193). It imparts a wonderful sweet taste that's not too heavy. It keeps indefinitely in the crock, but sometimes it hardens, depending on the temperature. Just place the crock in a little hot water to soften before using. Honey is a good substitute.

Mo-er Mushroom. See Chinese Edible Fungi

Mushrooms, Black

Black mushrooms have a meaty, smoky flavor and are chewy in texture. They are dried and must be soaked in hot water until soft and the hard stems cut off (see

page 66). The most expensive mushrooms are the biggest, best-looking ones; for dishes in which the mushrooms are going to be sliced or chopped you can buy the less expensive ones.

Mustard Greens. See Chinese Mustard Greens

Noodles. See Transparent Noodles

Oil

Cooking oil is used for stir-frying and deep-frying. The oil itself can be made from corn, peanuts, soybeans, cottonseed, or a combination, as long as it can withstand high heat without smoking. Peanut oil is preferred, because it has a high smoking point and clean flavor. Butter and olive oil cannot be used. Sesame oil (see page 38) is primarily used as a flavoring.

Okra. See Chinese Okra

Oyster Sauce

This highly savory sauce is made from oysters and spices. It has a light brown caramel color and a meaty

aroma. A good brand is not fishy at all. Oyster sauce comes in bottles and in large cans; once the cans are opened, the sauce should be transferred to bottles or jars. It is sometimes used as a dip for dishes like White-Cut Chicken (page 107) or Steamed Chicken in a Yunnan Pot (page 132) and to add its rich color, flavor, and sheen to vegetables and sauces. It should have a slightly thick consistency. Oyster sauce keeps in the refrigerator indefinitely. There is no real substitute for it.

PARSLEY. See Chinese Parsley

Peppercorns, Sichuan

Sichuan peppercorns are very aromatic, purple-brown in color, and have a fragrance not unlike lavender. They are spicier than regular black peppercorns and actually numb the tongue. They add an incomparable fragrance to dry marinades (see Smoked Tea Duck, page 174), sauces (see Braised Egg Dumplings, page 304), forcemeat mixtures, such as for wontons (page 307) or meat balls (page 208), and Sichuan-type dishes. In Chinese they are called "flower peppers" because

they look like flower petals opening up. They should be roasted before being used (see page 69) to bring out their full flavor, then coarsely crushed and stored in a tightly covered jar ready to use. Try them sparingly in any sauce that calls for peppercorns and in marinades for meats destined for the grill. They are usually sold in cellophane or plastic bags in Chinese markets or in gourmet food shops.

Pickled Vegetables and Rinds

These are an assortment of vegetables (such as cucumbers, melon rinds, and ginger) cooked in a spicy sugar syrup and packed in bottles and jars. The sweet, thick

syrup can be used right out of the bottle or can in sauces such as Sweet-and-Sour Sauce (page 200). The vegetables can be served cold as sweet, crunchy appetizer nibbles. They are also used in Squirrel Fish (page 244) and could be added to Sweet-and-Sour Pork (page 200).

PICKLES. See Chinese Pickles

Plum Sauce (Duck Sauce)

This is a thick, preserved, jamlike sauce made of plums, preserved ginger, chili, spices, vinegar, and sugar. Although in this country it is served as a table condiment, in China it is used only as a cooking ingredient. When serving it as a dip for spring rolls, meat

balls, fried wontons, or other appetizers, dilute it with a lighter preserve—orange marmalade or red currant jelly, for example. It is delicious used in place of black beans and garlic to make Braised Spareribs (page 206).

PRESERVED TURNIP BUNDLES. See Turnip Bundles

RADISH. See Chinese Radish

RED BEAN CURD. See Bean Curd

Rice

Of the many kinds of rice used in China, there are really only two main types: long-grain white rice and short-grain glutinous rice. Any long-grain rice works fine, except for converted rice, which has had too much rice starch removed and is not sticky enough. Long-grain rice is simply boiled and eaten with meals, the leftovers made into Rice Porridge (page 282) or Fried Rice (page 280) or into crusts for Sizzling Rice Soup (see pages 285 and 327) and the like.

Glutinous rice (also known as sweet rice) is short, round, and pearly, creamy in color, with a dull surface and a sweet, rich taste. Do not confuse it with rice powder, which is finely ground and used in Chinese pastries. Glutinous rice is used in many stuffings (see, for example, Whole Stuffed Chicken Skin, page 120) because it holds up very well through long cooking and absorbs the flavor of neighboring ingredients. It is also used to make Fermented Wine Rice (page 289). The rice must be soaked for about 2 hours before

being used. Try glutinous rice in your everyday stuffings whenever rice is called for. Just soak it for a little while and cook it in stock.

SAUSAGE. See Chinese Sausage

Scallions (Green Onions)

Scallions, a member of the onion family, are an essential ingredient of Chinese cuisine. They are used as a garnish (see Peking Duck, page 176), as a cooked ingredient in many dishes (see Spicy Chicken with Peanuts, page 145), or in stuffings (Whole Stuffed Chicken Skin, page 120) or marinades (Beggar's Chicken, page 124). They have a mild flavor. Scallions are widely available in supermarkets throughout the year and are easy to grow. They keep in the vegetable bin of the refrigerator for at least a week.

Sesame Oil

This rich, thick oil is made from roasted sesame seeds. It has a nutty flavor and is very aromatic. Sesame oil is not used for cooking—it is too strongly flavored—but as a condiment and seasoning. A dash is often added at the last moment to finish a dish. It is often added to soups just before serving (see, for example, Sizzling Rice Soup, page 280) to heighten their aromatic appeal. There's a light brown and a dark brown sesame oil (the darker is thicker and stronger). It is sold in bottles and should be kept in a cool, dark place, but not in the refrigerator. Sesame oil is wonderful for marinating, but it should be used carefully, as the flavor is quite strong. Dilute a small quantity with peanut or any other mild-flavored salad oil to add a special flavor to your salads.

The light-colored variety found in natural-foods stores and Middle Eastern markets is not made from toasted seeds and is not an adequate substitute.

Sesame Seeds

Sesame seeds—both white and black—are used primarily as a coating to add a crunchy and attractive appearance and a nutty flavor to foods (see, for example, Fried Sesame Seed Fish, page 240, and Spun Apples, page 334).

Shaoxing (frequently spelled Hsao Shing) Wine (Rice Wine)

Produced in Shaoxing, Zhejiang province, this wine is one of China's oldest and most popular alcoholic drinks. It is brewed from glutinous rice and has a bouquet like a rich sherry. A special yeast in the manufacturing process contributes to its unique flavor, and good spring water plays an important part. It is made in six steps. First, the rice is soaked, steamed, and made to ferment. The resulting mash is pressed and

the liquor decanted and sealed in jars. The entire production cycle lasts about 100 days. The wine is usually aged from three to five years, during which time the wine increases in aroma and fragrance. It is during storage that the wine acquires clarity, body, and sweetness. In China the wine is usually sealed in carved ceramic jars.

For cooking, the use of Shaoxing wine is incomparable. Once the alcohol is cooked off, the wine leaves a rich and mellow flavor. Dry sherry can be substituted, but if you can you should get the real thing. Since the resumption of trade with China, Shaoxing wine is readily available in the United States. It can be stored at room temperature, and a bottle will last for quite a while. You need to use only a little in each dish. Mirin, a sweetened Japanese rice wine, or sake is not a good substitute.

Shrimp Chips (Shrimp Slices)

These are thin slices of a dried dough made from shrimp and starch, not to be confused with dried shrimp. They are irresistible as appetizers, hors d'oeuvres, and snacks, and are quick and easy to prepare. They make a wonderful garnish for other types of deep-fried appetizers like Fried Wontons (page 313) and a good accompaniment to soups or porridge. They

come in cans or boxes and have a dull, pebbly texture. When they are deep-fried in hot oil (see page 68), they puff up dramatically and become crisp and brittle, like potato chips. Although they are made from shrimp, they do not have a heavy fish taste, but are light, delicate, and slightly sweet.

SICHUAN PEPPERCORNS. See Peppercorns, Sichuan

SICHUAN PRESERVED VEGETABLES. See Chinese Pickles

Snow Peas

This familiar vegetable combines a tender, crisp texture and a sweet, fresh flavor. Snow peas are delicious simply stir-fried, with a little oil and salt, or combined with other ingredients. Shredded they add a crisp texture and sweet taste to stuffings (for example, in Spring Rolls, page 315) and other dishes. Blanched and tossed in a dressing, they produce a crunchy, tender, unique salad. Before they are cooked, the ends should be trimmed (see page 96). Snow peas are widely available in supermarkets. Look for pods that are firm with very small peas, which means they are tender and young. They keep for at least a week in the vegetable bin of the refrigerator.

Soy Sauce

Soy sauces are made from fermented soybeans, wheat, yeast, salt, and sugar. There are two main types of soy: light and dark. Light, or thin, soy has a light, clear brown color and is the saltier of the two, but is lighter in flavor. It is used in dips and combined with other sauces, vinegar, and strong-tasting aromatics such as scallions. Dark, or black, soy is rich and thick and is frequently used to make braising liquids. It has a deeper aroma and darker color that gets absorbed by the poultry or meat being braised. Light and dark soy sauces are often used together in marinades. When cooked in a dish they are usually used in conjunction with other ingredients such as rice wine, chicken stock, or sugar.

There are other variations of soy available—mushroom soy, shrimp soy, and the like. Many of the brands from the People's Republic of China are quite good. Japanese soy sauce, however, is not a good substitute. Soy sauce comes in bottles and large cans. Keep the container tightly closed and in a cool place.

Star Anise (Anise, Whole Anise)

This star-shaped, licorice-flavored spice is the dried pod and seeds of the anise bush. It is an ingredient in five-spice powder and is used in braised dishes and marinades. You can make an anise beef stew by adding a little more anise to the Chinese Beef Stew recipe on page 217, or prepare an anise-flavored duck by adding anise to the smoking ingredients for Smoked Tea Duck (page 174). Its flavor is strong and, again, a little goes a long way. Star anise is widely available. It comes in cellophane or plastic packages and keeps indefinitely.

SUGAR. See Malt Sugar; Chinese Sugar

Transparent Noodles (Cellophane Noodles, Chinese "Vermicelli," Bean Threads)

Although these are called noodles, they are actually made from green soybeans, starch, and water. They come dried and look like thin, brittle, opaque threads. They are often tied into fluffy bundles and packaged in cellophane. They are never eaten alone, but are used in soups (try them in a consommé) or deep-fried like shrimp chips to make a beautiful crisp garnish. Before being used in soups, they must be soaked in warm

water for 5 minutes to soften. When soaked, they acquire a slippery, light, and appealing texture. They will absorb the flavor of any rich broth and become quite tasty. One package (about 100 grams or 3½ ounces) should be enough for two people or for a garnish.

TREE EARS. See Chinese Edible Fungi

subtle. If you substitute Western for Chinese, use less. Chinkiany vinegar is black with a mild, distinctive flavor almost like Italian *aceto balsamico* vinegar. Chinese vinegars are delicious as dips, too, as they are mild. They come in bottles and keep indefinitely at room temperature. Try them on a selective basis in salads for a change in flavor.

Water Chestnut Powder (Water Chestnut Flour)

This finely ground flour made from water chestnuts is used for coating deep-fried foods such as Fish Roll (page 251) or for thickening sauces. You can buy it in small boxes or in cartons. Though it is more expensive when used in place of cornstarch, for example, it makes an exceptionally light, crisp coating. Stored in a tightly closed jar, it keeps indefinitely. Don't be put off by its slightly "off" smell; it vanishes after cooking.

Water Chestnuts

Sweet, crisp water chestnuts have been eaten in China for centuries. They are especially popular in the south, where they are sometimes grown between rice plants in paddies. (This is why they are often muddy.) They are also grown commercially in large tanks as a single crop. They are being cultivated in Florida, Texas, and California and are appearing in supermarkets all over. They are basically an edible root that forms in the mud at the base of the stem.

Turnip Bundles

A turnip bundle is actually a dried, compressed packet made up of the cut-up leaves, roots, and tops of turnips. For more information on how to use them, see page 72.

Vinegar

Chinese vinegars come in many forms. They are generally sweet, pungent, strong, and fragrant. Their sour, spicy, and tart flavor is essential to many Chinese dishes. Western vinegars tend to be sharper and less

Canned water chestnuts are a pale version of the fresh ones because both the crispness and the flavor are lost in the canning process. Try to get fresh ones, or eliminate them altogether. When buying fresh ones, look for a firm, hard texture. The skin should be tight and taut, not wrinkled. If they are mushy, they are too old. Feel them all over for soft, rotten spots. If you peel them in advance, cover them with cold water to prevent browning, or store them in the refrigerator.

41

If you keep them for more than a day, change the water every 24 hours. Stored unpeeled, loosely packed in a plastic bag, good ones will keep in the refrigerator for up to 10 days.

Wine Ball (Wine Yeast, Wine Cube, in a different form)

Wine balls are compressed balls of dried, powdered yeast. The balls are crushed into a powder, mixed with flour, and combined with glutinous rice to make Fermented Wine Rice (page 289). They will keep indefinitely at room temperature.

WOOD EARS. See Chinese Edible Fungi

Basic Techniques

WE BEGIN WITH the most basic techniques used constantly in Chinese cooking and show you in pictures what words sometimes cannot describe: exactly how food is prepared—how wide to make the slices, how to refresh dried ingredients, how to deep-fry fish or slice meat or butterfly a chicken breast, how much oil to put in a wok to cook vegetables just right, how to score a fish, fry noodles, or stir-fry a simple and perfect meal. Once you learn these, you can tackle any recipe in any Chinese cookbook, confident in your ability to accomplish what you have set out to do. Beyond that, you will gain the confidence to add your own touches, to make each dish your own. You'll understand the significance of this ability the first time you substitute, say, zucchini for bok choy and realize that the technique that worked for bok choy works for dozens of other vegetables as well. And so it goes with all the basic techniques that follow.

You will want to refer back to these pages over and over again as you progress to the more complex preparations in this book, as the most complex dish is nothing more than several simple techniques, ingeniously combined.

The basic techniques travel with the Chinese everywhere in the world, readily adapting to a tremendous variety of foods. With these techniques, a Chinese cook can use whatever is available—and in many cases, what is most economical—to make something delicious, which is what we hope you will do, too.

BASIC CUTTING

Using the Cleaver

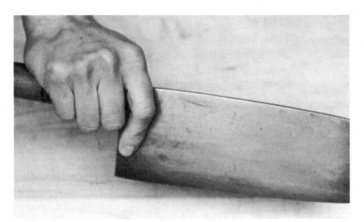

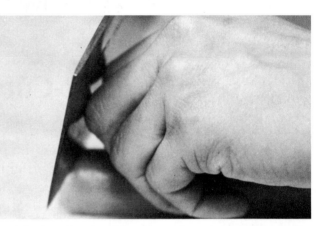

1. If you are right-handed, rest the palm of the right hand on top of the handle of the cleaver, index finger curled over the blade on one side and the thumb on the other to guide the cutting edge firmly. The remaining fingers curl under the handle, gripping it. (Left-handers, use your left hand.)

2. Hold the food with the other hand, fingertips turned under so that they are safely out of the way. The knuckles act as a guide for the blade. Different cutting techniques require different motions, but you should never lift the cutting edge of the blade higher than the knuckles of the hand holding the food, unless that hand is safely out of the way.

Slicing

1. Holding the cleaver perpendicular to the cutting board, cut straight through the food, down and away from your body. Use the knuckles of the hand holding the food as a guide for the blade.

2. Move the hand along the food slightly after each cut. Still holding the side of the cleaver against the knuckles, make another slice.

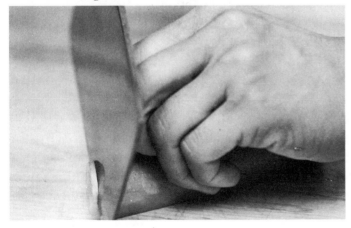

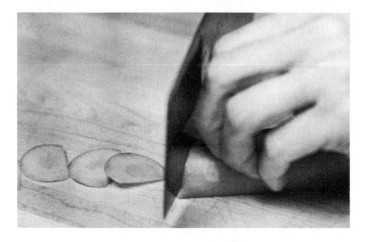

3. Repeat the procedure, regulating the thickness of the slices by how far you move the hand holding the food. With a little practice, you can develop a rhythmic slicing style.

Slant-Cutting

Slant-cutting is used for long, thin vegetables, such as asparagus or string beans, or for thin pieces of meat which if cut in the ordinary manner would form small, insignificant slices. Slant-cutting creates larger pieces that actually cook faster than smaller pieces because more of their surface is exposed to the heat.

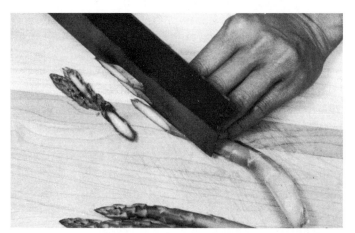

1. Hold the food from the side, so that the cleaver, held against the knuckles, cuts the food at a 60-degree angle.

2. Slice the food one piece at a time. (Don't try to line up several pieces to cut at once.)

Roll-Cutting

Roll-cutting is often used for bulky, tubular vegetables such as Chinese radish, zucchini, turnips, and carrots. It is both an aesthetic approach—the Chinese way of "turning" vegetables—and a technique that enables vegetables to cook faster, impart their flavor to sauces more readily, and acquire the tastes and flavors of seasonings. It creates three exposed surfaces instead of two.

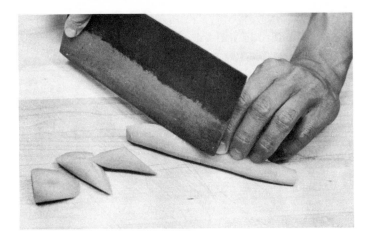

Every time you make a slant cut, roll the piece of food 180 degrees so that the next slant cut crisscrosses the angle of the first, making V-shaped pieces.

Shredding and Fine Dicing

1. Cut the food into sections about 2½ inches long.

2. Holding the sections on end, cut thin slices.

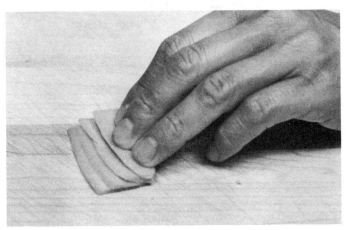

3. Stack the slices.

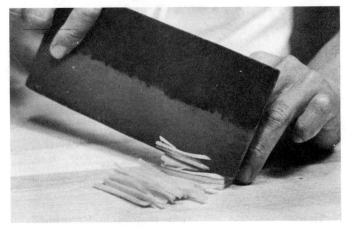

4. Slice the stacks thin, lengthwise.

5. To make tiny dice (for minced squab, for example), line up the shreds and thinly slice them crosswise. For larger dice, cut larger matchstick slices in step 4.

Slicing Meat

You will find it's much easier to slice meat or poultry uniformly if you partially freeze the meat, just long enough to stiffen it (about 10 to 15 minutes). If the meat is untrimmed, it is important first to pull off the membrane (or skin) that is attached to the top. Otherwise, the skin impedes cutting. (The Chinese prefer to buy untrimmed meat and use the trimmings for their

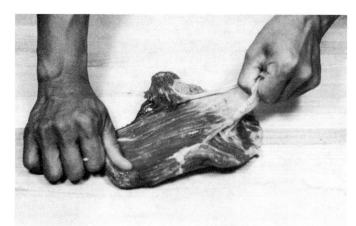

1. Peel off the membrane.

2. Cut the meat lengthwise into strips 1½ inches wide.

3. Gather the strips together. Hold them together with the tips of the fingers turned under.

4. Thinly slice the meat against the grain, on a slight slant.

flavor and texture in other dishes.) Flank steak, which we are using here, is the favored American beef cut.

Mincing Meat

This is a fast, simple way to produce chopped meat that doesn't lose its texture, which so often happens when it's ground.

1. Slice the meat, following the steps in the preceding technique, then spread the meat out flat on the cutting board. Using two cleavers alternately, chop the meat, turning the mass occasionally.

2. Within 1 minute, the meat is sufficiently chopped.

Splitting Horizontally (Parallel-Cutting)

Similar to Western butterflying, this technique is used to split a flat piece of food into two thinner pieces, which are then used to wrap around a stuffing. Freeze the meat partially to stiffen it (10 to 15 minutes) before you begin.

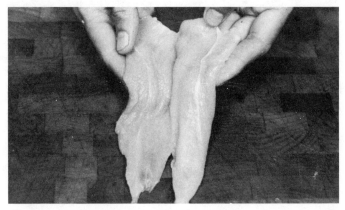

1. Hold the cleaver parallel to the cutting board. With a gentle sawing motion, cut into the edge of the piece of food. Continue cutting, keeping the blade parallel to the board.

2. Stop cutting before the food separates into two pieces; leave about ¼ inch. The meat should unfold like a book.

Scoring

Scoring helps whole fish cook evenly and quickly, and it tenderizes tough seafood like squid.

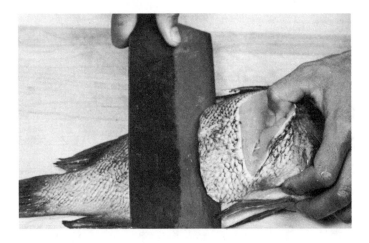

Make shallow cuts about halfway through the food on the diagonal. Take special care not to cut all the way through.

Other Uses of the Cleaver

Using the Cleaver As a Spatula

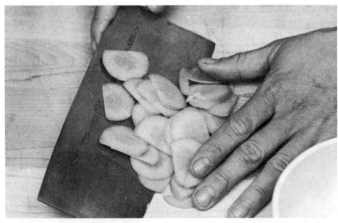

1. Slide the blade of the cleaver under cut-up ingredients.

2. Transfer them to another spot, and push the food off the cleaver with your fingers. Always keep your hand (or fingers) parallel to the blade to prevent cutting yourself.

Smashing with the Cleaver

Use the side of the cleaver to smash small pieces of food, such as ginger or garlic, to release their flavor.

1. Raise the cleaver to shoulder height, the blade parallel to the work surface, and bring it down with a whack, striking the food decisively.

2. Smashing loosens the skin, making the food easier to peel, and flattens it, making it easier to chop.

3. If you are not so bold, lay the cleaver on the food and strike the cleaver smartly with your fist.

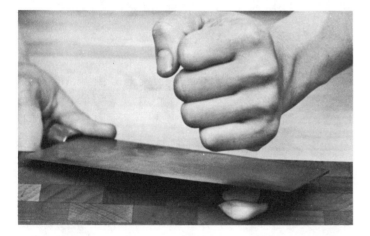

With less force, the same technique is used to crack the shells of crab, lobster, and other shellfish.

Using the Cleaver As a Mortar

Use the handle of the cleaver to grind spices in a small bowl.

BASIC COOKING

Stir-Frying

The wok is used for many forms of cooking, but its primary use is for stir-frying. It is uniquely suited for this technique, in which food cut into manageable pieces is cooked over high heat in a little fat or oil while being tossed about with a wide spatula. Because the food cooks quickly, you should organize the ingredients before you begin.

1. Turn the heat up under the wok to its highest level. When the wok is very hot, the bottom few inches begin to shimmer with subtle rainbow colors, somewhat like the reflection of light from oil. The Chinese call this "turning red." Depending on how hot the flame is, it can take anywhere from 20 seconds to more than a minute to reach this stage.

2. When the wok is hot enough, add the oil. For most dishes, 2 to 3 tablespoons is sufficient. Pour the oil so that the stream hits the side of the wok about halfway up and dribbles down the side to the center. Move the stream around the wok as you pour.

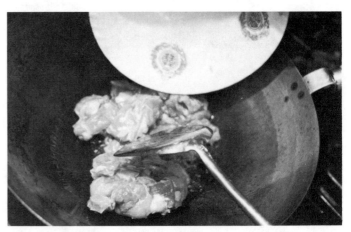

3. The oil heats in a few seconds. When the surface ripples slightly, it is hot enough to add seasonings to flavor the oil—sliced ginger root, crushed garlic, dried chili peppers, or, in some dishes, salt. Press ginger or garlic with the spatula to release the flavors. The pieces of ginger and garlic can be removed or left in, to your own taste. Work quickly, so that the pieces of ginger or garlic do not burn and become bitter.

4. Add the main ingredient to brown and begin to cook in the flavored oil. Meat and poultry must be left untouched for a few seconds to begin browning properly.

5. Vegetables must be kept moving from the moment they hit the wok. It is not necessary to work rapidly, but do work smoothly.

6. Remember, the main heat source is at the center, so keep tossing the vegetables from the center of the wok up onto the sides so that they don't burn. If the heat source seems too hot, lower it and add a couple of tablespoons of water or stock to cool the oil down a bit. This is a matter of judgment that comes with experience; follow your intuition.

Completing Dry-Fried Vegetables
Fragile, high-moisture vegetables, such as bok choy and zucchini, and leafy vegetables like spinach cook very quickly and can be "dry-fried"—stir-fried without the addition of more liquid. They should be cooked over high heat, which seals in juices. Low heat steams the vegetables and extracts moisture.

1. Continue to stir-fry over high heat.

2. Test by tasting a piece, removed from the wok with long chopsticks. Add water, stock, or rice wine if the vegetables seem too dry and need a little moisture to keep from burning. Since the vegetables continue to cook a little longer in their own heat, remove them from the wok when they are slightly crunchier than you actually want.

53

Completing Sauced-Fried Vegetables

Harder, low-moisture vegetables, such as broccoli, carrots, or Chinese radish, start out as stir-fried but end up with a quick boil.

1. Stir-fry the vegetables over high heat until they are partially cooked, then add the premixed sauce ingredients—stock, water, or whatever the recipe calls for. Let the vegetables boil until they are almost done; taste a piece to be sure. If the recipe calls for a thickened sauce, push the vegetables up the side of the wok to leave a pool of liquid in the bottom. Because the side of the wok isn't as hot as the bottom, the food won't overcook.

2. Add cornstarch dissolved in stock or water to the pool of liquid (the recipe will specify the amount). Let the liquid return to a boil, then stir the ingredients back into the sauce to coat them. The sauce should be just thick enough to coat the food lightly. You can also thicken the sauce by reducing it. In this case you should remove the vegetables while you let the sauce boil down.

Completing Braised Vegetables

Vegetables that need longer cooking, such as eggplant, bitter melon, or celery cabbage, are browned, then simmered gently over low heat. Braised vegetables can be cooked ahead of time and reheated, or served cold as a sort of salad.

1. Stir-fry the vegetables until they are partially cooked, then add the premixed sauce ingredients. When they come to a boil, reduce the heat so that the sauce simmers.

2. As the food simmers, the sauce is reduced in volume somewhat. Again, taste the vegetable to make sure it has cooked enough.

Stir-Frying Meat, Poultry, or Fish with Vegetables

In a stir-fried meat and vegetable dish the meat is browned and removed from the wok, then the vegetables are cooked. The meat is returned to the wok only at the last minute to avoid overcooking.

1. When the meat has browned, remove it from the wok and set it aside. Wipe the wok clean. Add 2 tablespoons oil to the wok. Add the vegetables and stir-fry them quickly, to coat them completely with the oil and keep them from cooking unevenly.

2. When the vegetables are coated, add the sauce ingredients. Bring them to a boil.

3. When the vegetables are not quite cooked through, add the meat and finish the cooking together in the sauce. (With quick-cooking vegetables, such as bok choy or zucchini, the meat must be returned to the wok as soon as the sauce comes to a boil. With longer-cooking vegetables, such as carrots or broccoli, wait until the vegetables cook for a few minutes and begin to soften.) Finish by thickening the sauce as described for sauced-fried vegetables (page 54).

Note: For dishes in which the meat is cooked with more than one vegetable, add the longest-cooking vegetable first. Add the remaining vegetables in reverse order of their cooking times, the quick-cooking vegetables last.

Deep-Frying

Proper deep-frying does not produce greasy food. The secret is the temperature of the oil: it must be hot enough to seal the surface of the food immediately to keep the oil from penetrating. The trick is to regulate the heat so that the surface of the food is sealed but does not brown so fast that the food remains uncooked at the center. This requires some practice, but it is not terribly difficult. The wok is an efficient piece of equipment for deep-frying. It uses less oil than a standard pot because of its bottom, which curves inward. Because the food floats to the surface, having a wide base of oil at the bottom is not important. Also, since the rim of the wok is so wide, it catches any splatters that occur.

The Oil
To deep-fry in a 14-inch wok you need between 4 and 6 cups of oil, the larger amount for large pieces such as whole chickens (see Whole Stuffed Chicken Skin, page 117) or whole fish (2 to 3 pounds).

The Chinese generally use peanut oil because it holds heat without smoking or burning. Other unflavored oils can be used, but not olive oil, which is too strong in flavor and burns at a relatively low temperature.

If you are cooking on an electric stove, you must watch the heat of the oil carefully. Because you can't instantly lower the heat as you can on a gas stove, equip yourself with an extra wok ring so that you can move the wok and oil to the unheated ring to cool.

Most oil can be reused and must be handled in the following manner:
1. Let the oil cool entirely so that it can be handled.
2. Strain it into a jar through a strainer lined with cheesecloth to remove particles that would burn if reheated and give the oil a bitter flavor.
3. Label the jar with what the oil has been used for and how many times it has been used.
4. Oil can be used a maximum of three times. After that it begins to break down.

Timing
Deep-frying is a lot quicker than most people think, though many factors are involved: how hot the heat source gets, what type of oil is used, whether a gas or an electric stove is used.

Delicate foods such as cut-up fish or chicken cook very quickly, from 5 to 8 minutes. Stuffed thin doughs and dumplings (such as wontons) take 3 to 4 minutes. Very thinly cut food (such as shredded chicken) takes less than a minute—just in and out. Very large pieces of food, such as a whole duck, chicken, or even fish, take 8 to 15 minutes. Cut-up pork takes about 8 minutes.

Learn to judge how well cooked the food is from its color as it browns and crisps.

1. Have the food to be deep-fried at room temperature. Dry its surface thoroughly. (Moist food spatters when it hits hot oil.)

2. Pour enough oil into the wok so that the food will be completely submerged. Do not fill the wok more than two-thirds full, however, or you run the risk of overflowing.

3. Heat the oil over a high flame. To test the temperature, drop a small piece of food or a cube of bread into the oil. If the food sinks to the bottom and doesn't bubble, the oil is not hot enough. If it sinks to the bottom but starts to bubble immediately, then floats to the surface within a few seconds, the oil is around 350 degrees (moderate), hot enough for large pieces of meat or fish. If the food floats to the surface immediately, the oil is about 375 degrees (hot), the correct temperature for quick-frying small pieces of meat or fish. This is as hot as the oil should get or it will start smoking. When the oil reaches the desired temperature, reduce the flame to keep the temperature constant.

4. If the food is to be dipped in a batter, make sure all the excess batter drips off before adding it to the oil.

5. Add the food without crowding the wok. The pieces should move around freely in the oil. Adding too much will lower the temperature of the oil excessively, which can make the food greasy. Adding any amount of food lowers the temperature slightly, however. To compensate for this, turn up the flame under the oil just before adding the food. Reduce the flame once the initial bubbling has subsided. (This requires a little practice and experience; most cooks pick it up after a very few tries.)

6. To tell when the food is done, remove a piece with long chopsticks or a sieve.

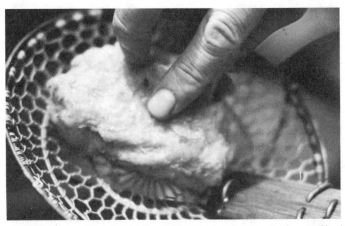

7. Cut it open to check for doneness.

8. If the pieces of food are large, such as whole stuffed chicken breasts, remove one from the oil and press it. If it feels soft and mushy, it's not done. When it feels springy, it's done.

Fried food can be kept in a warm oven on trays covered with paper towels for up to 15 minutes.

Deep-Frying Large Pieces of Food
When you deep-fry a whole chicken, duck, or fish, never attempt to turn it in the oil. It is too fragile and can break apart or cause the oil to splash dangerously.

1. When the oil is hot, slide the well-dried food gently into the wok to avoid splashing.

2. If the food is not fully immersed, ladle hot oil over it. Baste the exposed portion with oil continually, until the entire surface is browned.

Steaming

Steaming cooks food gently in moist heat. Since few Chinese homes have ovens, the steamer is the piece of equipment most often used in its place. Even breads are steamed. Steamed food tends to be subtler in taste than the same food cooked in other ways. Steaming is generally used for delicate and easily abused foods like fish. It is also a fine way to extract fat from duck, or to warm cooked foods without drying them out, or to prepare foods that are easily overcooked.

1. Put some water in the bottom of the wok. Use enough that it won't boil away, but not so much that it touches the steamer basket or the plate on which the food to be steamed is to be placed.

2. The food must be suspended at least 1 inch above the water level. Small pieces of food can be placed in a bamboo steamer basket lined with cheesecloth. The cheesecloth keeps the food from sticking to the steamer and ensures that the bamboo won't flavor the food.

3. Larger pieces, such as whole fish, can be steamed on a plate. Put the plate on a trivet, inverted heatproof bowl, or empty metal can opened at both ends, to keep it more than 1 inch above the water level. Bring the water to a boil before putting the food in the steamer.

4. Cover the wok tightly so that the steam is captured under the lid and can circulate freely around the food.

5. Keep a kettle of water on hand to replenish the steaming liquid in the wok if the level gets too low. Be careful not to pour the water onto the food. Food takes about twice as long to steam as it does to boil.

Other Cooking Techniques

The following techniques are explained in greater detail in the sections dealing with the food to which they are characteristically applied.

Steeping

This is the Chinese equivalent of poaching; the food is put into simmering liquid, covered, and the heat turned off. The food steeps in the hot liquid, the heat penetrating slowly and gently. The food retains its juiciness. This technique is used for delicate foods like chicken (White-Cut Chicken, page 107) and fish (West Lake Fish, page 237).

Simmering

The liquid is brought almost to a boil, but not quite; only the surface shimmers. Occasionally a small bubble may break the surface. This gentle cooking technique is used to make stocks (see page 325). (In braising, the liquid stays at a slightly more vigorous simmer, and the food is usually browned first.)

Red-Cooking

Simmering food in dark soy sauce or a dark broth with seasonings gives the food a reddish-brown color; hence the name. The food takes long cooking to absorb the color and flavors of the braising liquid. See Soy Sauce Chicken (page 112).

Browning

Browning is a first step in many recipes. The food is tossed in a very hot wok to sear its surface. At the same time, bits of the brown surface adhere to the wok; they will flavor any liquid added later. The technique is used in making Chinese Beef Stew (page 217) and Braised Spareribs (page 206).

Roasting

Traditionally, the Chinese roast meats by suspending them over an open fire or in a pit. This is hard to do in home ovens because they are not tall enough. To approximate the procedure, place the meat on a rack in the oven. The objective is to cover as little of the meat as possible so that the bulk of it is exposed to direct heat, producing a crisp outer surface and juicy interior. Convection ovens, like open fire pits, provide a steady flow of circulating hot air and so can be used for Chinese roasting. If they are large enough, like restaurant models, even ducks can be hung in them. See Peking Duck (page 176) and Barbecued Pork Strips (page 193).

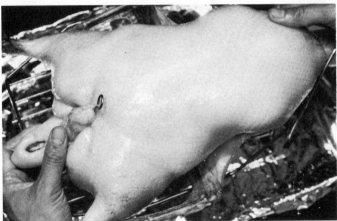

Smoking

By enclosing the food in a container with a smoky fire, the food is infused with the flavor of the smoke as it cooks. Often the aromatic qualities of the smoke are enhanced with citrus peel, tea leaves, or raw rice (see Smoked Tea Duck, page 174). A standard domed outdoor barbecue grill is the perfect piece of equipment for doing this at home.

Twice-Cooking

Twice-cooking infuses meats with flavors that a marinade can't; it renders fat from fatty meats, making them more enjoyable to eat; and it alters the texture of the meat. First, the meat is simmered. Then it is sliced and stir-fried until it is crisp and the fat is rendered. Then other ingredients are combined with the meat. Twice-cooking is most often done with pork (see page 203).

Blanching

Contrary to popular belief, Chinese cooks rarely steam vegetables. When they cook with moist heat, they blanch. The vegetable is plunged into boiling water for a few minutes, just long enough to soften it slightly. It is then drained and served right away (see Blanched Chinese Broccoli with Oyster Sauce, page 75). The technique is also used to precook harder, longer-cooking vegetables for later stir-frying. Sometimes poultry and meats are blanched to rid them of scum and to cook them partially.

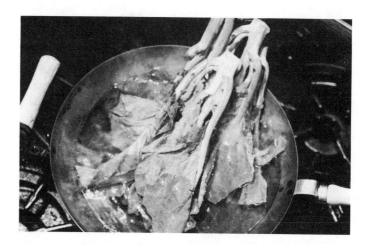

Barbecuing

Barbecuing is a variation of traditional roasting, in which marinated meat is suspended over an open fire and an open container of water is placed under the meat to keep the air around it moist. The meat is also basted. In modern kitchens, hanging the meat from the top rack of an oven approximates the technique. See Barbecued Pork Strips (page 193).

Shallow-Frying

When flat pieces of food must be browned evenly, they are fried in a flat skillet rather than in a wok. This is the same as Western pan-frying. See Stuffed Bean Curd (page 91).

Pot-Steaming

This is done in a special Yunnan clay pot, a small casserole with a chimney in the middle and a lid. Food is placed in the pot, and the pot is then placed in a covered wok with enough water to produce steam. The steam rises through the chimney and disperses in a fine mist that slowly cooks the food. See Steamed Chicken in a Yunnan Pot (page 132).

Flavor-Potting

Flavor-potting is a technique for braising in stocks or sauces flavored with bags of seasonings. Often the same braising liquid is reused—supplemented as necessary by stock or sauce—so that the flavor pot becomes richer and more flavorful and so does the food that cooks in it. See Five-Spice Braised Duck (page 168).

VEGETABLES

Stir-fried Chinese okra with oyster sauce, page 99

Steamed Stuffed Bitter Melon, page 84

Stuffed Bean Curd, page 91

CHICKEN
AND OTHER
SMALL POULTRY

Parchment Chicken, page 140

Beggar's Chicken, page 124

Dark-Meat Chicken with Shallots, page 154

Whole Stuffed Chicken Skin, page 120, garnished with blanched bok choy

Steamed Chicken with Sausage, page 131

Steamed Chicken in a Yunnan Pot, page 132

Minced Squab with Lettuce Cups, page 161

CHICKEN AND OTHER SMALL POULTRY (cont.)

Chicken Shreds with Hot Peppers, page 147, garnished with pepper fans, page 102

Phoenix and Dragon, page 137

Eight-Jewel Duck, page 187, garnished with Chinese parsley and tomato roses, page 104

Cantonese Roast Duck, page 171

Smoked Tea Duck, page 174, served on a bed of watercress

DUCK

Peking Duck Dinner, page 176: duck skin and breast meat with traditional garnish of pancakes, scallion brushes, and hoisin sauce; Stir-Fried Roast Duck meat; Peking Duck Soup

Chinese Beef Stew, page 217

Beef with Asparagus, page 220

Deep-fried Stuffed Meat Balls, and Steamed Pearl Balls, pages 208 and 210

Roast Suckling Pig Banquet, page 214: roast pig, pancakes, hoisin sauce, scallion brushes, tomato roses

MEAT

Sweet-and-Sour Pork, page 200

Fish Roll, page 251, with lemon wedges and roasted salt and pepper, page 70

Shrimp Balls, page 256, garnished with Dry-Fried Crayfish, page 263

FISH AND SEAFOOD

Fish Cakes, page 248, stir-fried with vegetables and ginger shreds

Shrimp in Lobster Sauce, page 261

Dry-Fried Crayfish, page 263

Fish Balls, page 246, and Watercress Soup, page 326

Phoenix Shrimp, page 259

Crystal Shrimp, page 254

FISH AND SEAFOOD (cont.)

Fried Wontons, page 313, served with shrimp chips, page 68, and plum sauce

Spicy Shrimp with Wine Rice, page 292, garnished with Dry-Fried Crayfish, page 263

RICE, DOUGHS AND NOODLES

Crisp Noodle Cake, with bok choy and Barbecued Pork Sauce, page 320

Steamed Pork in Rice Crumbs, page 288

Fried Rice, page 280, garnished with a tomato rose, page 104

Spring Rolls, page 315, served with hot dry mustard and plum sauce

Deep-fried Onion Cakes, page 299, cut into serving wedges

Braised Egg Dumplings, page 304, with sauce

Steamed Wonton Dumplings, page 311, in bamboo steamer

Wontons for Soup, page 309

Deep-fried Rolled Onion Cakes, page 300

SOUPS

Egg-Flower Soup, page 329

Sizzling Rice Soup, page 327

DESSERT

Spun Apples, page 334

BASIC INGREDIENTS AND PREPARATIONS

Peeling and Chopping Garlic

1. Place a single clove of garlic on a cutting board and gently tap it with the side of a cleaver. This loosens the skin.

2. The loosened skin should slip off easily.

3. With the other hand out of the way, chop rapidly, keeping the cleaver perpendicular to the board. Stop occasionally to push the bits of garlic that have stuck to the cleaver back onto the board.

Shredding Ginger

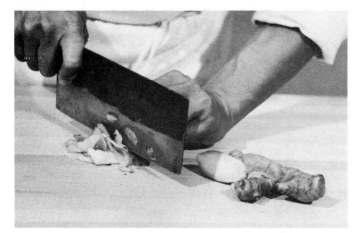

1. If the ginger is fresh, it is not necessary to peel it; simply wipe it clean with a damp cloth. Cut thin diagonal slices from the knob of ginger.

2. Cut the slices into thin shreds.

Preparing Dried Mushrooms

Because of lack of refrigeration in China, many ingredients are dried to preserve their flavor so that they can be stored for use any time of year. Most dried ingredients must be soaked in warm water for 20 to 30 minutes to restore them before use. Do not use the soaking water in cooking.

1. Put the dried mushrooms in a bowl large enough to allow them to double in size as they soak. Pour in boiling water to cover.

2. When the mushrooms are soft (after about 20 to 30 minutes), lift them from the water, leaving behind any sand and grit that has sunk to the bottom.

3. Squeeze the mushrooms dry.

4. Cut off the tough stems and slice, shred, or use the mushrooms whole.

Shredding Lily Stems

Soak and squeeze the lily stems, following the instructions for preparing dried mushrooms. Then break off and discard the ends and pull the stems apart with your fingers to shred them. This makes them tender and releases their fragrance.

Preparing Tree Ears and Cloud Ears

1. Put the dried tree or cloud ears in a bowl large enough to allow them to double in size as they soak. Pour in boiling water to cover. When they are soft (after about 20 to 30 minutes) lift them from the water, leaving behind any sand and grit that has sunk to the bottom. Squeeze the pieces dry, and cut off the hard stems.

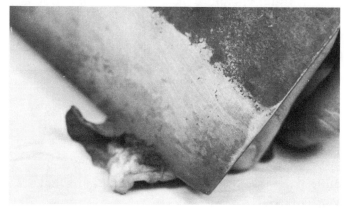

2. Tree and cloud ears are usually shredded so that their texture will spread throughout a dish. To shred, stack several together.

3. Slice them thin.

Frying Shrimp Chips

Do not confuse shrimp chips with dried shrimp. Shrimp chips look like dried disks and are available in white or pastel colors. They can be fried ahead of time and kept in a plastic bag for a few days.

1. In a wok heat 2 cups oil to at least 325 degrees. Test the oil with one chip to make sure it's hot enough. If the oil is not hot enough and the chips take too long to puff, they will come out greasy. Add all the chips at once.

2. Immediately after the chips are added to the oil, they begin to puff.

3. Within a few seconds the chips are completely puffed. Remove them from the oil and drain them. Use as a garnish.

Frying Transparent Noodles

When used as a crisp garnish or as a base for a sauced dish, transparent noodles are deep-fried.

1. Heat 2 cups oil to 325 degrees. Plunge the bundles of noodles into the hot oil.

2. Within a few seconds the noodles expand to many times their volume. Remove them from the oil before they brown. Drain and serve.

Roasting Sichuan Peppercorns

Roasting brings out the fragrance and flavor of these peppercorns.

1. Put the peppercorns in a skillet or a wok over high heat. Shake the pan occasionally. Roast for a minute or so, until their fragrance becomes strong, then turn off the heat.

2. Crush the peppercorns in a bowl with the handle of a cleaver or in a mortar and pestle. A blender or food processor does a good job, too. Do not overprocess. The peppercorns should just be coarsely ground.

Roasting Salt and Pepper

Roasted salt and pepper make a delicious dip that goes very well with deep-fried foods, such as Crisp Soy Squab (page 157) or Fish Rolls (page 251). Once roasted, the mixture can be stored indefinitely in a tightly closed jar. Try roasting salt with other types of peppercorns for a variety of tastes.

1. Place 1 tablespoon Sichuan peppercorns and 3 tablespoons coarse (kosher) salt in a moderately hot wok without any oil. Stir until the salt begins to brown.

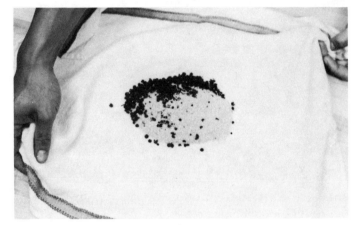

2. Remove to a clean towel.

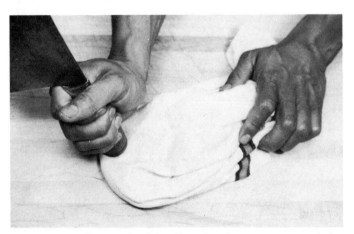

3. Use a mallet or the handle of a cleaver to pound the mixture until crushed. This can also be done in a blender, but a food processor doesn't seem to get the peppercorns fine enough.

4. Roasted and ground salt and pepper.

Preparing Dried Salted Fish

Dried salted fish is soaked, boned, and minced, and then it's ready to use.

1. Soak the fish in warm water for about 30 minutes, until it is softened. Discard the water.

2. Holding the fish bone side up, press on the backbone from underneath to make it pop out.

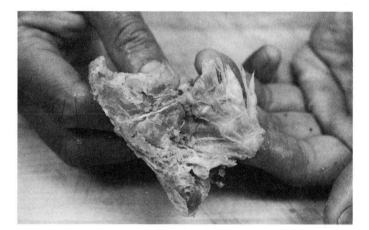

3. Remove the bone and mince the fish. Add it to the other ingredients as specified in the recipe (see, for example, Steamed Pork Cake, page 211).

Preparing Turnip Bundle

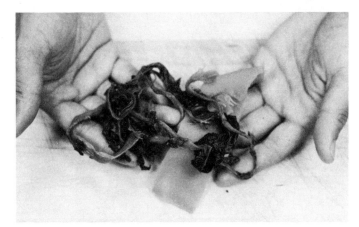 

1. Unravel the bundle, rinse, then chop the stringy tops.

2. Slice the thick stems and, if the recipe calls for it, finely mince them as well.

Vegetables

IF YOU WERE TO GO TO A CHINESE MARKET, you would find a great variety of vegetables unknown to Western cooks. Not only do the Chinese enjoy many different types of vegetables, but they employ many techniques for cooking them. Vegetables are enjoyed with a relish equal to that for poultry and fish. In recent years, stir-frying vegetables has become popular all over the world. This is a basic, quick way of cooking vegetables that preserves their flavor and freshness with a minimum amount of cooking. Often stir-frying is done in oil that is flavored with garlic (see Stir-Fried Bok Choy in Garlic Oil, page 77), but ginger is also used to bring out special flavors.

Vegetables are sometimes quickly stir-fried, cooled, and served for lunch or as a salad course (cucumbers are often used; see page 80), or blanched and served as part of the main course (see Blanched Chinese Broccoli with Oyster Sauce, page 75).

A cheap source of protein throughout China is bean curd, a soybean derivative. It may be eaten alone, stir-fried with other vegetables, or used in a marinade. It can be stuffed (see page 97) or cut into cubes and used in Sizzling Rice Soup (see page 327). Making bean curd is a commercial specialty, and a variety of bean curd products is now available in supermarkets and specialty shops.

What vegetables you prepare depends partly on the season, on where you live, on your personal preference, and on your imagination. Substitute whenever and however you choose for any technique demonstrated, but we urge you to try new, unfamiliar vegetables like winter melon, bitter melon, Chinese okra, and bok choy—whenever possible. Try them alone or combined with more familiar foods. They are no more difficult to prepare than broccoli or green beans. Remember to concentrate on cutting carefully and uniformly.

MAIN-INGREDIENT VEGETABLES

Chinese Broccoli

Chinese broccoli tastes vaguely like the milder Western broccoli. More elongated in shape and with fewer flowerets, it is very crunchy and slightly bitter, rather like chard.

The recipe that follows calls for blanching the broccoli, a very simple cooking method that produces the simplest and freshest-tasting vegetables. Other leafy vegetables like mustard greens and spinach can also be served in this manner. Instead of oyster sauce, soy sauce or other condiments such as chili sauce with garlic or even a warm vinaigrette may be used, to taste.

The broccoli is blanched whole. For stir-frying it should be slant-cut or prepared like Bok Choy (page 76) so that it cooks evenly.

Blanched Chinese Broccoli with Oyster Sauce

1 pound Chinese broccoli
1 quart boiling water with 2 teaspoons salt added
¼ cup oyster sauce

METHOD: Blanching (page 63)
SERVES 4 as an accompaniment to meat, fish, or fowl.
SUGGESTED BEVERAGE: Dry Chenin Blanc or Soave

1. Plunge the broccoli into the boiling water. Return to the boil and let it cook until tender-crisp (about 5 minutes).

2. Drain the broccoli well and put it on a platter.

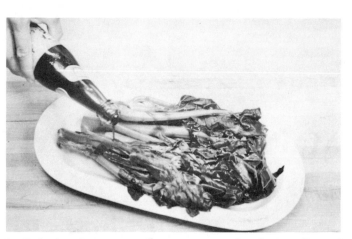

3. Drizzle the oyster sauce over the broccoli and serve. Pull off pieces with chopsticks.

Bok Choy

Bok choy is a very versatile vegetable, one of the most popular in Chinese cooking and one of the oldest in the world. Bok choy is actually the Chinese name for several varieties of Chinese cabbage; it looks like a cross between romaine lettuce and celery. Basically, you will find it in three different sizes. The large-stalked bok choy commonly found in supermarkets is used mainly for soups, though it stir-fries fairly well. The thinner, younger bok choy is sweeter and more tender; it is best stir-fried or blanched. Tiny bok choy, no more than 3 inches long, are wonderfully crisp and sweet, but they are rarely available commercially and are expensive when they are.

Bok choy stems, peeled and sliced like broccoli stems so that they will cook evenly with the rest of the cut-up stalks, are the tastiest part. The yellow flowers of young bok choy have a delicious mustardlike flavor. Bok choy goes well with virtually all meat and poultry, either as a side dish or stir-fried with the main ingredients.

Preparing Bok Choy

1. With a thin cleaver, cut off the base of the stalks to separate them.

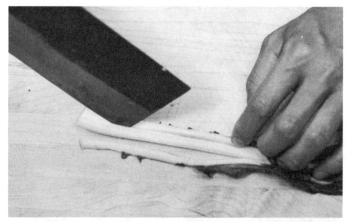

2. Holding each stalk by the leaf, run the point of the cleaver through each stalk to divide it lengthwise.

3. Line up the stalks and cut them into 2-inch pieces. Thus, all the pieces are more or less the same size and will cook evenly.

4. Peel the base to remove the tough outer layer. The interior is the most flavorful part of the vegetable. Cut it thinly on the diagonal so that it will cook evenly.

Stir-Fried Bok Choy in Garlic Oil

3 tablespoons peanut oil
1 teaspoon salt
3 or 4 cloves garlic, lightly crushed and peeled
1½ pounds bok choy, cut into 1-inch pieces (see above)

METHOD: Stir-frying (page 52)
SERVES 2 as a main vegetable course, 4 as an accompaniment to meat, fish, or
      fowl.
MAY BE PREPARED in advance and served cold.
SUGGESTED BEVERAGE: Dry Sauvignon Blanc or Sancerre

1. Heat the wok over a high flame for 1 minute. Add the oil, and when the oil is very hot (this will take just a few seconds; pass your hand over it to feel the heat, or look for a wisp of smoke), add the salt and garlic to flavor the oil. A common mistake is to skimp on oil in stir-frying vegetables, which makes them dry out and burn. Use enough to coat the vegetables thinly but thoroughly.

2. Remove the garlic when it has browned. Add the bok choy and stir-fry, working smoothly and rapidly, keeping the vegetables moving.

3. Taste a piece of bok choy to see if it is done. It should be crisp but should not taste raw. When it reaches that stage, transfer it to a serving dish. Stir-fried vegetables should glisten with brilliant color; never let them fade in the wok.

4. Variation: Chinese mustard greens are very good prepared in a similar manner. Substitute 4 ¼-inch-thick slices of fresh ginger root for the garlic and 1½ pounds mustard green stems (see pages 34 and 31), cut into 1-inch pieces, for bok choy and proceed as above.

Chinese Cucumber

Chinese cucumbers are difficult to find in this country, although you can find seeds for them and grow your own. They are longer and narrower than the cucumbers found in most American supermarkets (the expensive "English" cucumbers are more similar), but our own supermarket variety can be used too.

Here the cucumbers are stir-fried with Flower Carrots (page 101) and allowed to marinate and wilt in the sauce in which they are cooked, then are refrigerated. Served cold, the cucumbers make an excellent first course or salad course, wonderful for summer eating. Both unusual and easy, the salad can be made way ahead of time; the more it marinates, the tastier it becomes.

Preparing Chinese Cucumber

1. Peel the Chinese cucumber and scrape out the seeds with a teaspoon.

2. Cut the cucumber into strips as wide as the vegetable is thick by running the point of a cleaver down its length.

3. Cut the strips crosswise into dice.

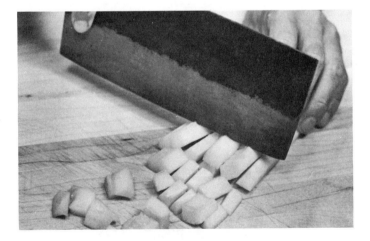

Spicy-and-Sour Cucumber Salad

2½ tablespoons peanut oil
4 dried chili peppers
2 cloves garlic, lightly crushed
1 medium carrot, cut into flowers (see page 101)
2 Chinese cucumbers, diced (see above)

SAUCE:
1 tablespoon thin soy sauce
1 tablespoon Shaoxing wine or dry sherry
2 tablespoons white vinegar
1 tablespoon sesame oil
Salt to taste

METHOD: Stir-frying (page 52)
SERVES 4 as a first course or salad course.
PREPARE AHEAD of time, refrigerate, and serve cold.
SUGGESTED BEVERAGE: Generic white wine or beer

1. Over a moderate flame, heat the oil in a wok. Add the peppers and the garlic to flavor the oil.

2. Stir-fry the carrots 1 minute.

3. Add the cucumbers and the sauce ingredients. Mix them well with the carrots for 30 seconds.

4. Remove the salad immediately to a serving plate. Season with salt to taste. Refrigerate the salad until ready to serve.

Chinese Eggplant

Chinese eggplant is smaller and narrower than the Western kind. In some cities, supermarkets sell it as Chinese or Japanese eggplant; Italian markets carry it as well. Since it is picked younger than Western eggplant, it tends to be less bitter. It contains less moisture and need not be salted. Leave the skin intact, as it holds the eggplant flesh together and provides a nice contrast in texture.

Eggplant is unique among Chinese vegetables in that quick cooking does not fully develop its flavor and texture. As with eggplant dishes of other cuisines, the vegetable must be thoroughly cooked. In the recipe that follows, the eggplant is browned in oil by stir-frying, then braised in a savory sauce until it is tender, absorbing the flavors of the sauce as it cooks. Eggplant takes well to braising, as it absorbs flavor like a sponge yet doesn't lose its character. It can also be stir-fried successfully with meat, but braise it before adding tender meats such as beef or chicken. Or braise it with ground pork or pork slices, which need a longer cooking time.

Braised eggplant reheats well. Chilled, it makes a wonderful alfresco dish, like a Chinese ratatouille. For a variation of the following recipe, eliminate the chili sauce and vinegar and add tree ears and lily stems to make eggplant "in the style of the fish," so called because it resembles a typical braised fish sauce.

Preparing Chinese Eggplant

1. The long and narrow shape of Chinese eggplant is ideal for cutting into chunks, each with a bit of tender skin attached.

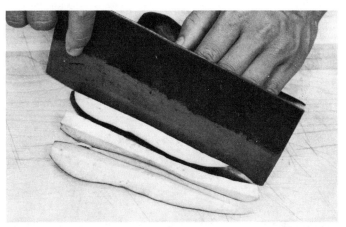

2. Without peeling the eggplant, cut off and discard the base and tip, then cut the eggplant lengthwise into quarters.

3. Line up the eggplant strips and cut them crosswise into 1-inch chunks.

Braised Sichuan Eggplant

3 tablespoons peanut oil
4 Chinese eggplants, or 1 large eggplant, about 1 pound, cut into 1-inch
 chunks (see above)
4 garlic cloves, minced
2 tablespoons minced fresh ginger root
4 whole scallions, minced

BROTH MIXTURE:
2 tablespoons chili paste with garlic
2 tablespoons Shaoxing wine or dry sherry
2 tablespoons thin soy sauce
½ teaspoon sugar
1 tablespoon Chinkiany vinegar, or 2 teaspoons cider vinegar or red wine
 vinegar
½ cup chicken broth
Salt to taste
2 teaspoons sesame oil

METHOD: Stir-frying (page 52), braising
SERVES 2 to 3 as a main course, 4 as a salad.
MAY BE PREPARED in advance and reheated, or served cold as a salad.
SUGGESTED BEVERAGE: Rosé or light red wine, chilled

1. Heat the wok, then heat the oil in it over a high flame. Stir-fry the eggplant pieces to coat them with oil. Add the garlic, ginger, scallions, and then the broth mixture. Mix well and let the mixture cook, stirring it occasionally to keep the pieces of eggplant from sticking.

2. After 3 minutes, reduce the heat, cover the wok, and let the eggplant braise until it is tender (10 to 15 minutes).

3. Taste the sauce to see whether it needs salt, transfer the eggplant and its sauce to a serving dish, and drizzle on the sesame oil. The dish can be served immediately, reheated, or served cold as a salad.

Bitter Melon

Bitter melon has no counterpart in the Western world. It has a slightly bitter flavor (which comes from quinine; in fact, the melon is often dried and used as a medicine in China), and like beer, which also has a bitter flavor, it is an acquired taste but one that's easy to develop. The vegetable is attractive, rather like a gourd with its bumpy surface. Dark green bitter melons are the youngest and least bitter. As they mature, they become yellow-green, bright yellow, and finally brilliant orange, growing progressively stronger in taste. Blanched and cooked in chicken broth, they make a refreshing soup, especially in their more mature stages.

In the recipe that follows, we stuff the melon, then steam it on a plate over water until it is tender. In Western cuisines, stuffed vegetables are usually baked in the oven or braised in a sauce, but the Chinese prefer steaming because it preserves the texture of the vegetable so that it contrasts with the texture of the stuffing.

Zucchini, cucumber—any vegetable suitable for stuffing—can be steamed in the same manner.

Steamed Stuffed Bitter Melon

[see photo in color section]

STUFFING:
½ pound pork, ground
4 fresh water chestnuts, peeled and finely minced
1 teaspoon minced fresh ginger root
2 tablespoons minced scallion
1½ tablespoons Shaoxing wine or dry sherry
½ teaspoon salt
½ teaspoon sugar
1 tablespoon thin soy sauce
1 egg, lightly beaten
1 teaspoon cornstarch

2 large bitter melons, about ¾–1 lb.

SAUCE:
2 tablespoons peanut oil
2 teaspoons minced garlic
1½ tablespoons fermented black beans
1 tablespoon Shaoxing wine or dry sherry
¾ cup chicken broth
Salt to taste

½ teaspoon cornstarch mixed with 1 teaspoon cold chicken broth
1 tablespoon sesame oil

METHOD: Steaming (page 59)
SERVES 2 as a main course.
MAY BE PREPARED in advance and reheated by steaming.
SUGGESTED BEVERAGE: Beer

1. Combine the stuffing ingredients in a large bowl.

2. Mix them thoroughly. The hands are the best tool for this job.

3. Cut the bitter melon into 1-inch slices; discard the end pieces.

4. With a paring knife, trim out the insides.

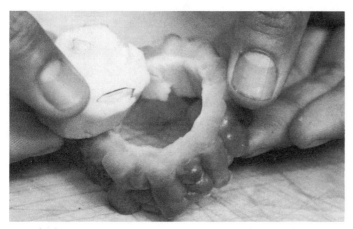

5. Lift them out.

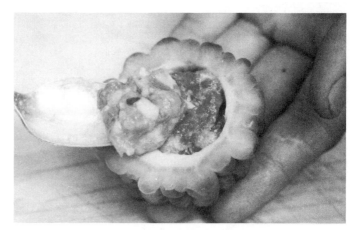

6. Stuff the cavity of each slice with a generous spoonful of stuffing.

7. Arrange the stuffed pieces of vegetable on a plate, and set the plate on a trivet in a wok over enough hot water to come within 1 inch of the plate. Cover the wok and steam the food for 20 minutes. Remove the platter and the trivet.

8. In a separate wok or pan, prepare the sauce. First heat 2 tablespoons peanut oil. Add the garlic and fermented black beans, stir for a minute, then add the Shaoxing wine, chicken stock, and salt. Add the liquid that results from the steaming of the melon. Bring the mixture to a boil. Thicken with the dissolved cornstarch and flavor with sesame oil.

9. Pour the sauce over the bitter melons and serve.

Chinese Mustard Greens

Chinese mustard greens are not as pungent as the Western variety. They have thicker stems, which are prized for their special slightly sweet flavor. In Chinese markets you can buy either stems alone or the whole vegetable. The stems and leaves can be cut up like bok choy (see page 76) and stir-fried or added to soups. They are especially delicious with fresh squid (see page 271). The stems only are used for pickling.

Next to drying, pickling is the most common Chinese technique for preserving vegetables. The sharp tang of pickled vegetables makes a marvelous addition to stir-fried dishes (try substituting them for the asparagus in Beef with Asparagus, page 220); they are particularly good in Rice Porridge (page 282). To pickle, you need a covered crock or glass container (metal containers react with the acidity of the brine). The vegetables simply soak in the brine, retaining their crispness but "cooking" in the same way a fish "cooks" in seviche. Although stems of mustard greens make a traditional pickle, other vegetables, such as carrots, Chinese radishes, red radishes,

Preparing mustard greens

1. With a thin cleaver, cut off the base and separate the thick leaves from the round core.

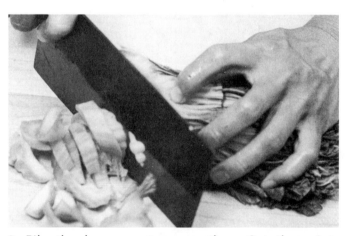

2. Pile the leaves on one another. Cut them into ¼-inch slices on the diagonal.

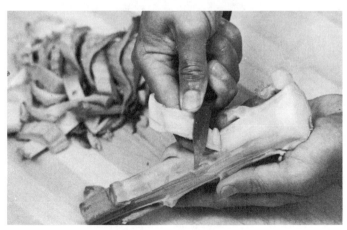

3. Peel the core with a paring knife.

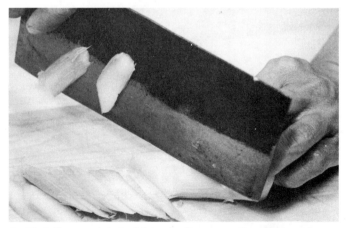

4. Cut the core into ¼-inch slices on the diagonal.

and turnips, can also be pickled. Keep the vegetables, once pickled, in the brine in glass jars in the refrigerator. Although the refrigerator slows down the pickling action, the longer you leave them, the sharper they get. To use pickled vegetables, rinse them and cut them as you would fresh vegetables.

Pickled Chinese Mustard Greens

2 pounds whole stems of Chinese mustard greens or whole vegetable

BRINE:
3 tablespoons salt dissolved in ½ cup boiling water
1 tablespoon sugar
1 tablespoon distilled vinegar

METHOD: Pickling

1. Totally immerse the vegetables in the brine in a ceramic pot.

2. Press the vegetables into the brine and add cold water to cover. Cover the pot and leave it at room temperature.

3. After 3 days, remove the vegetables from the brine, drain them, and store them in the refrigerator. They should keep for up to two months.

MAKES 4 cups.
MAY BE STORED in the refrigerator for up to two months. Served as a condiment, in soup, or stir-fried with meat, seafood, or fowl.
SUGGESTED BEVERAGE: Beer

Bean Curd

Chinese cooks seldom deep-fry fresh vegetables; however, bean curd takes well to this cooking method. There is no need for a batter, as the curd's natural starchiness forms a crust automatically. Frying changes its texture completely, making it crisp on the surface and soft inside, like bread. Once fried, it acts like a sponge, absorbing the flavor of whatever sauce accompanies it. It makes a great contrast to the heaviness of Roast Suckling Pig (page 214) and can be added to any stir-fried meat, poultry, fish, or vegetable dish. With vegetables, it completes a nutritious one-dish vegetarian meal. It can also be sliced, shredded, or cubed and added to soups.

The frying may be done well ahead and the curd stir-fried to heat through before serving.

Fried Tofu with Vegetables and Cooked Meat

4 cups peanut oil for deep-frying
½ pound tofu, cut into 1-inch cubes
1 cup sliced or shredded roast pork or other cooked meat

SAUCE:
1 tablespoon Shaoxing wine or dry sherry
2 tablespoons oyster sauce
½ cup chicken broth
1 teaspoon cornstarch dissolved in 1 teaspoon cold chicken broth

5 whole scallions, cut into 3-inch lengths

METHOD: Deep-frying (page 56), stir-frying (page 52)
SERVES 2 as a main course, 4 to 6 as an accompaniment.
MAY BE PREPARED in advance through step 3.
SUGGESTED BEVERAGE: Dry Gewürztraminer

1. Heat the oil to about 375 degrees (medium hot). The tofu should begin to brown as soon as it hits the oil. Drop the tofu cubes into the oil one by one to keep them from sticking to each other. (See page 56 for more about deep-frying.)

2. When the tofu cubes float to the surface, turn them with long chopsticks to brown them evenly. The surface of the tofu blisters and puffs slightly.

3. When the cubes are golden brown (about 2 minutes), remove them from the oil and drain them on paper towels. This much can be done well in advance.

4. Drain the oil from the wok and add 2 tablespoons oil over high heat. Stir-fry the meat just to coat it with the oil, then add the sauce ingredients. Bring the mixture to a boil, then add the scallions. Just before serving, stir in the tofu to heat it through. It loses some of its crispness, but it also absorbs the flavor of the sauce.

Stuffed Bean Curd

[see photo in color section]

Stuffed bean curd is unusual and delicious. The flavors of the stuffing contrast with the blandness of the curd. Each bean curd is cut into triangles that are hollowed out carefully and stuffed with shrimp paste (fish paste may be used as well). The triangles are pan-fried to firm up the surface, making a light crust to hold the packages together. The flat pieces of bean curd brown better in a flat skillet than in a curved wok. The dish reheats well, so it can be made ahead. If triangles seem too risky, try hollowing out squares instead. For this technique, firm Chinese bean curd is a must; the Japanese type is too soft.

4 large squares Chinese tofu
½ recipe Basic Shrimp Paste (page 256)
3 tablespoons peanut oil, or more

SAUCE:
1 tablespoon thin soy sauce
1 tablespoon Shaoxing wine or dry sherry
1 cup chicken broth
2 teaspoons sesame oil
2 tablespoons minced Chinese parsley

METHOD: Shallow pan-frying
SERVES 2 as a main course, 4 as a side dish.
MAY BE PREPARED ahead of time and reheated in the sauce.
SUGGESTED BEVERAGE: Dry Sauvignon Blanc or Graves

1. Cut the squares of tofu diagonally into triangles. Use a paring knife or a butter knife to etch a thin outline for the pocket on the diagonal surface of the triangle, leaving a ½-inch margin.

2. Working slowly and carefully, gently begin to "chisel" out a pocket.

3. Keep in mind that the tapering sides of the triangle mean you'll have to dig deeper at the center than at the sides.

4. When the pocket is hollowed out as much as possible, gently press the shrimp puree into it with your finger.

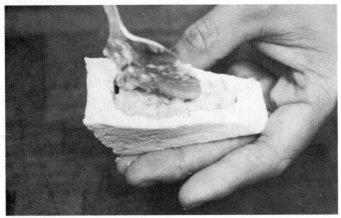

5. Use a spoon to push the puree gently into the corner of the triangle as far as it will go. Work carefully to avoid splitting the piece of tofu.

6. Heat the oil in a flat skillet and brown the triangles in it, starting with the stuffed edge. This keeps the stuffing in.

7. Brown the triangles lightly on all sides.

8. Add the sauce ingredients and simmer the dish for 5 minutes.

9. This can be prepared ahead and gently reheated in the sauce.

COMPLEMENTARY VEGETABLES

Some vegetables, such as water chestnuts, rarely get to star in their own dishes. Instead, they function as a supporting cast, contributing their characteristics to a more complex preparation. Water chestnuts, for example, add crispness and sweetness. Their milky-white color provides contrast with dark, colorful foods. Just as most Americans know that carrots must be well scrubbed or scraped, Chinese cooks know that water chestnuts must be peeled a certain way before they can be used. Likewise, snow peas must be snapped and strung. The following techniques show how these vegetables are prepared for cooking, at the same time introducing them and offering suggestions on how best to use them.

Water Chestnuts

Fresh water chestnuts have an incomparably light, crisp texture and a delicate, sweet flavor. Canned water chestnuts, widely available, are but a pale ghost of the fresh ones and not worth using. If you can't find fresh ones, substitute *jícama* (a Mexican root), found in Mexican and Chinese shops and some supermarkets. It lacks the sweetness of water chestnuts, but matches them in texture. When shopping for fresh water chestnuts, look for a firm, hard texture. Reject any that feel mushy (too old) or that have any rotten spots. Store them in a plastic bag left untied. If you peel them in advance, immerse them in cold water to prevent browning, and keep them refrigerated, changing the water every 24 hours. Fresh, unpeeled water chestnuts will keep refrigerated up to 10 days. Once you have peeled them, try to use them within a day or two.

Preparing Water Chestnuts

1. Slice off and discard the top and bottom. Holding the water chestnut on edge like a wheel, cut thin slices of the skin around the edge. Rotate the chestnut toward you as you peel until all the skin is removed. Always slice *away* from you at an angle. Wipe the cleaver after peeling each water chestnut to keep it from making the next one dusty. Keep the peeled vegetable in cold water.

2. Place a water chestnut flat side down on a cutting board. Holding the cleaver vertically, slice the water chestnut. This is the one form in which the vegetable is used.

3. For shredded water chestnuts, line up the slices and slice them again lengthwise.

4. For diced water chestnuts, align the shreds and cut them crosswise.

5. To make minced water chestnuts, continue chopping. They are often used in this form for fillings and stuffings.

Snow Peas

Snow peas grow on a vine like ordinary peas, only the pod is smaller and thinner. The whole pod is edible, offering a crunchy texture and a mildly sweet, grassy-fresh taste. They take very little cooking, in most cases only 10 or 20 seconds, so they retain their crunch. When cooked, they turn a brilliant emerald green. Stir-frying in garlic oil (see page 52) is a delicious way to serve them alone as a side dish. Shredded or whole, they add character to soups and stir-fried dishes. Shredded, they add texture and sweetness to stuffings, like the one for Spring Rolls (page 315). Shop for small, crisp pods; large ones can be tough.

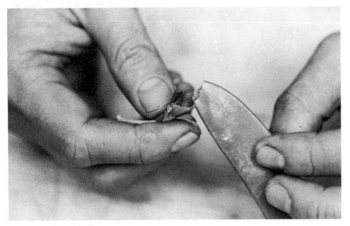

1. Break off the stem.

2. Pull the string along the straight edge as far as you can.

3. Start at the tip and pull the string along the same edge from the other direction. Rinse the snow peas well. Leave them whole, or shred them.

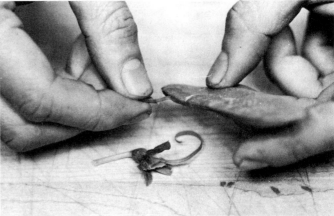

Gingko Nuts

Canned gingkos come already shelled and cooked, but fresh ones have a chestnutlike texture and purer flavor. They must be shelled and blanched to loosen the skin so that it can be peeled. As an ingredient, gingko nuts add a soft texture to stir-fried vegetables. They are added to soups, but their greatest contribution is to stuffings. Unshelled and unpeeled gingkos can be kept refrigerated up to three weeks. Freshly peeled gingkos are preferred.

Preparing Gingko Nuts

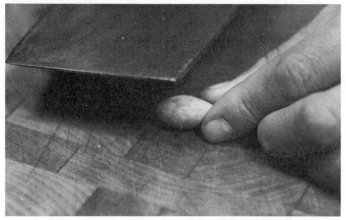

1. With the blunt edge of a cleaver, tap lightly to just crack the shell. Don't crush the nut.

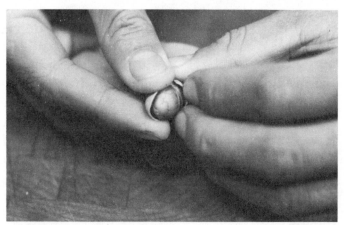

2. Pull the hard shell apart.

3. Remove the nut.

4. Drop the nuts into boiling water and turn off the heat. Let them sit for 10 minutes to loosen the skins.

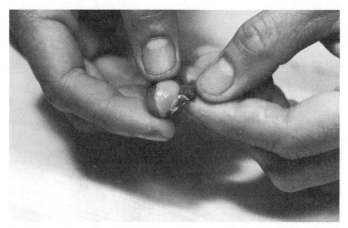

5. They should peel right off.

Chinese Radish

Historically regarded as healthful, with a reputation for stimulating the appetite, this vegetable often turns up in medicinal brews. The roots average a foot long and an inch wide. They are light and crisp in texture, like the smaller red radish, but are slightly milder in flavor. Skilled chefs sculpt elaborate figures from Chinese radishes for banquets. They are roll-cut and added to braised dishes such as Chinese Beef Stew (page 217), or sliced, then blanched, and added to stir-fried dishes. Grated, they make a tangy addition to salads; try using them in Spicy-and-Sour Cucumber Salad (page 80). The size and type of the cut should harmonize with the other ingredients in a dish: larger chunks for braised beef, grated for salads, sliced for quick stir-fried dishes. They are also very good pickled (see pages 87–88). In non-Chinese markets, this vegetable is often referred to as Daikon or Japanese radish.

Preparing Chinese Radishes

1. Cut off the stem end.

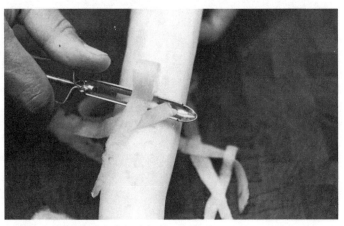

2. Peel the vegetable like a carrot.

3. Roll-cut to retain the texture.

Chinese Okra

[see photo in color section]

Chinese okra is probably not an accurate name for this vegetable because it does not taste like American okra at all. It has the watery texture of zucchini but is more like cucumber in taste. One of the most popular methods of cooking Chinese okra is stir-frying. As a side dish, stir-fry or blanch it and serve just with a lightly thickened oyster sauce. Chinese okra can be cooked with cucumbers for a hot-and-sour salad (see page 80) or simmered briefly in soup. It cooks quickly and can simply be sautéed in butter and shallots for an unusual Westernized accompaniment to a main dish. It has a slightly bitter flavor that is concentrated in the ridges that run lengthwise along the vegetable. These are usually pared off. Shop for firm Chinese okra.

Preparing Chinese Okra

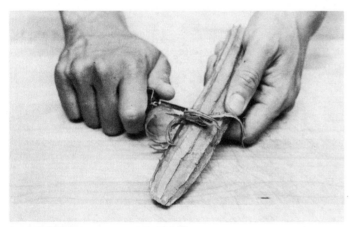

1. Peel the bitter-tasting ridges.

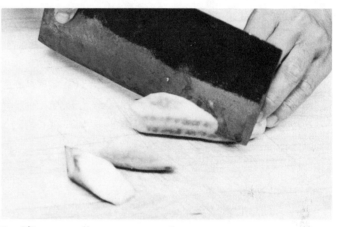

2. Slice or roll-cut, as you choose.

3. Stir-fry or blanch.

99

Chestnuts

The Chinese use the same Western chestnut with its sweet flavor and soft, mealy texture in stir-fried dishes and stews like Chinese Beef Stew (page 217) and in stuffings. Shop for large, dark brown chestnuts in the fall, when they are in season. Dried chestnuts, once soaked, can be used like fresh chestnuts.

Preparing Chestnuts

1. Boil the chestnuts for 30 minutes, shells on.

2. Peel the outer skin first.

3. Peel the inner skin, revealing the golden meat. Chestnuts are usually used either whole or split in half.

FANCY-CUT VEGETABLES

The Chinese are masters at creating beautifully sculptured food, and there are chefs who are specially trained for that function. However, there are a few easy fancy-cut vegetables that you can make to add that special touch to your Peking Duck dinner or to garnish that special dish. Some, such as Flower Carrots, can be used as ingredients. Others, such as Tomato Roses, function as a pretty and edible garnish. (The Chinese never waste anything.) Scallion Brushes serve a double function: they look pretty as a garnish, and they serve as a means of conveying hoisin sauce from its bowl to a pancake for wrapping Peking Duck (page 176) or Roast Suckling Pig (page 214).

Flower Carrots

Any time a dish calls for sliced carrots, you can use a few extra strokes of the cleaver to convert them into delightful flower shapes. Carrots must be blanched before they are incorporated into stir-fried dishes or soups, unless they are sliced very thin.

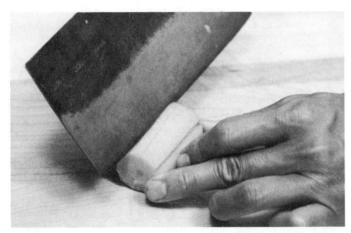

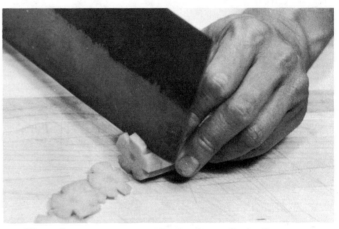

1. Cut scraped carrots into 3- or 4-inch chunks. Angling the cleaver, cut V shapes ⅛ to ¼ inch deep into the side of the carrot. Repeat the procedure, spacing the grooves evenly around the outside of the carrot. (Make four or five cuts, depending on the size of the carrot.)

2. Slice the carrot crosswise to form little flowers.

Pepper Fans

Given a few simple cuts with a sharp cleaver, ordinary green peppers make a particularly attractive garnish for dishes containing shredded ingredients, or peppers, or both. Blanch or stir-fry the peppers gently to develop their deep green color and to cook them partially.

1. Cut the pepper in half lengthwise and remove the seeds. Cut the halves again to make quarters.

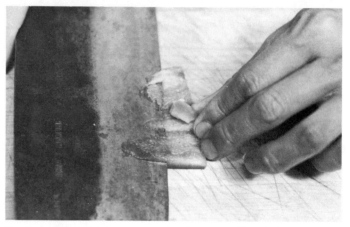

2. Parallel-cut to remove the inner walls of the pepper, and trim the quarters to make flat rectangles.

3. With the point of a cleaver, shred the peppers, but not all the way to the end, to make a fringe.

4. Pepper fans make an attractive garnish. Here they add color to Chicken Shreds with Hot Peppers (page 147).

Scallion Brushes

These are used to garnish roast duck and roast pig. Use with Peking Duck (page 176) and Mu Shu Pork (page 196) to convey the hoisin sauce from the bowl to the pancake in which the duck or pork is wrapped.

1. Trim the scallions, cutting off the stem end and leaving them in 3-inch lengths. Make a 1-inch cut through one end.

2. Rotate the scallion on its axis and make another 1-inch cut, perpendicular to the first. Make a third and fourth cut at an angle to the first two.

3. The result resembles a flower bud opening. Repeat the procedure at the opposite end.

4. Drop the scallions into ice water.

5. After a minute or two, the ends curl attractively.

Tomato Roses

Red, symbolizing happiness and prosperity, is a favorite color in China. A red garnish, thus, is quite festive.

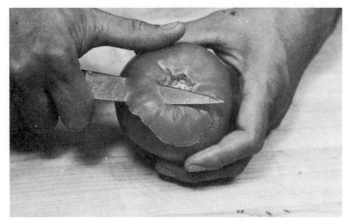

1. Use a ripe but still firm tomato. Start paring at the crown, cutting a thin strip about ½ inch wide.

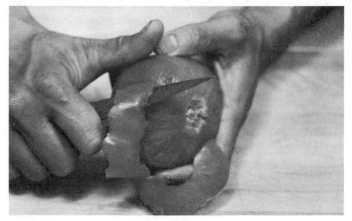

2. Continue paring the long strip for two or three revolutions.

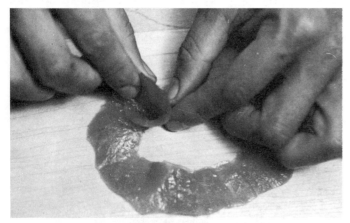

3. Roll the strip skin side out into a tight spiral.

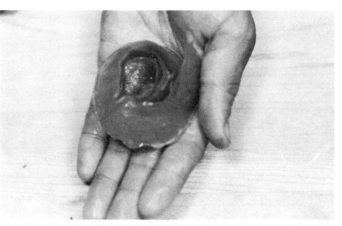

4. The spiral will naturally be narrower on one side. Hold the wide side in the palm of your hand.

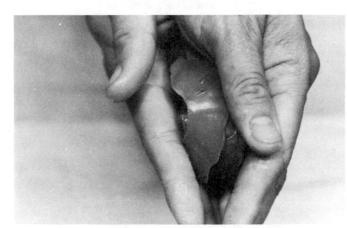

5. Put your other hand over the rose.

6. Transfer it to the other hand. It forms a rose automatically. Use it to garnish Fried Rice (page 280) or any plain, light-colored dish.

Chicken and Other Small Poultry

CHICKEN IS PERHAPS THE MOST VERSATILE OF FOODS. The widest variety of techniques is used in its preparation; they constitute the largest section in this book. Chicken is invariably a part of any Chinese meal.

Chicken breasts can be butterflied and stuffed (page 135), shredded and stir-fried with chili peppers (page 147), or velveted for a special texture (page 143). Wings can be marinated and stuffed, then deep-fried for an extraordinary appetizer (page 150). The dark meat is especially prized for stir-fried dishes (page 154) or for steaming. The feet are braised or used in stock for their rich flavor, the gizzards cut up and deep-fried. The Chinese cook makes use of every part of the chicken.

When you shop, look for chickens that weigh at least 3 pounds. We prefer larger roasting chickens of 4 to 5 pounds because they are richer in flavor and are easier to bone. Larger chickens also have a higher meat-to-bone ratio. Be sure that you are buying a roasting chicken, however, and not a stewing or a baking hen; hens are tough and cannot be steamed or stir-fried.

THE WHOLE CHICKEN

Slow-Steeping Chicken

This technique is used for delicate foods, such as chicken or fish. It applies the gentlest possible heat so that the flesh of the chicken or fish remains extremely moist with a satiny texture the Chinese call "smooth."

The food simmers in liquid for a few minutes, then the heat is turned off, the pot tightly covered, and the food left to steep to finish cooking. Slow-steeping produces a texture quite different from that of foods cooked at a constant simmer. It takes longer, but the results are worth the extra time.

This is a good technique to use when you are preparing many dishes on a small stove. Once it starts steeping, the pot can be removed from the stove.

White-Cut Chicken (White-Cooked Chicken)

Slow-steeping in water flavored only with ginger and scallion produces a chicken of incomparably delicate flavor. The gentle heat makes the chicken retain its moisture, and one last step ensures that the chicken will remain juicy—the cooked chicken is plunged into ice water to firm the flesh and trap the juices. For maximum juiciness, the Chinese prefer chicken with the bones still red and the flesh satiny. This simple dish is usually served cold or at room temperature with a dipping sauce, soy sauce, or oyster sauce. This makes it an easy first course, served perhaps on a bed of watercress, or, for summer dining, a light main course. It can be prepared a day ahead and cut up at the last minute. The water in which the chicken cooks can be saved and added to stock. White-Cut Chicken can be used in chicken salad, chicken in aspic, or as a substitute for cold poached chicken. As a variation, instead of scallions and ginger, flavor the water with sliced carrots, yellow onions, celery, parsley, bay leaf, and thyme.

1 roasting chicken, 4 to 4½ pounds (see note)
2 whole scallions
2 slices fresh ginger root
1 teaspoon salt
3 quarts water, approximately
3 trays ice cubes

METHOD: Steeping
Note: Smaller fryers can be used. Adjust cooking time accordingly.

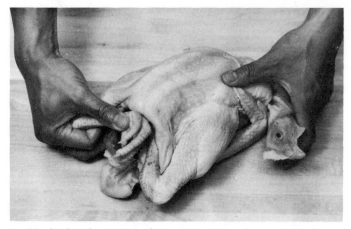

1. Tuck the feet into the cavity to make a more compact package.

2. Add the scallions, ginger and salt to a pot containing enough water to cover the chicken.

3. Place the chicken in the pot. If the water level is too low, add more.

4. Bring the water to a simmer. As the water heats, skim off the scum that rises to the surface. When the scum is gone (about 10 minutes), cover the chicken and let it simmer gently for a total of 20 minutes. Turn off the heat and let it steep, still covered, 40 minutes longer. (Steep 15 minutes longer if you want the bones to lose their red color and the chicken to be more well done.)

5. Fill a large bowl with equal parts ice cubes and water. Lift the chicken from the pot with a large strainer and plunge it into the ice water.

6. This forces the juices to retract into the chicken meat, making it extremely juicy.

7. Turn the chicken in the ice water to chill it thoroughly. Then pat it dry with paper towels and wrap it in plastic wrap. Keep it refrigerated until time to serve it, or at room temperature up to 1 hour.

Cutting a Chicken into Pieces

White-Cut Chicken is cooked whole to maintain its juiciness; just before serving, cut it into bite-sized pieces. This is a popular way to do that.

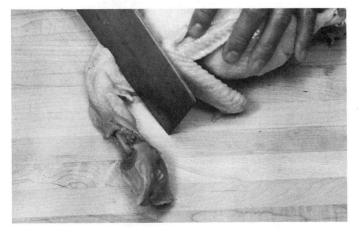

1. Cut off the neck with a cleaver.

2. Cut the wings off at the body. Set them aside.

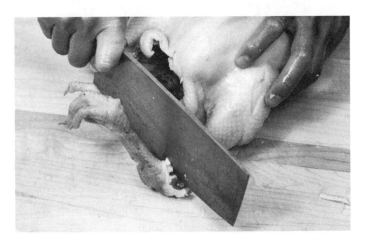

3. Cut the feet off at the drumstick. Set them aside.

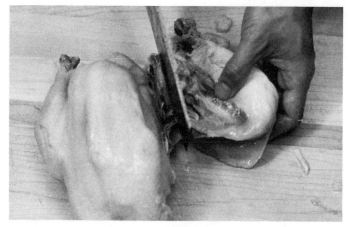

4. Cut around the skin at the thigh joint. Pull it back with your hand to expose the thigh joint, and sever it from the carcass with the cleaver.

5. Holding the carcass by the backbone, cut through the series of joints attaching the ribs to the back, separating the back from the breast. Chop the back crosswise into three pieces. Arrange the pieces in a line on a serving plate.

6. Position the cleaver over the keel bone, which runs down the center of the breast. Hit the back of the cleaver with your free hand to drive it through the breast, splitting it in two.

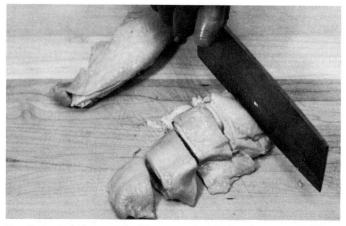

7. Cut each breast half crosswise into about six pieces 1 inch thick.

8. Arrange the pieces on the plate, reassembling them as neatly as you can.

9. To cut up the wing, first cut crosswise just above the joint, leaving a V-shaped piece.

10. Trim off the wing tip, but keep the parts together so that they look like a whole wing when you put them on the plate.

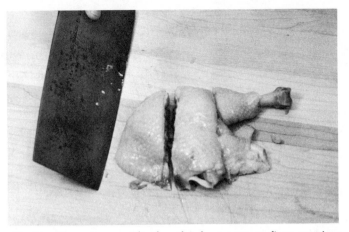

11. Do the same with the thigh quarter, first cutting crosswise just above the joint, leaving a V-shaped piece. Then cut through the rest of the pieces with one or two whacks of the cleaver.

12. Prepare a dipping sauce (see page 112) and serve it with the cold chicken arranged neatly on a plate.

DIPPING SAUCE

The pure, simple flavors of White-Cut Chicken call for a suitably pungent counterpoint in the dipping sauce. Scallions and ginger root, jolted to their full fragrance by a quick dousing of hot peanut oil, offer the perfect flavors.

4 scallions, white part only, shredded
2 teaspoons finely minced fresh ginger root
2 tablespoons thin soy sauce
1 tablespoon salt
4 tablespoons peanut oil

SERVES 4 as a main course, 6 as an appetizer.
MAY BE PREPARED up to a day ahead of time and cut up at the last minute. Serve cold with a dipping sauce.
SUGGESTED BEVERAGE: Chardonnay or Macon Blanc

1. Combine the scallions, ginger, soy sauce, and salt in a small bowl.

2. Heat the peanut oil in a small saucepan until it begins to smoke. Immediately pour it over the scallions to release their fragrance.

Soy Sauce Chicken (Red-Cooked Chicken)

Though this chicken is slowly steeped, just like White-Cut Chicken, the contrast between the two finished dishes is startling. Soy Sauce Chicken is cooked in sauce that is at once slightly salty from the two types of soy sauces; sweet from the sugar; spicy on account of the peppercorns, anise, and fennel seed; and mellow and winy from the rice wine.

This is a good dish to serve cold; it is even better made a day in advance because the spices continue to flavor the chicken. Chinese delicatessens and markets generally sell precooked Soy Sauce Chicken in halves, cutting up each half only on request so that the chicken remains juicy. Whenever you need only half a chicken at home, don't cut up the other half until you are ready to serve it.

SOY SAUCE BRAISING LIQUID:
2 cups dark soy sauce
2 cups light soy sauce
½ cup Chinese rock sugar or brown sugar
1 tablespoon whole Sichuan peppercorns, roasted
1 whole star anise
½ teaspoon fennel seed
2 slices fresh ginger root
2 cups chicken broth
½ cup Shaoxing wine or dry sherry

1 roasting chicken, 4 to 4½ pounds
Sesame oil (optional)

METHOD: Red-Cooking

Put the braising liquid ingredients into a pot large enough to hold the chicken. Add the whole chicken and heat to simmering.

1. Turn the chicken several times in the sauce while it simmers so that it colors evenly. Simmer for 20 minutes, then turn off the heat and let the chicken steep in the spices for 1 hour. The liquid can be saved and reused.

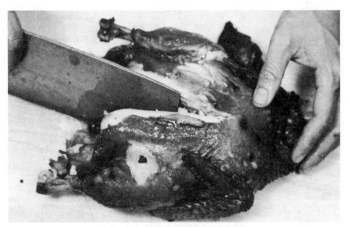

2. Cut through the chicken lengthwise, dividing it in half. The chicken is quite easy to cut when cooked.

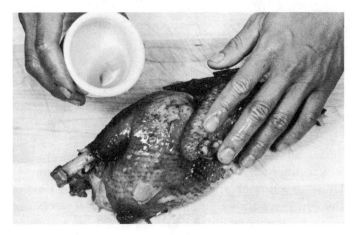

3. *Optional:* Rub each half with sesame oil to give the chicken an attractive gloss and heighten the flavor.

Cutting Chicken Halves into Pieces

SERVES 4 as a main course, 6 as an appetizer.
BEST PREPARED a day in advance and cut up at the last minute. Serve cold.
SUGGESTED BEVERAGE: Light Zinfandel or Gamay

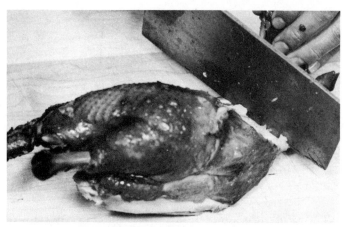

1. Cut off the wing at the body joint.

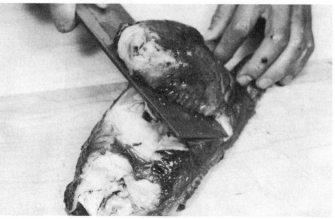

2. Cut off the thigh at the body joint.

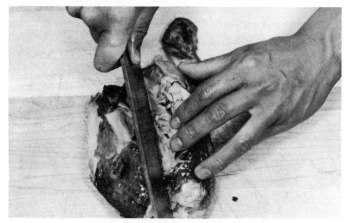

3. Cut the carcass, which is mostly breast, in half lengthwise.

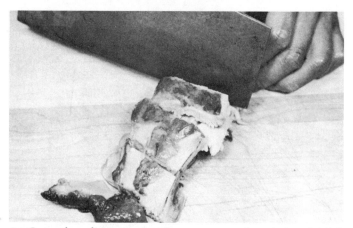

4. Cut the breast sections crosswise into 1-inch pieces.

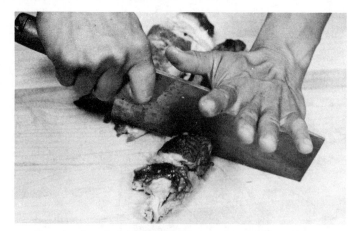

5. Cut the back sections crosswise into 1-inch pieces. These are bonier and require more pressure on the cleaver. Place the edge of the cleaver where you want to make the cut, and hit the back of the cleaver to chop through it.

6. Cut the thigh and wing as described for White-Cut Chicken (page 107), and reassemble the chicken on a platter. Serve the cut-up chicken with roasted salt and pepper for dipping (page 70), or with a little of the braising liquid, or just plain.

Skewering Poultry

We use this technique of sealing the cavity of a chicken or duck to entrap internal marinades, secure stuffings, and keep air from escaping in preparations such as Peking Duck (page 176).

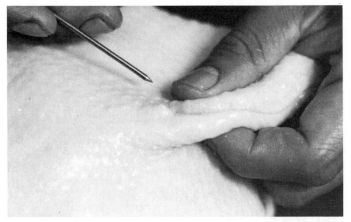

1. Thread a poultry skewer through the skin flaps over the tail vent, rolling the skin in repeated S-curves.

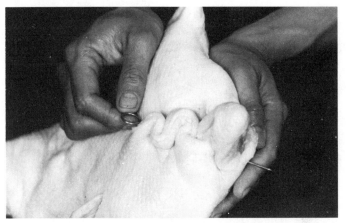

2. Insert the skewer through the tail.

3. To make the closure airtight, tie a string around the skewered area, looping it several times.

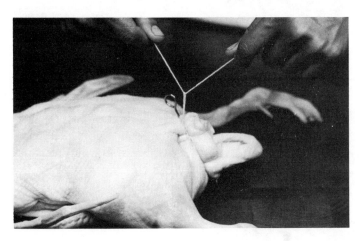

Salt-Roasting Chicken

Chicken roasted in salt is totally unexpected—not salty at all, but rather tender and flavorful, because the salt seals it completely as it roasts. The chicken's cavity is filled with a tasty marinade, then the chicken is wrapped in caul fat to keep it moist. This is a dish that is equally delicious hot and cold. Restaurants and shops that make it usually use rock salt, but coarse salt works as well. It may be prepared up to a day ahead; take the chicken out of the salt, wrap it in plastic wrap or aluminum foil, and refrigerate. Keep the marinade inside to keep the chicken moist. It should not be reheated; serve it at room temperature.

Salt-Roasted Chicken with Marinade

1 roasting chicken, 4½ to 5 pounds
1 recipe Cantonese Roast Duck marinade (page 171)
1 large piece caul fat or cheesecloth soaked in oil
5 to 6 pounds coarse (kosher) salt or rock salt

METHOD: Salt-roasting

SERVES 4 to 6 as a main course.

MAY BE SERVED hot or cold; if cold, the chicken may be prepared up to a day in advance.

SUGGESTED BEVERAGE: Pinot Noir or Burgundy

Fill the chicken with the marinade, skewer it shut (see page 115), and allow it to dry for 1½ hours.

1. Wrap the chicken in a large piece of caul fat or cheesecloth soaked in oil.

2. Heat the salt in a pot on top of the stove over a low flame or in the oven at 350 degrees for at least 1 hour. Pour off some of the salt, leaving just enough to cover the bottom of the pot. Lay the chicken on top of the salt in the pot and cover it with the remaining salt. Cover the pot and bake the chicken at 350 degrees for 1½ hours.

3. Remove the chicken from the salt.

4. Pull off the salt that remains caked on the chicken. Be careful, because the salt is hot.

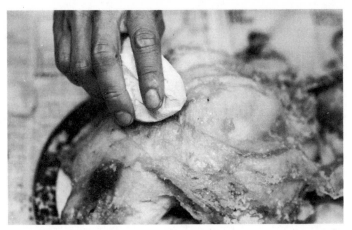

5. With a paper towel, wipe away the remaining salt. (The salt left in the pot can be reused.)

6. Peel off the caul fat, drain the marinade, and cut the chicken into bite-size pieces, using either of the methods described on pages 109 and 114.

Skinning Whole Chickens

The Chinese delight in making something seem to be what it isn't. Here the whole chicken skin is removed intact, without ever cutting into the skin. (We call it "chicken pajamas" at this stage.) Then the skin is stuffed and reshaped like a chicken, and—the surprise for the eaters—there is no chicken at all. The result is quite spectacular.

Chicken is ideally suited to this type of treatment because the skin is flexible and can withstand a certain amount of stretching, yet it is delicate. Of course, this is a treat for those of us who can never get enough skin.

Use a large roasting chicken (about 5 pounds) so that you can really stuff it. Also, the skin of large chickens is thicker and therefore less likely to tear.

Once the stuffing has been distributed inside the skin so that the chicken looks like a chicken again, the next step is to steam it to firm it up and render the fat. This much can be done hours, even a day, in advance. Finally, the chicken is brought to room temperature, then deep-fried for 5 to 10 minutes to brown and crisp the skin. The stuffing can be almost anything. In a fit of extravagance, we once stuffed it with lobster, truffles, and *foie gras*. Here we use a rich and delicious glutinous rice and pork stuffing. The effect is rather like a French galantine.

Use a large wok for deep-frying, and make sure the oil is absolutely hot. If there are any small holes in the skin, the hot oil will seal them.

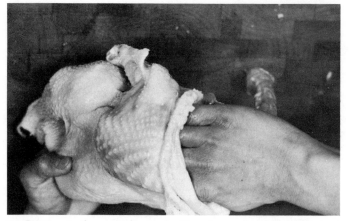

1. Start at the neck end. Reach under the skin to loosen it along the breast.

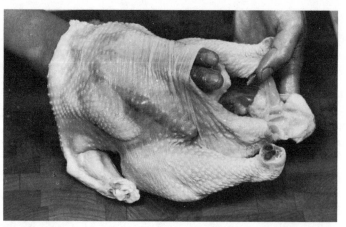

2. Slowly work your fingers all the way to the other end. Gently separate the skin where it is attached to the breast.

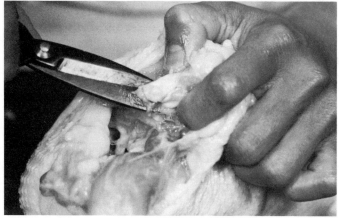

3. Find the joint where the wing is attached to the body. With poultry shears, cut the outer part of the joint, exposing the ligaments.

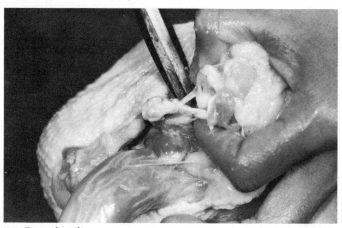

4. Cut the ligaments apart to sever the wing. Make sure all the ligaments are severed.

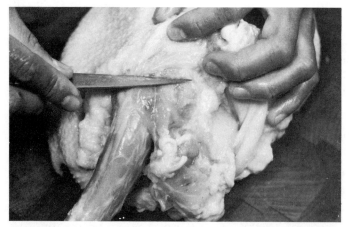

5. Start at the back of the neck to loosen the skin along the back. Use a paring knife, the edge always toward the bone, tip resting against the bone as well. Pull the skin away gently with one hand, freeing it from the neck with the knife where necessary.

6. As the skin is loosened, pull it gently over the chicken to turn it inside out. It is now attached only at the lower back and at the thighs.

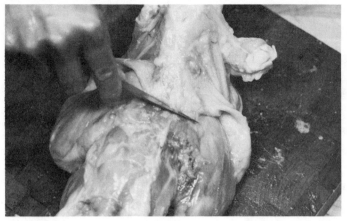

7. Continue cutting against the bone and gently pulling off the skin at the back.

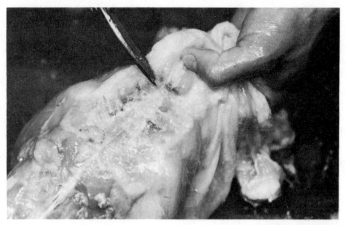

8. Use poultry shears or scissors to remove the tail from the carcass, leaving it attached to the rest of the skin. The tail reinforces the tail vent when you sew it closed, and it heightens the illusion that the re-formed chicken still has bones.

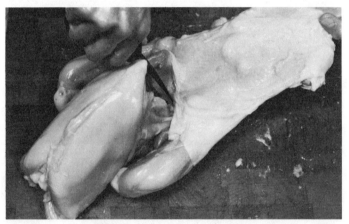

9. Turn the chicken breast up. Pull the skin gently over the thighs and drumsticks.

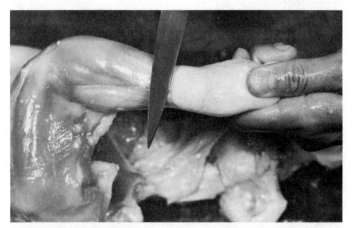

10. Using a paring knife, scrape the small fibers at the base of the drumstick to free the skin.

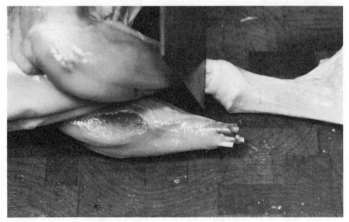

11. Chop the drumstick off just above the joint, leaving the joint attached to the skin. (This also makes the stuffed skin look more realistic.) Repeat with the other thigh and drumstick.

12. Turn the skin right side out. (Use the meat for other dishes.)

Whole Stuffed Chicken Skin
[see photo in color section]

1 recipe Glutinous Rice Stuffing (page 284)
1 whole chicken skin from a 5-pound roasting chicken (see above)
6 cups peanut oil for deep-frying

METHOD: Skinning, steaming (page 59), deep-frying (page 56)
SERVES 6 as a main course.
MAY BE PREPARED up to a day in advance through step 7. Deep-fry just before serving, and serve hot.
SUGGESTED BEVERAGE: Cabernet Sauvignon or Bordeaux

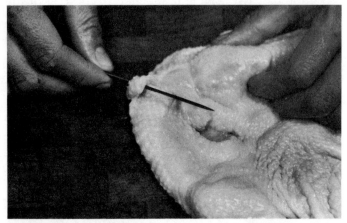

1. Prepare the stuffing. Sew the neck opening of the chicken closed.

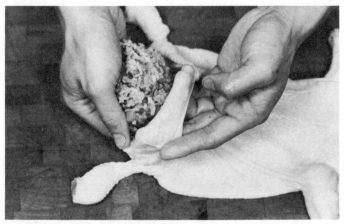

2. Start adding the stuffing through the tail vent. Push it all the way up into the neck.

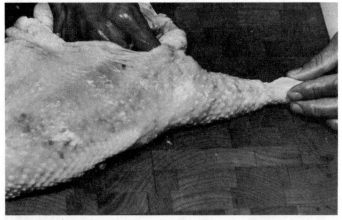

3. Simultaneously push it into the legs and thighs. The idea is to "build" a new chicken, forming it with stuffing to fill the skin. Do not overstuff. Fill the chicken, but keep the stuffing loose.

4. Sew up the tail vent carefully; the skin is thin.

5. Form the chicken on a plate that fits in the wok.

6. Steam the chicken 1 hour.

7. Pour off the liquid that has accumulated in the plate. At this point the chicken can be cooled and refrigerated for up to a day.

8. Heat the oil for deep-frying in a wok. When it reaches 375 degrees, lower the chicken into the oil with a strainer, breast up. Use the ladle to baste the breast with the oil until the chicken is brown and quite crisp (5 to 7 minutes).

9. Lift it out of the wok with a strainer. Let it drain, and serve it on a platter.

10. Serve the chicken whole. Eat by poking the skin with chopsticks to get at the stuffing, tearing off bits of skin at the same time.

Boning Whole Chickens

Boning a chicken for the first time is inevitably quite an undertaking. It may seem to take forever, but keep at it. Even if you mangle it slightly, it will still look fine once it's stuffed and cooked. With practice, boning becomes not too time-consuming. The Chinese do not cut a seam down the back the way others do, which eliminates sewing and makes it easier to form the chicken back to its original shape with stuffing.

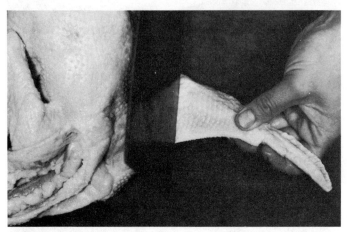

1. First, cut off the wing tips and second joints.

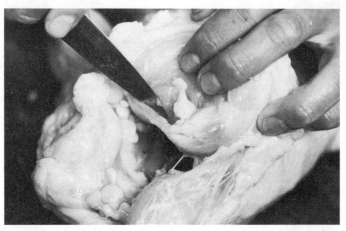

2. With a paring knife, find the wishbone and remove it.

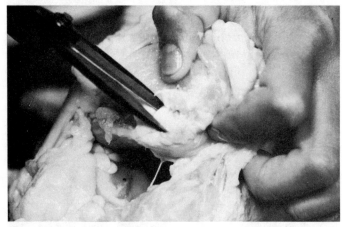

3. With scissors or poultry shears, find the joint where the wing joins the collarbone and clip it apart.

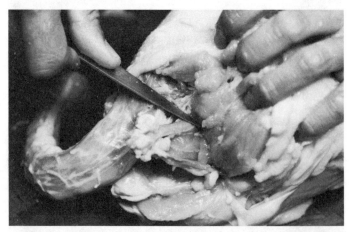

4. With a paring knife, find the keel bone, which runs down the middle of the breast. Start peeling the meat away from the side of the bone—but not the top ridge —cutting against the bone with the knife to loosen the meat.

5. Keeping the knife against the bone and pulling the meat away with the other hand, work toward the tail as far as you can without stretching the skin, about halfway.

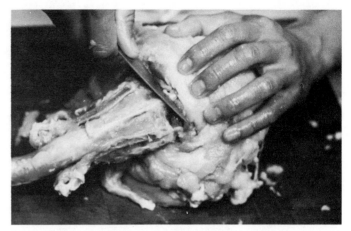

6. Turn the chicken over. Starting from the neck, work down the back with a paring knife, keeping the blade against the bone to separate it from the meat. Gradually, the carcass will begin to emerge.

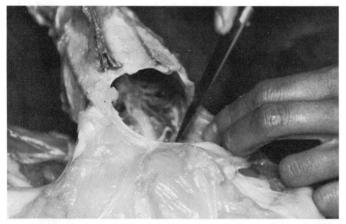

7. Once the top half of the carcass is free down to the end of the breastbone, feel for the joint where the thigh is attached to the body. Cut it free with scissors and continue to work toward the tail with the paring knife.

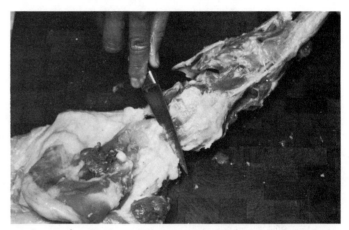

8. Once the entire carcass is exposed, cut it free at the tendons near the tail. Leave the tail attached.

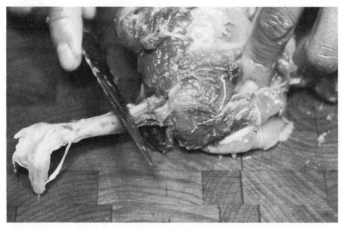

9. Make a slit down the inside of the drumstick to expose the bone. Scrape the meat away from the bone all the way around, and from the joint where it meets the thigh.

10. Cut the tendons that attach the drumstick to the thigh, but do not sever the meat.

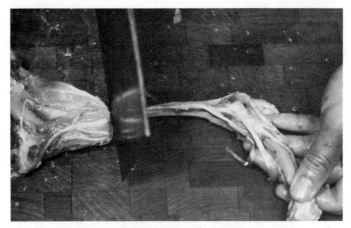

11. Continue scraping away the meat to expose the thigh bone. Remove the bones and set them aside for the stockpot. Repeat the procedure for the other thigh and drumstick.

12. Cut around the base of the wing drumette to free the meat.

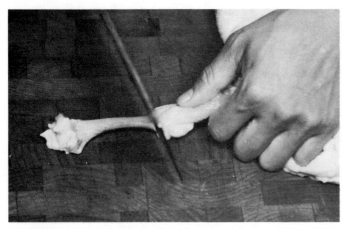

13. Then simply pull the bone away, turning the drumette inside out. This can be done with the fingers. Chop the wing bone near the body joint.

14. A small stub remains. This heightens the illusion that the stuffed boned chicken still has bones.

Beggar's Chicken
(BONED STUFFED CHICKEN BAKED IN CLAY)
[see photo in color section]

Of several legends concerning the origin of this recipe, the most common is that a beggar, having stolen a chicken and thinking he had eluded his pursuers, started to cook the chicken over a campfire by a river. When the chicken was half cooked, he heard his pursuers in the distance. In a panic, he buried the chicken in the mud. The pursuers arrived, but could not find the chicken and departed. The beggar retrieved the chicken, which by now was encased in mud, finished cooking it, and cracked it open—to discover an incredibly succulent meal.

Although it may seem complicated, Beggar's Chicken is only a series of simple steps, most of which can be done well in advance. A boned chicken is marinated; stuffed with ground pork, water chestnuts, ham, and scallions; wrapped in lotus leaves and clay, then baked. The effect is stunning when the guest of honor cracks the clay to release the heady aroma. The lotus leaves are optional, if dramatic, and a clay pot can be used instead of wet clay.

Consult an art-supply store for a porous, quick-drying type of clay that can take intense heat. If you cannot find the special clay, take the precaution of wrapping aluminum foil around the chicken before applying the clay so that the juices will not moisten the clay and cause it to crack.

1 roasting chicken, 4½ to 5 pounds, boned (see above)

MARINADE:
2 tablespoons Shaoxing wine or dry sherry
2 tablespoons thin soy sauce
2 teaspoons sesame oil
2 tablespoons finely minced fresh ginger root
2 tablespoons minced scallion

STUFFING:
6 Chinese black mushrooms, soaked, squeezed dry, and coarsely chopped
¼ cup tree ears, soaked, squeezed dry, and coarsely chopped
½ cup preserved Sichuan vegetables, coarsely chopped
6 fresh water chestnuts, peeled and coarsely chopped
2 scallions, coarsely chopped
½ pound pork, coarsely ground or chopped
¼ pound Smithfield ham, coarsely chopped
2 tablespoons peanut oil
2 tablespoons Shaoxing wine or dry sherry
1 tablespoon thin soy sauce
2 teaspoons sugar
Fresh caul fat for wrapping
Clay pot, or 2 large lotus leaves, soaked (or aluminum foil), and 6 pounds moist ceramic clay

METHOD: Boning, baking

SERVES 6 as a main course.

THE CHICKEN should be boned and marinated the night before, then stuffed and baked just before serving.

SUGGESTED BEVERAGE: Pinot Noir or Burgundy

Marinate the boned chicken overnight. To make the stuffing, stir-fry the vegetables, pork, and ham in the 2 tablespoons of oil; add the rice wine, soy sauce, and sugar, and mix all the ingredients well.

125

1. Stuff the mixture into the chicken until it is plumped up to its original shape. The caul fat and clay will hold in the stuffing, so you need not skewer the chicken shut.

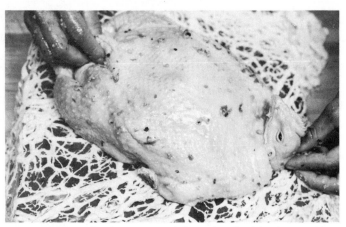

2. Wrap the chicken in caul fat. This holds the stuffing in as well as imparts richness to the chicken.

3. If you are using a clay pot, soak the pot in cold water according to manufacturer's directions, drain it, and put the chicken in it. Cover the pot and bake the chicken for 2 hours at 350 degrees.

4. To make Beggar's Chicken the authentic Chinese way, first wrap the chicken in the soaked lotus leaf or aluminum foil.

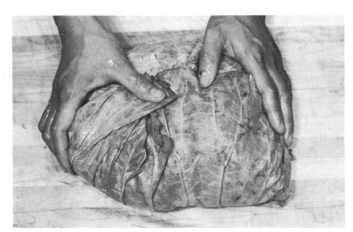

5. The chicken should be completely enclosed.

6. Double-wrap with the second leaf or sheet of foil.

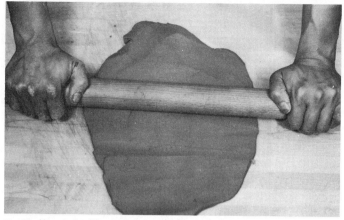

7. Roll out half of the moist ceramic clay to a thickness of ½ inch.

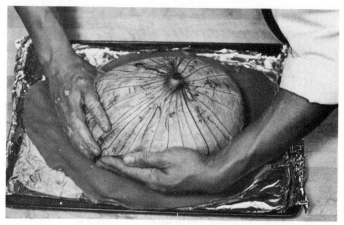

8. Lay it on a baking pan lined with aluminum foil. Set the lotus-wrapped chicken on the clay.

9. Roll out the other half of the clay on a sheet of waxed paper. Cover the chicken with the clay. (The waxed paper should be on the outside so that it can be peeled off.)

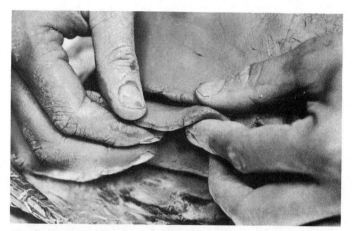

10. Bring up the edge of the bottom piece of clay and press it to the chicken.

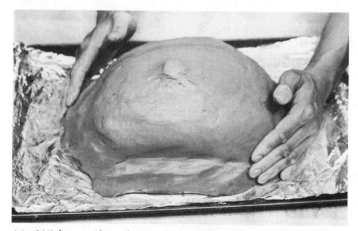

11. With wet hands, seal the clay all the way around. Press tightly to seal it well. Bake the chicken for 2 hours at 350 degrees.

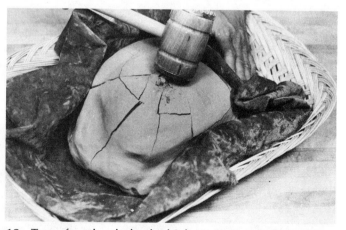

12. Transfer the baked chicken to a serving platter cushioned with a thick towel. Crack the clay with a mallet.

13. Peel away the lotus leaves or foil.

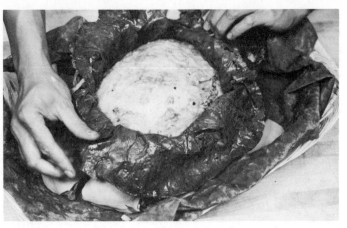

14. The peeled lotus leaves expose the tender, succulent chicken inside.

15. Traditionally, everyone eats the chicken by picking bite-sized pieces with chopsticks.

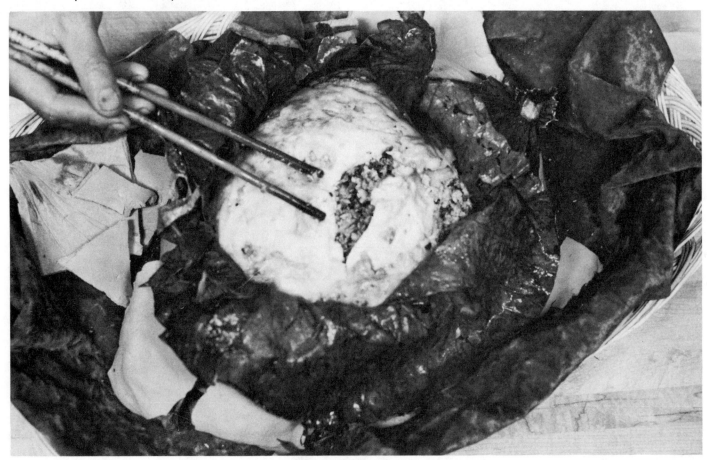

SECTIONED WHOLE CHICKENS

Cutting Up Raw Chickens

Chinese cooks begin cutting up raw chicken the same way Western cooks do, but they take it a few steps further, ending up with close to twenty pieces. Remember, the result will be eaten with chopsticks, so the pieces must be bite-sized. The Chinese take pleasure in picking around the bones, for the good flavor they impart and for the simple fun of it. This method of cutting up chicken is used for steamed dishes, such as Steamed Chicken with Sausage (page 131), and stir-fried dishes such as Beef with Asparagus (page 220) when chicken pieces are substituted for beef.

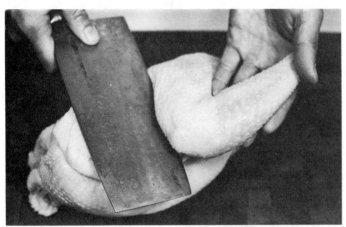

1. Pull the thigh away from the body of the chicken with one hand while cutting through the skin with the cleaver to expose the thigh joint. Cut through the thigh joint where it is attached to the body.

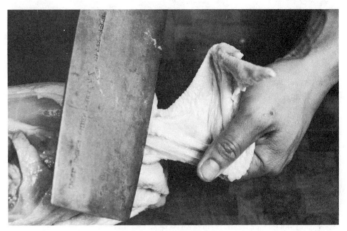

2. Cut off the wings at the body.

3. Cut the wings apart at the joint.

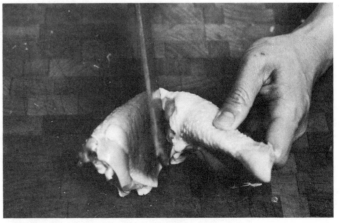

4. Cut the drumstick and thigh apart.

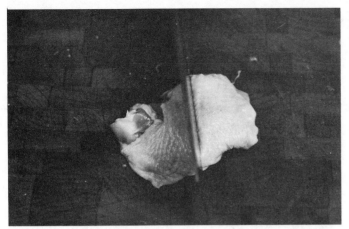

5. Cut the thigh in half. Either whack down hard on the thigh to break the bone, or set the cleaver on the right spot and hit the back of the cleaver hard with the back of the other hand or with a mallet.

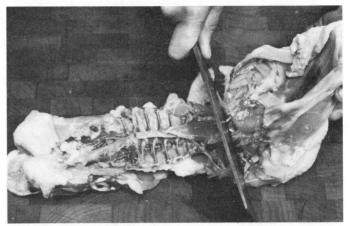

6. Split the chicken where the breast ribs meet the back ribs, separating the back from the breast.

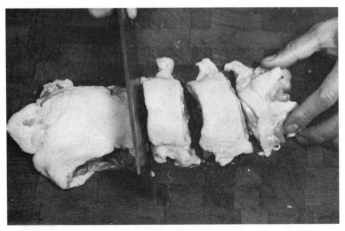

7. Chop the back into 1½-inch pieces.

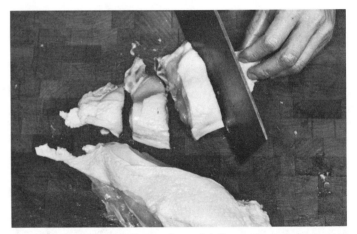

8. Split the breast down the middle and cut it into 1½-inch pieces.

Steaming Chicken

Steamed chicken is very delicate and a good vehicle for subtle flavors that enhance the chicken taste without the new flavors dominating as they do when stir-fried. The following recipe uses sausage, but equally nice are slices of lemon, fermented black beans, dried fruit peel, dried chrysanthemum flowers, black mushrooms, pickled vegetables—or just plain, with soy sauce and rice wine.

Steamed Chicken with Sausage

[see photo in color section]

1 roasting chicken, 4 to 4½ pounds, cut up (see page 129)
4 Chinese pork sausages, thinly sliced diagonally

SAUCE:
2 tablespoons thin soy sauce
2 tablespoons Shaoxing wine or dry sherry
1 tablespoon sesame oil
1 teaspoon sugar
Pinch of salt

METHOD: Steaming (page 59)
SERVES 4 to 6 as a main course.
SUGGESTED BEVERAGE: Light Zinfandel or Beaujolais

1. Arrange the back pieces on a plate.

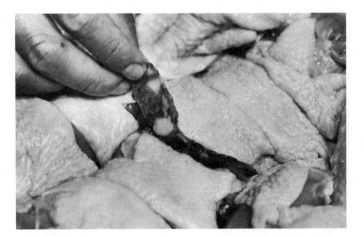

2. Surround them with the rest of the chicken pieces. Between the pieces, insert thin slices of pork sausage. Put the breast meat on the bottom, so that it is surrounded by the longer-cooking dark meat.

131

3. Pour the flavoring sauce over the chicken.

4. Place the plate in a steamer set in a wok for 60 to 70 minutes, or until the chicken feels firm rather than mushy when pressed.

5. Serve the chicken on the platter with the sausage.

Steamed Chicken in a Yunnan Pot
[see photo in color section]

This is a delicious soup with substance. The chicken is cut up, then quickly blanched to rid it of any scum so that the finished broth will be clear, rich, and delicate, very much like a double consommé. It is similar to a French *pot-au-feu,* but without chunky vegetables. The dish cooks and comes to the table in a specially designed ceramic pot with a chimney in the middle. The pot itself is placed in water in another covered pot or a wok. The steam condenses off the lid of the pot and back onto the chicken in a gentle mist. This differs from the usual method of steaming, in which the steam surrounds the food and the plate. Pot-steaming is more gradual and subtle. However, if you do not have a Yunnan pot, you can steam this dish in the usual way. Just cut the steaming time to 1½ hours. The dipping sauce for White-Cut Chicken (page 112) makes a delicious accompaniment.

1 roasting chicken, 4 to 4½ pounds, cut up (see page 129)
3 slices fresh ginger root, cut into 2-inch sections
3 scallions, cut into 2-inch sections
Salt to taste
¼ cup Shaoxing wine or dry sherry
Chicken broth to cover

METHOD: Pot-steaming

SERVES 4 as a main course.

SUGGESTED BEVERAGE: Dry Sauvignon Blanc or Sancerre

1. Blanch the chicken in boiling water for 2 minutes to float away some of the scum. Drain the chicken and rinse it well.

2. Arrange the chicken in the Yunnan pot with the ginger, scallions, salt, and Shaoxing wine, and pour in enough broth to cover the chicken.

3. Cover the pot and set it in a wok with enough hot water to come halfway up the pot. Steam it for 2 hours. Check the level of the water from time to time and add more if necessary.

4. Serve the chicken in its dish in the broth.

CHICKEN BREASTS AND WINGS

Boning Chicken Breasts

Boning chicken breasts is much easier than most people think. It takes little practice, and it can be applied to any type of cooking, not just Chinese. Remove the tendon because it tends to shrivel up the filet when it cooks. Boned chicken breasts are wonderful stuffed, particularly in the two styles that follow here. Boning breasts is the first step in the wonderful cubed and shredded chicken dishes described on pages 142 and 147. Beginners should partially freeze the breast for about 15 minutes, to firm the meat and make it easier to work with. Save all bones for stock.

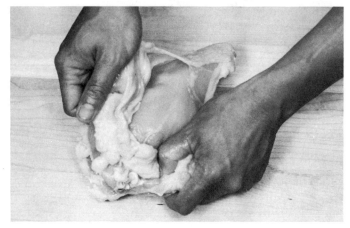

1. Pull off the skin.

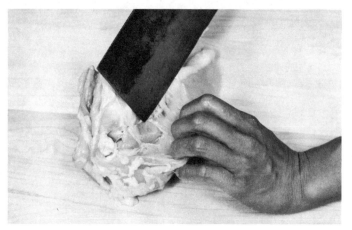

2. Starting with the keel bone (the center of the breast), pull the meat away from the bone, using the cleaver more as a guide than as the main means of separating the breast meat from the bone. Always keep the blade edge against the bone, and cut parallel to the ribs.

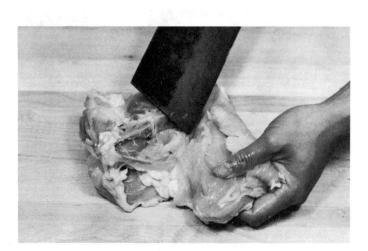

3. Work slowly and gently, finally pulling the entire breast away from the bone.

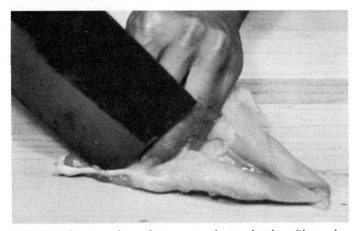

4. Find the tendon that runs through the filet, the long, narrow muscle nestled inside the breast. It must be removed so that the breast doesn't shrivel when cooked. Cut the meat to expose the end of the tendon.

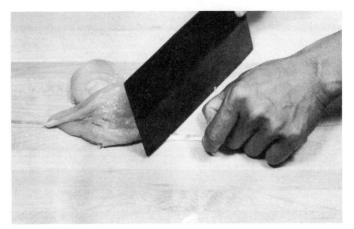

5. Hold the end of the tendon in one hand. Lay the cleaver against the chicken breast to hold it in place while you pull the tendon out of the filet. (At first you may find it easier to grasp the end of the tendon with a paper towel to get a better grip.)

Stuffing Chicken Breasts

Whereas a Western cook might stuff a chicken breast by pounding the boned meat thin and wrapping it around a filling, a Chinese cook butterflies the breast with a single cut parallel to the cutting surface. Then the breast is folded around the filling and deep-fried. Most deep-fried dishes use a batter to form a protective coating, but chicken has such a delicate flavor that we prefer to leave it plain. The stuffing keeps the chicken moist, and when the chicken is cut crosswise into bite-sized pieces it provides a contrast in colors.

Butterflying a Boned Chicken Breast

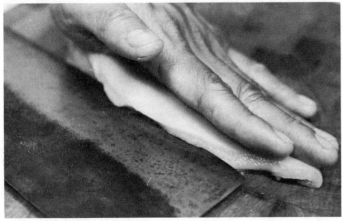

1. Hold the boned breast flat on the cutting board. With the cleaver parallel to the board, parallel-cut to butterfly the breast.

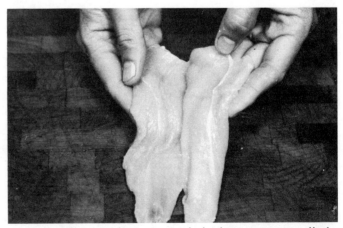

2. Stop the cut about ½ inch before you cut all the way through. Try to keep the halves of equal thickness.

We offer two styles of stuffed chicken breasts. The first, made with shrimp paste, is excellent stir-fried with vegetables. (First stir-fry the vegetables, then add the fried and sliced stuffed breast to heat through.) The second has a stuffing of Smithfield ham and is served with a vegetable sauce as an elegant main course or as appetizers without the sauce.

Chicken Breasts Stuffed with Shrimp

1 recipe Basic Shrimp Paste (page 256) or Basic Fish Paste (page 246)
4 large chicken breasts, boned (see page 134) and butterflied (page 135)
4 cups peanut oil for deep-frying

METHOD: Boning, parallel cutting, deep-frying (page 56)
SERVES 4 as a main course, 6 as an appetizer.
SUGGESTED BEVERAGE: Chardonnay or Macon Blanc

1. Spoon some of the paste onto one half of a butterflied breast, but not so much that the breast can't be folded over to enclose the filling completely. Fold the breast to enclose the filling. Seal in the stuffing by pressing the two edges together. Repeat for the other breast.

2. Heat the oil in a wok to 350 degrees (medium hot). Slide the stuffed breasts into the oil one at a time.

3. Deep-fry the breasts until they are brown (about 5 minutes). Test by pressing one; if it is mushy, the chicken is not yet done.

4. Remove the stuffed breasts from the wok, drain them on paper towels, then cut on the diagonal into ½-inch slices.

5. Arrange on a serving platter in pinwheel fashion and serve.

Phoenix and Dragon
[see photo in color section]

4 thin slices Smithfield ham
1 whole chicken breast (about 1 pound), boned (see page 134) and
 butterflied (page 135)
4 pieces fresh caul fat
¼ cup water chestnut powder, flour, or cornstarch
4 cups peanut oil for deep-frying

METHOD: Deep-frying (page 56), stir-frying (page 52)
SERVES 4 as a main course, 6 as an appetizer.
MAY BE DEEP-FRIED ahead of time, then warmed through in the sauce just
 before serving.
SUGGESTED BEVERAGE: Sauvignon Blanc or white Graves

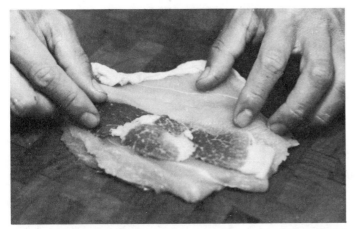

1. Lay 2 slices of ham on one side of the butterflied breast. Refold the breast, enclosing the ham. The ham flavors the chicken from the inside.

2. Lay the breast on a sheet of caul fat.

137

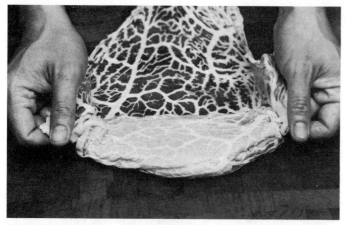

3. Roll it up tight. The caul is sticky, so it needs nothing to seal it.

4. Dust the surface with water chestnut powder, flour, or cornstarch. Shake off the excess.

5. Heat the oil in a wok to 350 degrees (moderate). Slide the chicken breasts into the oil one by one. When they have browned (about 5 minutes), remove one from the oil and press it. If it feels mushy, it needs further cooking. Remove and drain the chicken.

6. Slice the chicken crosswise diagonally into ½-inch pieces.

VEGETABLE SAUCE
2 tablespoons peanut oil
2 whole garlic cloves, lightly crushed
2 slices fresh ginger root
4 fresh water chestnuts, peeled and sliced lengthwise
½ cup bamboo shoots, sliced lengthwise
4 whole scallions, cut into 3-inch sections
1 tablespoon thin soy sauce
1 tablespoon Shaoxing wine or dry sherry
½ cup chicken broth
1 teaspoon cornstarch dissolved in 1 tablespoon cold chicken broth

Heat the oil in a wok and flavor it with garlic and ginger. Remove the garlic and ginger and add the water chestnuts, bamboo shoots, and scallions to

7. Arrange the pieces over vegetable sauce (see below) in a pattern to show off the contrast in colors and shapes.

the wok. Stir-fry them for 30 seconds, then add the soy sauce, wine or sherry, and chicken broth. When the liquid comes to a boil, stir in the dissolved cornstarch to thicken the sauce. Spread the sauce on a platter as a bed for the sliced chicken breast.

Cooking in Paper

The standard Chinese restaurant way of doing this—wrapping chicken with hoisin and soy sauces in aluminum foil—doesn't approach the classic preparation. In this, a thin slice of chicken is sandwiched between many layers of texture and flavor in a package of parchment or cellophane and deep-fried. The chicken actually steams in its package, although the parchment browns. As the packages cook, the ham flavors the marinated chicken, while the bamboo shoots and water chestnuts protect it from cooking too fast. The ham adds smokiness, the bamboo shoots and water chestnuts add sweetness and crunch, parsley adds perfume, and scallions add spiciness. Once you master the folding technique, you may find yourself making these often. Parchment Chicken makes a great appetizer or first course.

Be sure to wrap the packages tight so that oil does not get inside. For variations, use thin slices of fish fillets (see page 238 for cutting) or Barbecued Pork Strips (page 193) instead of chicken.

Parchment Chicken
[see photo in color section]

1 pound chicken breasts, boned (see page 134), thinly sliced diagonally

MARINADE:
1 tablespoon dark soy sauce
1 tablespoon Shaoxing wine or dry sherry
2 teaspoons sugar
1 teaspoon sesame oil
2 tablespoons oyster sauce
1 tablespoon Scallion-Ginger-Garlic Marinade (see below)

Parchment or cellophane cut into 30 to 40 6-by-6-inch squares

FILLING:
2 fresh red peppers (hot or sweet), shredded
1 bunch Chinese parsley, stemmed
4 large pieces bamboo shoot, thinly sliced
¼ pound Smithfield ham, thinly sliced
1 bunch (5 or 6) scallions, shredded
8 fresh water chestnuts, peeled and thinly sliced

6 cups peanut oil for deep-frying

METHOD: Cooking in paper, deep-frying (page 56)

Marinate the chicken breast 1 hour or more; remove and drain.

140

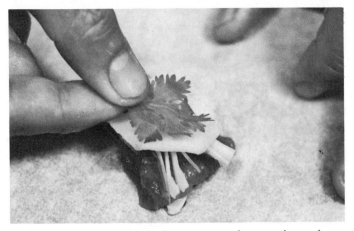

1. Place a piece of parchment on the work surface, point toward you. In the center, pile up the following, one atop the other, in this order:

A sliver of red pepper
A Chinese parsley leaf, light side up
A slice of bamboo shoot
A slice of marinated chicken
A slice of Smithfield ham
A few slivers of scallion
A slice of water chestnut
A Chinese parsley leaf, dark side up

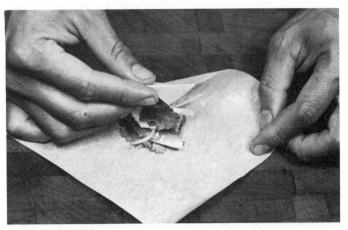

2. To fold the package, first fold up the point facing you.

3. Then fold in the sides.

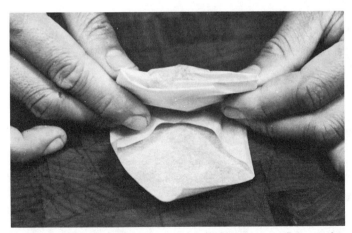

4. Fold the entire package in half, leaving a flap at the point away from you.

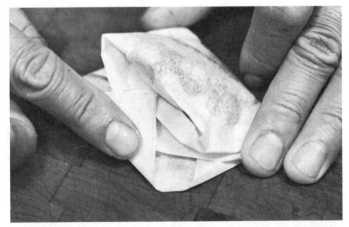

5. Tuck the flap in to secure the package. Repeat the procedure until all the parchment and ingredients are used up.

6. Heat the oil in a wok to 350 to 375 degrees, and deep-fry the packages about a dozen at a time. The chicken is so thin that it cooks almost instantaneously. After a minute or so, when the packages begin to brown, remove them from the oil and drain them, open side up.

7. To eat them, unfold the paper at the table and pick up the contents with chopsticks.

SCALLION-GARLIC-GINGER MARINADE
This delicious and versatile marinade is used to flavor Parchment Chicken. It can also be used in other chicken recipes, fish dishes, and on grilled meats, such as pork chops, lamb chops, and steak.

4 whole scallions
4 slices fresh ginger root
4 cloves garlic
¼ cup Shaoxing wine or dry sherry

Puree all the ingredients in a blender or food processor. Strain the marinade through a fine sieve, pressing the solids with chopsticks or a spoon to extract all the juices. Makes about ¼ cup.

MAKES 30 to 40 packages. Serves 6 to 8 as an appetizer, 6 as a first course.
SUGGESTED BEVERAGE: Light Chardonnay or Pinot Blanc

Cubing Chicken Breasts

A few easy cuts transform a boned chicken breast into small, uniformly-shaped cubes that stir-fry evenly and quickly. For visual harmony, cubed ingredients should be combined with other chunky ingredients, such as nuts, not with sliced or shredded vegetables. Cubed chicken breast can be stir-fried with cubed cucumbers for a variation of Spicy-and-Sour Cucumber Salad (page 80). In fact, it is excellent in any salad, Chinese or not. Or mix it

1. Lay a boned breast of chicken (see page 134) flat on a cutting board. Cut it into ½-inch strips, lengthwise.

2. Line the strips up and cut them crosswise at ½-inch intervals to make cubes.

with diced carrots, cashew nuts, zucchini or other crisp vegetables, or snow peas. Use it in soups, as a garnish for broth (page 325) or in wonton soup (page 309), for a more substantial meal. Cubed chicken should be blanched in boiling water for 30 seconds before it is added to soup.

Velveting Chicken Breasts

Velveting is a standard step in the preparation of numerous stir-fried chicken breast dishes. It involves coating the chicken pieces in a mixture of egg white and cornstarch and partially precooking them in *warm* oil or hot water. The coating and preliminary blanching give the chicken a velvety smooth texture; hence the name. Velveting does not brown the chicken; it only firms it up before a final stir-frying with other ingredients, and can be done in advance. Try making the recipe that follows for Spicy Chicken with Peanuts twice, once with velveted chicken and once with raw chicken cubes, and notice the subtle difference. Incidentally, this is not to be confused with Chicken Velvet (page 333), a totally different process used for soup.

1 whole chicken breast, boned (see page 134) and cubed (see page 142), about 1 lb.
1 tablespoon cornstarch
½ egg white
2 cups peanut oil

143

1. Toss the chicken cubes to coat with the cornstarch and egg white, mixed together. Let the chicken marinate at least 10 minutes.

2. Heat the oil until it is warm. Check the temperature by adding a piece of chicken to it. If it floats, the oil is hot enough. Immediately turn off the heat so that the oil does not get too hot. The object is not to brown the chicken at all, but to cook it so that it comes out glistening white. Add the chicken.

3. Stir the chicken pieces in the oil with chopsticks so that they don't stick to each other. Let them cook for 15 seconds, just until they turn opaque on the surface.

4. Set the chicken aside until you are ready to use it. *Note:* The oil can be saved, but it must be labeled "for use with chicken only." It should be reused only twice.

Spicy Chicken with Peanuts

With the chicken cubed and velveted well in advance, this dish goes together quickly. Typical of the Sichuan region, where it originated, the flavors are robust with garlic and scallions and hot with chili peppers. The contrast in tastes and textures is unbeatable. For variations, try cubed pork (not velveted), beef, or shrimp.

¼ cup raw unsalted peanuts
3 tablespoons peanut oil
4 whole dried chili peppers
4 scallions, thinly sliced
3 cloves garlic, thinly sliced

SAUCE:
1 tablespoon chili paste with garlic
2 tablespoons dark soy sauce
1 teaspoon sugar
1½ tablespoons Shaoxing wine or dry sherry
1 tablespoon Chinkiany vinegar, or 2 teaspoons red wine vinegar or cider
*   vinegar*
1 teaspoon sesame oil

1 teaspoon cornstarch mixed with 1 tablespoon cold chicken broth
1 whole chicken breast, cubed and velveted (see above)

METHOD: Velveting (page 143), stir-frying (page 52)
SERVES 2 as a main course.
CHICKEN MAY BE cubed and velveted in advance.
SUGGESTED BEVERAGE: Medium-sweet sherry or beer

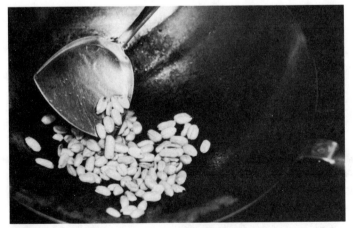

1. Stir-fry the peanuts over a high flame in 1 tablespoon of the oil until they develop a golden-brown color. This brings out their flavor. Take care not to let them burn. Remove them and set them aside.

2. Lower the flame to medium. Add the remaining 2 tablespoons of oil and flavor it with the peppers.

3. With the oil still at medium heat, add the scallions and garlic. Stir-fry them for 10 to 20 seconds, until their aroma rises from the wok.

4. Add the sauce ingredients. When the sauce comes to a boil, add the cornstarch dissolved in broth. The sauce must be thick enough to coat the chicken pieces. Since the chicken is not seasoned, the sauce is the seasoning.

5. Add the chicken pieces and the peanuts. Quickly toss to coat them well. Stir and toss the chicken for 10 to 30 seconds, or until the pieces are cooked through.

6. Turn the chicken out on a serving plate. The flavor should be quite spicy, but not so hot that you cannot taste the chicken. It is the interplay of flavors and textures that makes this such a superb dish.

Shredding Chicken Breasts

Long strips of shredded breast meat are attractive on the plate, cook in seconds, and are simple to prepare and have at hand to make a multitude of dishes. Combine them with other shredded ingredients, not with chunks, whether it be in a stuffing for Spring Rolls (page 315) or for a simple stir-fry.

1. Cut the breast crosswise into ¼-inch slices.

2. Cut the slices into ¼-inch shreds.

Chicken Shreds with Hot Peppers
[see photo in color section]

This is one of those dishes that is equally good hot and cold. Since the pepper seeds are removed, the spiciness is subtle, but nevertheless present. If you velvet the chicken ahead of time, the dish can be cooked at the last minute. You could also prepare it entirely ahead of time and serve it at room temperature with a squirt of fresh lemon as a spicy chicken salad, Chinese-style. The red and green peppers are shredded like the chicken.

2 small fresh hot red peppers, seeded and shredded
6 small fresh hot green peppers, seeded and shredded
2 tablespoons peanut oil

METHOD: Shredding, stir-frying (page 52)

1. Over moderate heat, stir-fry the peppers in the oil until they soften (about 30 seconds).

2. Add the sauce ingredients and the chicken. Mix well with the peppers, then add the cornstarch paste. Allow the sauce to thicken a few seconds, then transfer the finished dish to a serving plate.

SAUCE:
1 teaspoon salt
1 tablespoon Shaoxing wine or dry sherry
3 tablespoons chicken broth
½ teaspoon sugar

1 whole chicken breast, about 1 pound, shredded (see above) and velveted
(see page 143)
1 teaspoon cornstarch dissolved in 1 tablespoon cold chicken broth

SERVES 2 as a main course.
MAY BE PARTIALLY prepared ahead and served hot, OR PREPARED ENTIRELY ahead and served at room temperature.
SUGGESTED BEVERAGE: Beer

Preparing Chicken Wings

The wings are among the tastiest parts of the chicken, and with a little effort you can make them easy to eat. A few strategic cuts convert the drumettes into lollipop shapes. Removing the two bones from the second joint leaves long, thin cavities that are perfect for stuffing. In the process of frying, the wings practically reseal themselves. The preparation can be done up to a day in advance and the wings allowed to sit in the marinade, then quickly fried for an appetizer or first course. (Bring them back to room temperature before frying.)

Shaping Chicken Wings

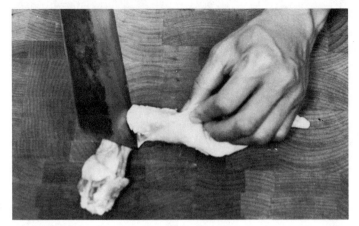

1. Cut the wing apart at the first joint, separating the drumette from the rest of the wing.

2. Cut off the wing tips; save them for broth, or braise them until they are soft so that even the bones are edible.

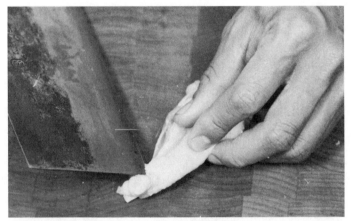

3. Cut through the tendons at the base of the drumette.

4. Scrape and push the meat toward the thick end.

5. Holding the meat down with the cleaver, pull the bone so that the meat wraps around the end.

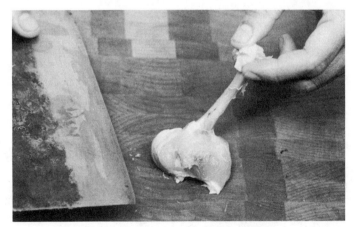

6. You should end up with a lollipop shape.

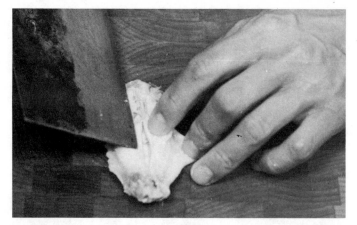

7. The second joints are difficult to work with when raw. The trick is to simmer them in water for 5 minutes to firm up the meat. When they are cool enough to handle, make a slice lengthwise down the middle of the back side.

8. Lift out the smaller bone.

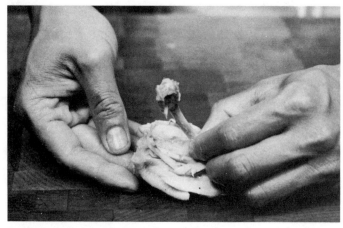

9. Carefully reach into the cavity, search out the larger bone, and pull it out.

10. Marinate the chicken wings, stuff the cavity, then form the wing back into its original shape.

Fried Chicken Wings

15 large chicken wings, prepared for stuffing (see above)

MARINADE:
2 tablespoons thin soy sauce
2 tablespoons dark soy sauce
1½ tablespoons sugar
1 tablespoon sesame oil
½ recipe Scallion-Ginger-Garlic Marinade (page 142)

STUFFING:
15 slivers Smithfield ham
15 leaves Chinese parsley or small spinach shreds or scallion slivers

BATTER:
2 eggs, beaten
1 teaspoon baking powder
4 tablespoons cornstarch or water chestnut powder
2 tablespoons water
1 teaspoon sesame oil
½ teaspoon salt

4 cups peanut oil for deep-frying

METHOD: Deep-frying (page 56)
SERVES 4 as an appetizer or first course.
THE WINGS MAY BE boned and marinated up to a day in advance, then stuffed
      and fried just before serving.
SUGGESTED BEVERAGE: Rosé wine or beer

Marinate the prepared wings at least 2 hours, then stuff the cavities with
the ham and Chinese parsley.

1. Using chopsticks, dip the stuffed wings into the batter and fry them in hot oil (375 degrees) for 3 to 4 minutes.

2. The hot oil seals them immediately, holding the stuffing inside. Remove the wings when they are nicely browned.

3. The drumettes need be dipped only at the meat end. The bone end can remain uncoated with batter. Deep-fry them 3 to 4 minutes.

4. Arrange the drumettes around the stuffed wings for
an elegant presentation.

DARK-MEAT CHICKEN

Boning Dark-Meat Chicken

The Chinese favor the dark meat of the chicken because of its rich flavor and juiciness. Some Chinese cooks even go so far as to use the dark meat for stir-frying and the rest of the chicken for stock. Dark meat is easy to bone and once boned it can be cut into bite-size cubes or shreds and used in any recipe for boneless chicken. Dark meat need not be velveted.

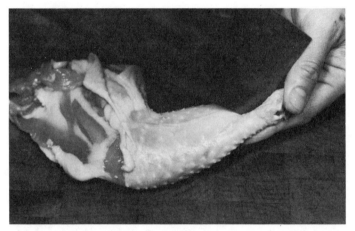

1. Hold the thigh quarter skin side down. Starting with the drumstick, make a slit down to the bone the length of the drumstick.

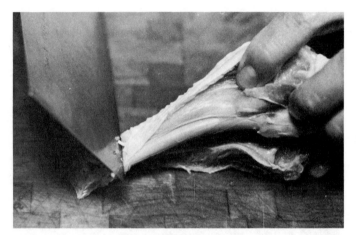

2. Do the same with the thigh.

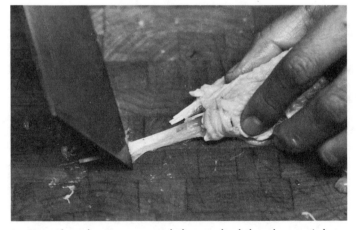

3. Run the cleaver around the end of the drumstick to free the skin. Pull the bone away from the tendons, holding the ends of the tendons in place with the cleaver.

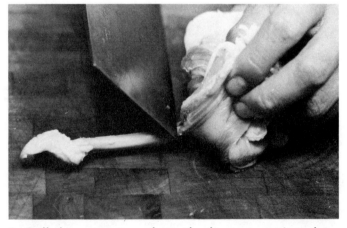

4. Pull the meat away from the bone, scraping along the bone with the cleaver, always holding the edge toward the bone.

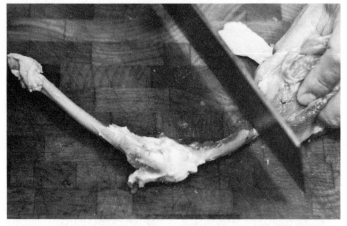

5. Keep going past the joint and do the same with the thigh.

6. Cut the boneless dark meat into 1-inch strips.

7. Cut the strips into squares.

Dark-Meat Chicken with Shallots
[see photo in color section]

Unlike light meat, dark meat can be reheated without worry of overcooking. Since there are no crisp vegetables in this dish to wilt, it can be prepared ahead and warmed just before serving. We prefer to leave the skin attached to the chicken to provide crisp texture and additional flavor, but the fat rendered from the skin should be spooned away. If you prepare the dish ahead, remove the skin before reheating or it will turn soggy. The skin can be shredded and stir-fried for cracklings.

*3 pounds chicken, thigh quarters (or all thighs), boned (see above) and
  cubed*

MARINADE:
1 egg, beaten
2 tablespoons Shaoxing wine or dry sherry
1 tablespoon thin soy sauce
Pinch of salt

154

¼ cup water chestnut powder or cornstarch
4 tablespoons peanut oil
4 tablespoons fermented black beans
2 tablespoons finely minced garlic
1 tablespoon finely minced fresh ginger root
15 small whole shallots, peeled
2 tablespoons chopped Chinese chives or regular chives

SAUCE:
1 tablespoon thin soy sauce
2 teaspoons sugar

METHOD: Stir-frying (page 52)
SERVES 4 as a main course.
MAY BE PREPARED ahead and warmed just before serving.
SUGGESTED BEVERAGE: Medium-bodied Zinfandel or Pinot Noir

Marinate the dark meat for 15 to 20 minutes.

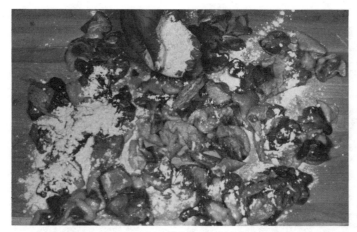

1. Dust the pieces of chicken (skin attached) with water chestnut powder or cornstarch. Shake off any excess.

2. Stir-fry the dark meat in the oil to brown it.

3. Make a well in the center of the wok by moving the pieces of chicken up the side of the wok where it is cooler, and spoon out the fat given off by the skin, leaving about 2 tablespoons.

4. Add the black beans, garlic, and ginger, mix them well, then add the shallots and the remaining ingredients. When the shallots have softened a little and the chicken is done (about 1 to 2 minutes), transfer to a serving plate.

SQUAB AND OTHER SMALL POULTRY

Braising and Deep-Frying Squab

The Chinese prize the rich dark-meat flavor and texture of squab, especially the Cantonese, who are famous throughout China for their ways with these little birds. This technique and the following one are both of Cantonese origin.

Here the squab is first braised to bring out its juicy texture and flavor, then the skin is allowed to dry, like duck for Peking Duck, so that the final deep-frying will crisp and brown the birds. You can braise and dry the birds up to a day in advance and reserve the final frying, which takes only a couple of minutes, for right before serving. The traditional garnish of lemon with roasted salt and pepper cuts the richness perfectly. Small Cornish hens (which are less expensive) can be prepared in the same way, as can quail.

Crisp Soy Squab

1 or more 1-pound squabs
1 recipe Soy Sauce Braising Liquid (page 113)
Malt-sugar mixture (1 part malt sugar or honey to 4 parts boiling water)
4 cups peanut oil for deep-frying

METHOD: Braising, deep-frying (page 56)

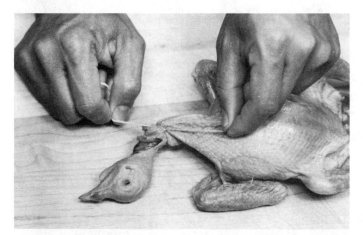

1. Tie a piece of string around the bird's neck to help you remove it from the braising liquid and to hang it to dry.

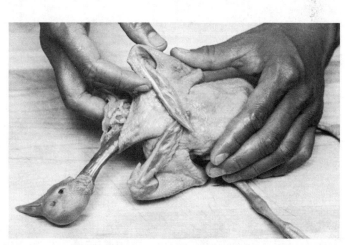

2. Tuck the wing tips in back to keep them from swinging free. This saves trussing.

3. Plunge the whole squab into boiling water for 2 minutes to rid the bird of scum and help pull the skin taut.

4. Drain the squab over the water. Braise in Soy Sauce Braising Liquid for 15 minutes. Hang the squab to dry over a bowl for 1 hour, then paint it with the malt-sugar mixture.

5. Just before serving, heat the oil in a wok. When it is moderately hot (350 degrees), add the squab. Deep-fry to brown the skin (about 5 minutes). (Save the strained oil for another use, but only with fowl.)

158

Cutting Up Small Poultry

Once cut into pieces that are manageable with chopsticks, the bird is re-assembled to look whole for presentation. Other small poultry, such as Cornish hens and quail, can be cut up in the same manner.

One squab per person as a main course.
MAY BE PREPARED in advance through step 4.
SUGGESTED BEVERAGE: Cabernet Sauvignon, rich Zinfandel, or Bordeaux

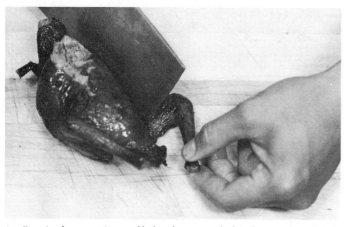

1. Begin by cutting off the legs and thighs at the thigh joint. Cut off the wings.

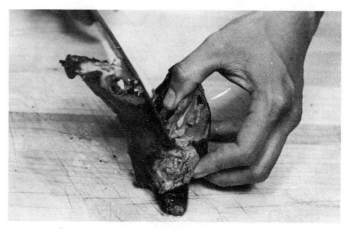

2. Cut the squab in half lengthwise, separating the backbone from the breast section.

3. Cut the back into 1-inch sections and set them on a plate.

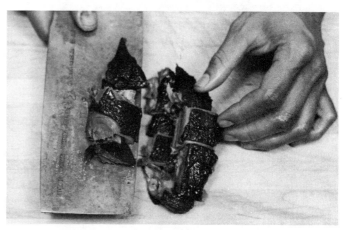

4. Cut the breast into 1-inch sections and set them on top of the pieces of back.

 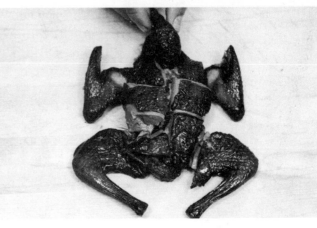

5. Reassemble the wings and thighs with the rest of the body.

6. Add the head.

7. Two squabs side by side on a serving plate, their parts reassembled, garnished with cut lemon. Roasted salt and pepper (page 70) is often served for dipping.

Mincing Squab

Mincing is a way to extend expensive ingredients, especially fowl and meat. And while being economical, it also makes an elegant presentation. In the recipe that follows, for example, with every ingredient finely chopped, the vegetables balance the delicate squab in an especially festive dish.

To mince, use a cleaver (or two alternately) to chop the food until the pieces are very tiny and even. Use the broad side of the cleaver to scoop the food toward the center. A food processor has a tendency to overmince, resulting in a pâté-like texture, so it is better to use the cleaver. The texture of the meat should be preserved. Vegetables are minced in the same way, but they require less force.

Minced Squab with Lettuce Cups
[see photo in color section]

Each guest wraps some of the squab mixture in a lettuce cup. In Chinese etiquette the package is eaten with chopsticks, but it is easier to handle with the hands. The dish usually is served as an early course, functioning as a sort of salad, served with deep-fried transparent noodles (page 40).

2 squabs, 1 lb. each
2 tablespoons peanut oil
2 cloves garlic, minced
10 fresh water chestnuts, peeled and minced
½ cup minced bamboo shoots
6 Chinese black mushrooms, soaked, squeezed dry, and minced
4 scallions, minced
6 dried oysters, soaked, squeezed dry, and minced (optional) or 4 duck liver sausages, minced
½ teaspoon minced fresh ginger root
½ cup chicken broth reduced with squab bones (see step 7)
1 teaspoon sugar
2 tablespoons thin soy sauce
2 tablespoons Shaoxing wine or dry sherry
1 tablespoon oyster sauce
1 teaspoon cornstarch dissolved in 1 tablespoon cold chicken broth
2 heads Bibb or iceberg lettuce, leaves carefully separated into lettuce cups

METHOD: Mincing (page 49), stir-frying (page 52)
SERVES 6 as an appetizer or first course, 2 as a main course.
MAY BE PREPARED in advance through step 12.
SUGGESTED BEVERAGE: Gamay, Beaujolais, or light Spanish red wine

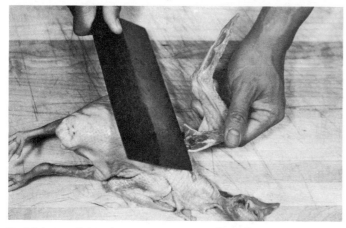

1. Using a thin cleaver, cut away the wings.

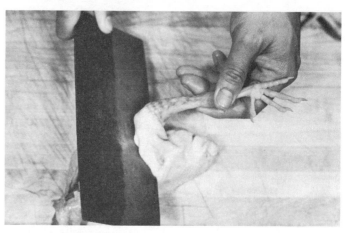

2. Cut away the thigh joints.

3. Pull off the skin, cutting it where necessary, and set it aside.

4. Bone the breasts. Scrape all the meat you can from the bone. Neatness does not count.

5. To remove the leg meat, make a slit the length of the leg to the bone.

6. Pull the meat away, cutting it off the bone where necessary.

7. Remove the small but tough tendon from each leg. Bone the second squab, then add the bones, feet, head, and wings to 1 cup chicken broth and reduce the liquid to ½ cup.

8. With two cleavers, start chopping the boned meat.

9. Chop until finely minced. Set aside.

10. Thinly slice the squab skin.

11. Stir-fry the skin in a little oil to render the fat and crisp the skin. This takes about 10 minutes.

12. As the skin browns, move it up the side of the wok. Set the crisped skin aside. The preceding steps can be done up to 8 hours in advance. Keep the minced squab refrigerated if it must stand longer than 1 hour.

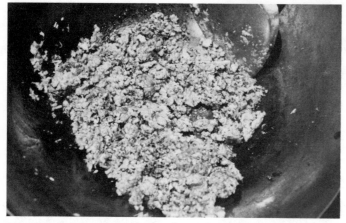

13. Stir-fry the squab in the oil with the garlic over high heat until it is browned lightly.

14. Add the remaining minced ingredients, mix them well, and add the reduced chicken broth, sugar, soy sauce, rice wine or sherry, and oyster sauce. Bring the mixture to a boil and stir in the cornstarch dissolved in broth.

15. Stir in the crisped skin and transfer the mixture to a serving plate.

16. Serve the dish surrounded by lettuce cups.

164

Duck

THE CHINESE LONG AGO put to rest the misconceptions that duck is greasy, hard to cook, and tough. The rich flavor of duck seems to be growing in popularity in this country. This is good, because properly cooked, duck is juicy, lean, and no more expensive than most good cuts of meat. It is considered quite an elegant selection, and the Chinese have perhaps one of the most varied and interesting assortment of techniques for preparing it in the world. These include the famous Peking Duck (page 176), considered by connoisseurs to be the single greatest technique for cooking duck; Smoked Tea Duck (page 174), a steamed whole duck finished with the incomparable flavor of smoking tea leaves; and a simple braised duck (page 168), which would be found in a home meal.

Such variety should not be surprising; after all, China was one of the first countries to domesticate the duck. Nearly all the ducks on the commercial market in the United States are descendants of the Chinese variety, called White Pekin and better known here as Long Island duck. Depending on how they are raised, the same variety can be quite fatty and full-breasted or relatively lean. Ducks raised in the East tend to be fatter than the Petaluma, California, ducks purchased in San Francisco's Chinatown for use in this book.

Another variety sometimes found in the United States is the Muscovy duck, a nonmigratory bird native to the jungles of Brazil. It has darker flesh and a stronger taste than Long Island (or Pekin) duck. The duck bagged by hunters is most often a mallard, which has a strong, gamy taste. The Chinese use these mostly with herbs to make medicinal broth.

The Chinese prefer to purchase poultry with head and feet attached, and this is especially helpful for Peking Duck. The long neck skin makes it possible to inflate the duck properly in an important preliminary step. It's possible to make Peking Duck with a trimmed and frozen duck.

Duck freezes better than other poultry. Duck fat seems to be more stable and suffers little loss of quality when frozen. Although a freshly killed duck with its head and feet attached is ideal, frozen duck produces a satisfactory result.

Trimming Whole Ducks

Frozen ducks come already trimmed, but if you buy a fresh duck at a farm or in a Chinese market, the head and feet will still be attached. The odds and ends must be removed to prepare the duck for braising and for some types of roasting.

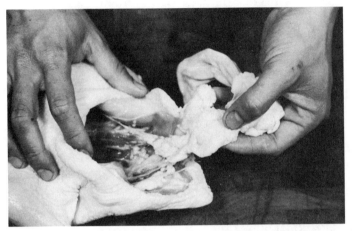

1. Remove the fat from around the tail. This fat can be rendered for stir-frying and refrigerated or frozen for future use.

2. Cut off the feet where they join the drumsticks. Reserve them for stock.

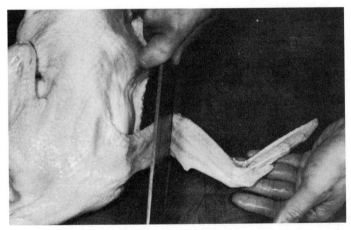

3. Cut off the wings at the second joint, leaving only the drumette attached.

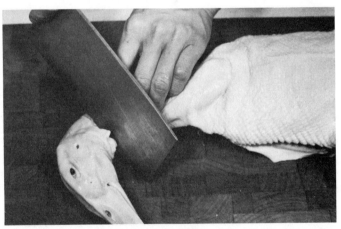

4. If the head bothers you, cut it off and reserve it for stock.

5. Cut off about half the neck and reserve it for stock. Leave a generous flap of skin around the neck.

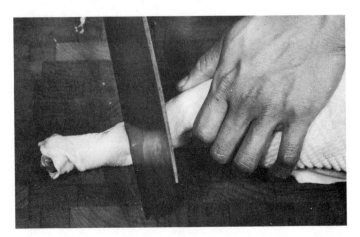

Braising Whole Ducks

Braising a duck results in an excellent duck "stew" that can be made a day ahead and reheated without loss of taste or quality. Deep-frying will harden the skin, making it less likely to come apart during the long cooking. Then it is simmered slowly in liquid. The duck becomes very tender—so tender, in fact, that it can be eaten whole with chopsticks, which makes it a favorite for informal meals.

It can also be cut into bite-size pieces like chicken (see pages 109 and 114), or boned and served with noodles in broth for a hearty cold-weather dinner, or shredded with cucumbers for a saladlike first course.

The braising liquid can be frozen for use at a later date.

Five-Spice Braised Duck

Here we use the Soy Sauce Braising Liquid from Soy Sauce Chicken and add a spice bag—a Chinese *bouquet garni*—to flavor the duck during braising.

1 whole duck, 4½ to 5 pounds, trimmed (see page 167)
1 recipe Soy Sauce Braising Liquid (page 113)
4 to 6 cups peanut oil for deep-frying

SPICE BAG:
2 pieces Chinese cinnamon
2 whole star anise
2 pieces dried tangerine peel
1 teaspoon five-spice powder
4 slices fresh ginger root
4 whole scallions

GARNISH:
4 bunches watercress
10 large whole black Chinese mushrooms, soaked

METHOD: Deep-frying (page 56), braising
SERVES 4 as a main course.
MAY BE PREPARED a day ahead, reheated, and served hot or at room temperature.
SUGGESTED BEVERAGE: Chianti Riserva or Barolo

Marinate the duck in Soy Sauce Braising Liquid for at least 2 hours.

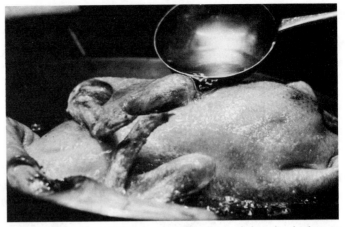

1. Pat the duck dry thoroughly. Reserve the braising liquid. Deep-fry the whole marinated duck in moderately hot oil (350 degrees) to brown it (about 10 to 15 minutes).

2. Ladle the hot oil over the portion of the duck that is not submerged in oil. When it has browned, lift the duck out of the wok, drain it well, and pat it dry with paper towels.

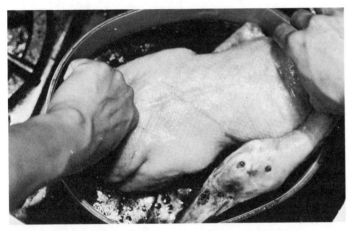

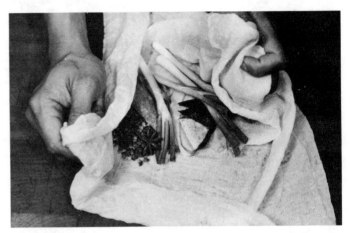

3. Put the duck and the marinade in a pot.

4. Put the spice-bag ingredients in a piece of cheese-cloth and wrap them tightly. Add this to the braising liquid, bring it to a simmer, and let it braise gently, covered, for 90 minutes.

5. Remove the duck from the braising liquid and drain it well. Set the duck on a platter. Add ½ cup braising liquid to 1 quart boiling water. Wilt the watercress in this mixture for a few seconds.

6. Surround the duck with the wilted watercress and serve it whole. Whole black Chinese mushrooms also make a good garnish. Cook them briefly in the diluted braising liquid.

Roasting Ducks with an Internal Marinade

This unusual way to flavor duck works from the inside rather than the outside. The cavity of the duck is filled with a pungent and delicious marinade. The method is ingenious, because not only does the marinade make a tasty duck, it also keeps the duck meat moist. The skin gets very crisp while the meat cooks through, but it never becomes dry. The duck's own juices combine with the marinade, creating a unique duck sauce. The recipe for the traditional Cantonese Roast Duck marinade follows, but you can also innovate with your own creations—for example, lemon and orange juice with spices. Cantonese Roast Duck marinade can also be used in Salt-Roasted Chicken with Marinade (page 116).

Cantonese Roast Duck is the duck that's so often seen in the windows of Chinese markets across the country.

Cantonese Roast Duck
[see photo in color section]

MARINADE:
3 slices fresh ginger root
3 whole garlic cloves, lightly crushed
3 whole scallions, cut into 3-inch sections
1 tablespoon peanut oil
1 tablespoon bean sauce
2 tablespoons thin soy sauce
1 tablespoon Shaoxing wine or dry sherry
1 tablespoon sugar
1 whole star anise
1 teaspoon whole Sichuan peppercorns, roasted
¼ cup chicken broth
8 whole stems Chinese parsley

1 whole duck, 5 to 5½ pounds, trimmed (see page 167) and inflated
* (optional, see page 178)*

BASTING LIQUID:
1 cup boiling water
¼ cup malt sugar or honey

METHOD: Roasting
SERVES 4 as a main course.
MAY BE SERVED immediately or prepared ahead and served at room temperature.
SUGGESTED BEVERAGE: Medium-bodied Cabernet Sauvignon or Bordeaux

1. Stir-fry the ginger, garlic, and scallions in the oil for a few seconds, then add the remaining marinade ingredients. Reduce the heat and simmer the mixture for 2 or 3 minutes, then pour it into a bowl to cool.

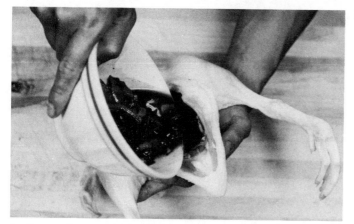

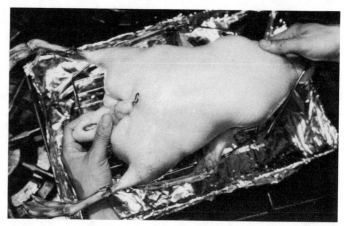

2. Pour the cooled marinade into the inflated duck through the tail vent. Skewer the tail shut (see page 115). Tie a string at the neck, and hang the duck to dry the skin for 1½ hours in front of a fan, 3 to 4 hours in a cool place. If you are not using duck with its head on, sew the neck flap closed and hang the duck from a hook through the neck.

3. Roast the duck on a rack over a pan of water according to this timetable:

15 minutes at 450 degrees, breast up
25 minutes at 350 degrees, breast up
35 minutes at 350 degrees, breast down
5 minutes at 450 degrees, breast down
10 minutes at 450 degrees, breast up
Total time: 1 hour 30 minutes
Baste after each interval with the basting liquid.

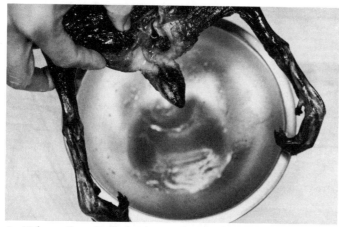

4. When the duck is done, open the tail vent and let the marinade drain into a bowl.

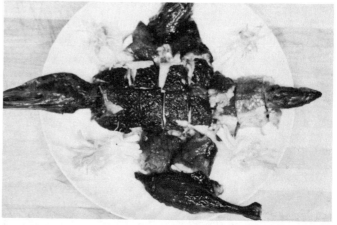

5. Cut up the duck Chinese-style (see pages 109 and 114). Arrange it on a platter. Serve the degreased marinade on the side or poured over the duck.

172

Dry-Marinating Ducks

Salt and five-spice powder make a fragrant dry marinade, which draws some of the moisture from the duck so that the spices penetrate the bird. The marinated duck is then steamed to firm it and cook it, then is finished by deep-frying or smoking. Chicken and squab may also be prepared this way.

3 tablespoons coarse (kosher) salt
1 tablespoon whole Sichuan peppercorns, roasted and crushed
2 teaspoons five-spice powder

METHOD: Dry-marinating (page 173), steaming (page 59), smoking

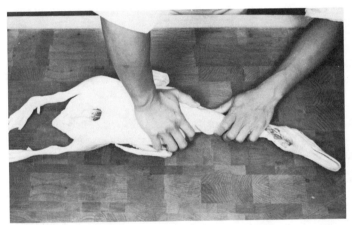

1. Press down hard on the duck's breastbone to flatten it.

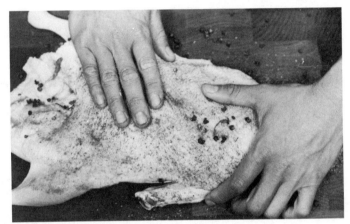

2. Rub the dry marinade over the trimmed duck.

3. Rub the dry marinade inside the cavity.

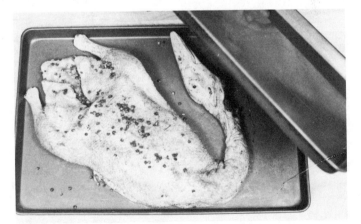

4. Put the duck on a baking sheet and cover it with another flat sheet.

5. Weight down the top sheet with a pot filled with water to flatten the duck and to make it release some of its own moisture. Let it marinate like this, in a cool place or in the refrigerator, for 2 days. Use the marinated duck to make Smoked Tea Duck, or steam it for 2 hours to cook and render all the fat. Let it sit at room temperature for several hours to dry, then deep-fry in about 4 cups oil until crisp.

Smoked Tea Duck
[see photo in color section]

This is a cold dish that can be prepared well in advance; in fact, we find that ducks smoked 2 days in advance are more flavorful. Chicken and squab can be dry-marinated and smoked in the same way. Reduce the steaming time according to the size of the bird; allow 15 minutes per pound for chicken, 30 minutes for squab.

The smoking process doesn't actually cook the duck. It adds flavor to a duck already cooked by steaming and changes the texture of the flesh to something similar to that of ham. A covered barbecue grill (such as any of the kettle-type barbecues on the market) is perfect.

1 whole duck, 5 to 6 pounds, trimmed (see page 167), dry-marinated for 2 days (see above)
6 slices fresh ginger root, cut into 3-inch sections
6 whole scallions, cut into 3-inch sections

FOR SMOKING:
1 cup raw long-grain white rice
1 cup dark Chinese tea leaves
½ cup brown sugar or hickory chips

METHOD: Steaming (page 59), smoking
SERVES 4 to 6 as an appetizer.
MAY BE SMOKED up to 2 days ahead of time and refrigerated until ready to serve. Allow to reach room temperature.
SUGGESTED BEVERAGE: Young, full-bodied Cabernet Sauvignon or Barolo

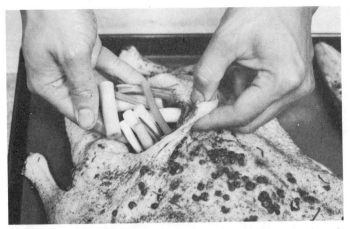

1. Stuff the cavity of the duck with the ginger and scallions.

3. Make a bed of charcoal in the barbecue and ignite it. When the surface turns to ash, set a metal pie plate containing the smoking ingredients on the coals.

2. Steam the duck (see Steamed Chicken with Sausage, page 131) for 1 hour 15 minutes (for a 5-pound duck) to 1 hour 30 minutes (for a 6-pound duck) to draw out the fat and to cook the duck gently, keeping it moist. Drain the duck and remove the ginger and scallions.

4. Cover it with a grate and set the duck on the grate.

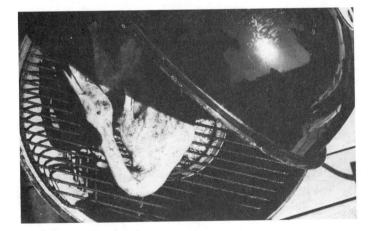

5. Cover the grill and smoke the duck for 45 to 50 minutes, turning it every 10 to 15 minutes to brown it evenly. Check the coals periodically to make sure they don't die down.

175

6. Serve the duck whole and cut it up at the table, or
cut it up Chinese-style (see pages 109 and 114).

Peking Duck
[see photo in color section]

In China, the roasting of Peking Duck is so highly regarded that chefs specialize in it, and some restaurants serve only Peking Duck dinners. Ducks are bred and raised especially for this dish: they are force-fed much as the French force-feed geese for *foie gras*. The birds' movements are restricted so that their flesh stays tender and juicy. The ducks are roasted in special ovens over a fire of dried jujube date, peach, and pear branches to give the skin and meat a unique fragrance. Then the duck is served in an elaborate, multicourse dinner that often includes special dishes made from the wings, webbed feet, and even the tongues.

Three courses are essential: first, the breast meat and crackling crisp skin are served with scallion brushes, hoisin sauce, and thin pancakes; second, the dark meat is stir-fried with vegetables; and third, a rich duck soup is made by simmering the bones in chicken stock.

The traditional method of making Peking Duck probably originated in the imperial kitchens during the Ming dynasty in the seventeenth century. In China one would not cook Peking Duck at home because a home kitchen simply is not equipped for it. Fortunately, the American oven makes it possible to come very close to the authentic dish.

Of all the elaborate banquet dishes in Chinese cuisine, this is the most glorious. It produces the ultimate duck—super-crisp skin with all the fat melted off, and meat that is tender and moist. Although it requires a great deal of preparation, much of it can be done well in advance and in easy stages. Because of the time and effort involved, prepare at least two ducks and invite as many guests as you can accommodate. Allow one duck for every four people. It takes little additional time to prepare a second duck.

The first step is to inflate the duck, forcing air between the skin and flesh so that the skin roasts crisp and the fat melts, basting the meat. This requires a duck with its head attached, so that the neck skin can be tied off to keep the duck inflated. In China, a sorghum stalk is used as a tube through which air is blown into the duck. An air compressor or a bicycle pump is much more effective, however. If you don't have one, or if you cannot obtain a duck with its neck intact, there is an alternate method: massage the duck all over, slowly working the skin away from the fat, taking care not to tear it. The skin won't be as evenly crisp, but it will be quite acceptable.

The second step is to scald the duck in boiling water, then hang it to dry. The scalded skin dries better. The duck is dried in front of a fan to hasten the process. It is then basted with malt sugar to give it a rich golden color and allowed to dry again before it is finally roasted.

Once the duck is roasted, it is ready for the final preparations: cutting up the breast meat and skin to serve with the pancakes, shredding the dark meat and preparing the vegetables for stir-frying, and putting the bones in a stockpot to make the third and last course, duck soup.

The inflating, scalding, and drying may be done the day before; the pancakes and the scallion brushes may be made in advance, too.

The proportions that follow are for two ducks that will serve eight people.

2 whole ducks, about 5 to 5½ pounds each, head and neck intact
¼ cup malt sugar or honey dissolved in 1 cup boiling water
16 pancakes (page 294)
16 Scallion Brushes (page 103)
1 can hoisin sauce

THE SOUP:
Bones from cut-up Peking-roasted ducks
8 cups chicken broth
2 pounds celery cabbage (Napa cabbage)
1 tablespoon thin soy sauce
Salt and pepper to taste
2 teaspoons sesame oil
4 tablespoons chopped scallion tops for garnish

THE STIR-FRY:
8 fresh water chestnuts, peeled and sliced
2 cups bean sprouts, plucked at both ends
3 tablespoons peanut oil
2 garlic cloves, crushed
2 tablespoons thin soy sauce
1 tablespoon dark soy sauce
2 tablespoons Shaoxing wine or dry sherry
Dark meat from 2 Peking-roasted ducks, shredded

METHOD: Roasting, stir-frying (page 52), braising
SERVES 8 as a three-course meal, more if part of a banquet.
SUGGESTED BEVERAGE: Well-aged Cabernet Sauvignon or Bordeaux

Inflating the Duck

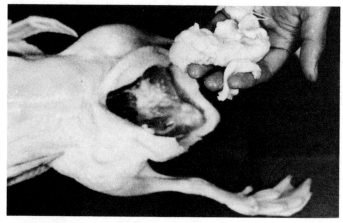

1. Pull the fat from the tail end. Discard it, or save it for sautéing or pâtés.

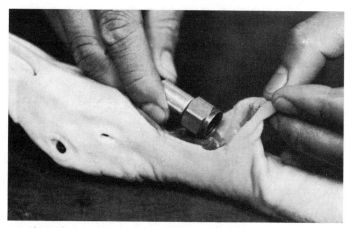

2. Slip the nozzle of an air compressor or bicycle pump under the neck skin.

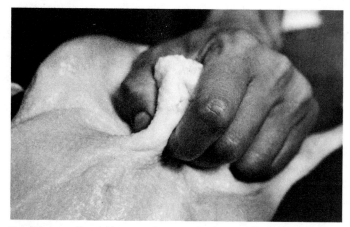

3. Clamp the tail vent shut with the other hand.

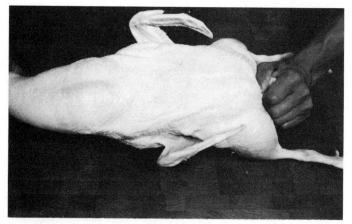

4. *S-l-o-w-l-y* start to pump air under the skin.

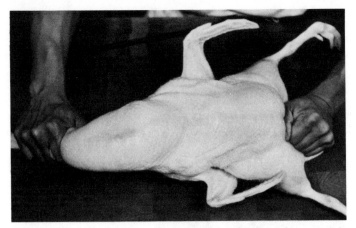

5. Continue to pump very slowly until the skin stands away from the body. (A duck will take quite a bit of air pressure, but sooner or later it can burst, so stop as soon as the skin is completely separated, about 30 seconds to 1 minute.) Release the tail vent and dry the duck with paper towels.

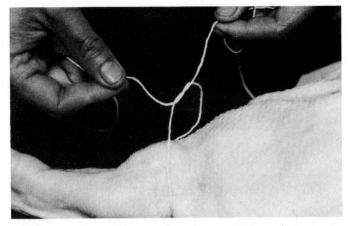

6. Skewer the tail vent shut (page 115) and tie it airtight. Loop another piece of string at the base of the neck; tie the knot, but leave it loosened.

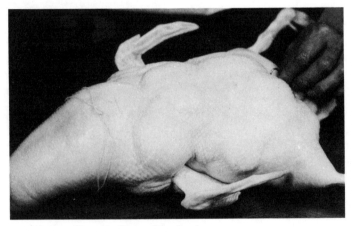

7. *S-l-o-w-l-y* reinflate the duck.

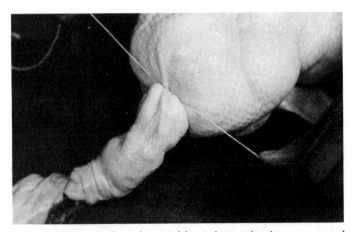

8. When it is inflated, quickly tighten the knot around the neck to make an airtight package. The loose end of the string can be used to hang the duck for drying.

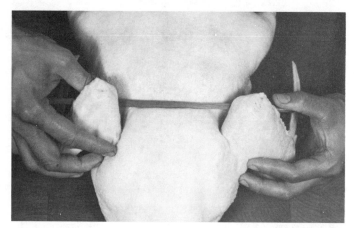

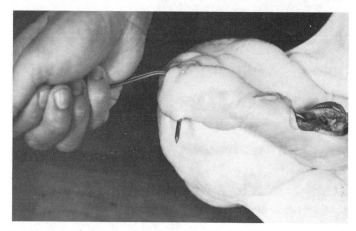

1. Hook a chopstick under the wing tips to hold the wings away from the body of the inflated duck. This allows the skin all over the body both to dry and to brown evenly. (Remove the chopstick before roasting, unless you have a Chinese oven.)

2. Insert a hanging hook in the neck, or hold the duck by its neck string.

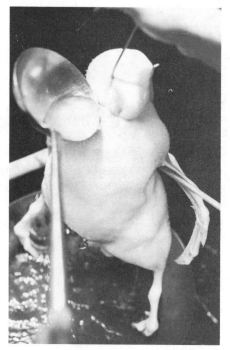

3. Hold the duck over a wok filled with boiling water. Ladle the boiling water over the duck for several minutes to rid it of its scum and scald the skin to make it taut. Hang the duck in a cool, airy place to dry. A pantry or a cooling closet, such as those one finds in old houses, is ideal. The duck may also be hung in front of an electric fan or air conditioner. With a fan, the drying process takes about 1½ to 2 hours; without, about 4 hours. The duck may deflate somewhat, but it will puff up in the oven later as the trapped air heats and expands.

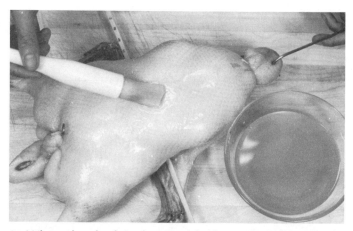

4. When the duck is thoroughly dry, it feels like parchment. Baste it with malt sugar or honey dissolved in boiling water. Hang it to dry again, for 2 hours if you are using a fan, for 4 hours if not.

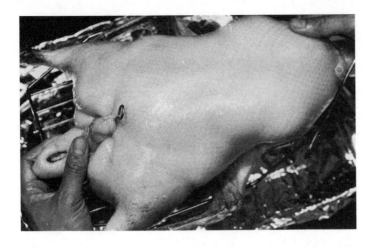

5. Set the duck on a V-rack, breast up, so that it is totally exposed to the oven heat. Follow this roasting timetable for a 5-pound duck:
15 minutes at 450 degrees, breast up
55 minutes at 350 degrees, breast up
20 minutes at 450 degrees, breast up
Total roasting time: 1 hour 30 minutes

Ideally, every part of the skin should roast crisp, which is why in China the ducks are hung from a pole rather than set on a rack. If you have a commercial-sized convection oven, you might try hanging the duck in it. The result is very close to authentic.

Final Preparations and Serving
The effort it takes to produce the perfect duck demands an elaborate presentation, something that shows why this dish was once served only to emperors. Although every chef has his own favorite presentation, the following one seems to suit the American knack for showmanship without requiring that too much time be spent away from the table.

Well before your guests arrive, make the pancakes and the scallion brushes, put the hoisin sauce on the table, and prepare the soup and the vegetables for stir-frying. As the ducks finish roasting, steam the pancakes so that they will be hot.

The first course should be served hot, while the skin is still crisp and the meat warm. So the first step, illustrated below, is to cut up the skin and the breast meat and send it out to your guests with the hot pancakes and scallion brushes. Before you join them, quickly shred the dark meat for stir-frying so that you don't have to clean the cleaver and cutting board a second time. Drop the bones into the broth to simmer, then you can join your guests in wrapping a slice of breast meat, a piece of crisp skin, a dab of hoisin, and a scallion brush in a pancake.

When you return to the kitchen, it takes only a couple of minutes to stir-fry the dark meat with the vegetables. By the time that is served, the broth with celery cabbage is ready to finish the meal.

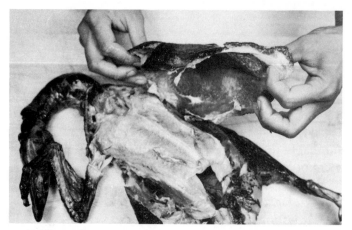

1. With a cleaver or a sharp paring knife, cut around the entire breast and lift the crisp skin off in one piece. (Notice that all the fat has dissolved.)

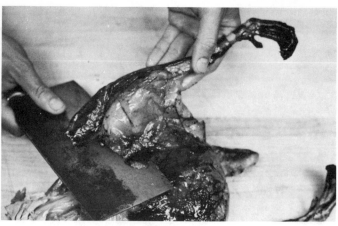

2. Cut the thighs off at the body.

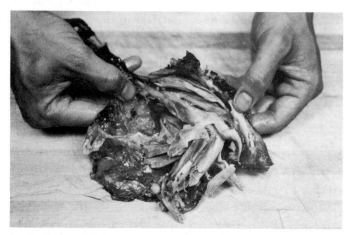

3. Pull the thigh meat away from the skin.

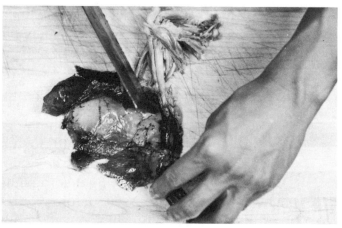

4. Remove the thigh skin in one piece.

5. Scrape the thigh meat off the bone and set it aside for stir-frying. Cut away the drumstick and reserve it for presentation with the breast meat. Add the bones to a pot of simmering chicken broth.

6. Shred the thigh meat.

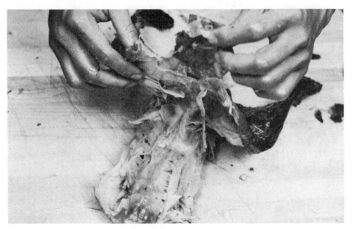

7. Lift the skin away from the back and set it aside.

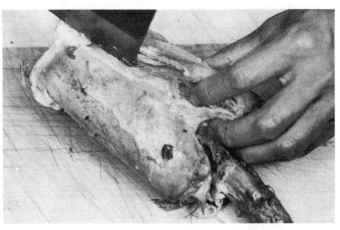

8. Bone the breast. First, cut along either side of the central keel bone.

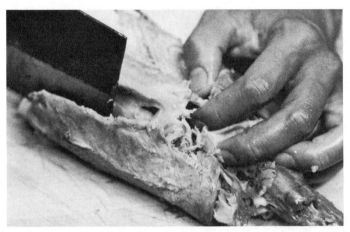

9. Then pull the breast muscles away, each in one piece. They should come away easily. Add the bones to the broth.

10. Slice the breast meat at a 45-degree angle into ¾-inch pieces. Keep the pieces aligned.

11. Pick up the entire sliced breast with the side of the cleaver. Arrange the breast meat in the center of a serving platter. Finish the platter with the drumsticks and the scallion brushes.

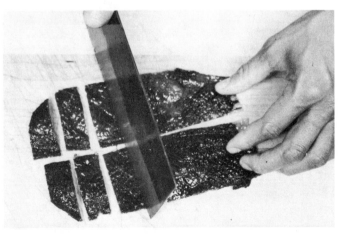

12. Cut the skin down the middle, then crosswise into rectangles about 1 by 2½ inches.

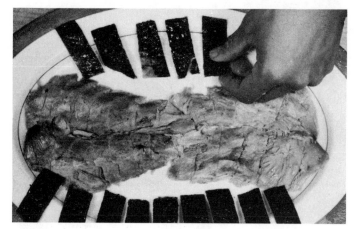

13. Arrange the pieces around the perimeter of the platter.

14. When the bones have simmered for 15 minutes, strain the soup and skim the grease. Add the remaining soup ingredients to the broth, and simmer for 5 minutes before serving it.

15. Stir-fry the vegetables in the oil flavored with garlic until they are just done (about 2 minutes).

16. Add the sauce ingredients and the shredded duck just to heat it through. Transfer it to a serving dish.

17. The Peking Duck dinner should be served in separate courses. *Clockwise from top:* Peking Duck Soup; pancakes, scallion brushes and hoisin sauce; skin with breast meat; stir-fried thigh meat with vegetables.

Boning Ducks

Duck is actually a little easier to bone than chicken, since the layer of fat reduces the likelihood that you'll cut through the skin. A sharp paring knife and a little patience are all that is necessary. The duck's anatomy requires a slightly different approach, which will also be of help to you if you ever bone a goose or a turkey.

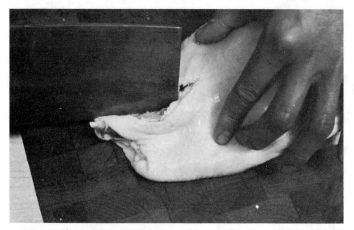

1. Trim the duck and cut a slit along the skin of the neck to expose the wishbone.

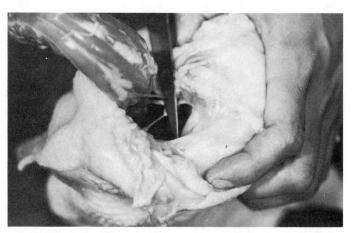

2. The wishbone ends at the wing joint. You may have to feel for it. The joints of a duck feel a little sharper, more angular, than those of a chicken.

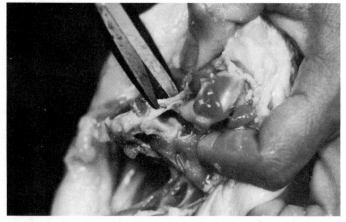

3. With poultry shears, cut the wing joint free.

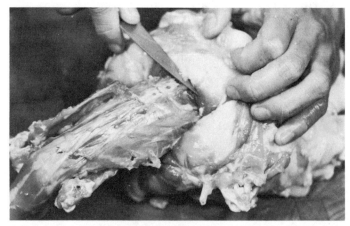

4. Because a duck is naturally fatter than a chicken, it is easier to pull the meat from the carcass. Work carefully, always keeping the knife edge toward the bone, pulling the meat away with the other hand.

5. When you reach the thigh joint, sever the joints to release the carcass.

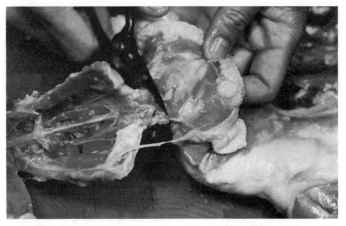

6. Keep the tail attached, and detach the rest of the backbone.

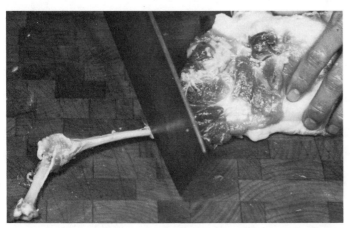

7. Scrape the meat away from the thigh and drumstick, as for chicken (see page 122).

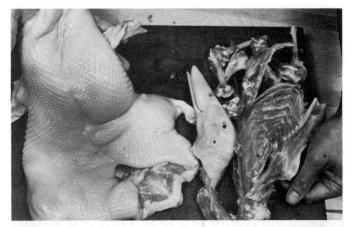

8. The boned duck, ready for stuffing, and its bones, ready for the stockpot.

Eight-Jewel Duck (Stuffed Boned Duck)
[see photo in color section]

Most of the preparation for this dish can be done in advance. All you must do at the last minute is brown the duck, either by frying it in hot oil (as described below) or by placing it on the top shelf of a very hot (500-degree) oven for 10 minutes. Choose stuffing ingredients that contrast in texture and flavor. The one used here—Eight-Jewel Duck—takes its name from the eight main ingredients in the stuffing: fresh water chestnuts, Smithfield ham, gingko nuts, black mushrooms, duck-liver sausages, chestnuts, bamboo shoots, and glutinous rice. Other stuffings, one of your own creation or the stuffing for Beggar's Chicken (page 124) or Whole Stuffed Chicken Skin (page 120), are just as delicious.

STUFFING:
2 tablespoons peanut oil
½ cup peeled and diced fresh water chestnuts
8 whole chestnuts, peeled and cut into quarters
½ cup diced Smithfield ham
2 tablespoons minced Chinese parsley
½ cup gingko nuts, fresh or canned (shelled if fresh)
¼ cup diced bamboo shoots
8 Chinese black mushrooms, soaked, squeezed dry, and diced
2 tablespoons minced scallion
2 tablespoons Shaoxing wine or dry sherry
1 tablespoon thin soy sauce
Salt to taste
*1 cup glutinous rice (soaked for 4 hours and drained), steamed for 30
    minutes with 4 duck-liver sausages (page 32)*

1 whole duck, about 5 pounds, boned (see above)

METHOD: Boning, steaming (page 59), deep-frying (page 56)
SERVES 4 as a main course.
MAY BE STEAMED in advance and refrigerated, then deep-fried just before
    serving.
SUGGESTED BEVERAGE: Cabernet Sauvignon, Bordeaux, or Nebbiolo

1. In the oil, stir-fry all the stuffing ingredients except the rice and sausage.

2. When they are thoroughly mixed (about 30 seconds), add the rice and sausage and combine well. Remove the stuffing from the heat.

3. When the stuffing is cool enough to handle, fill the boned duck with it through the tail.

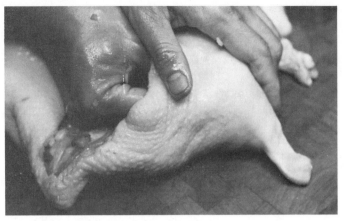

4. Fill the legs and thighs as well.

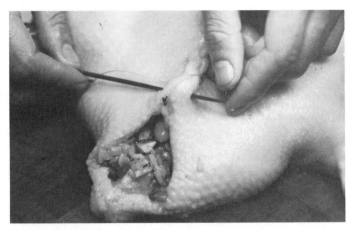

5. Sew the tail and neck shut.

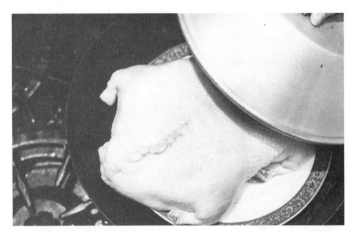

6. Steam the duck on a plate in a wok for 1¼ hour. Let it cool and dry, then dust it with water chestnut powder or cornstarch and, just before serving, deep-fry to brown it. (The stuffed steamed duck can be refrigerated if prepared ahead. Bring it to room temperature, dust with chestnut powder, then deep-fry.)

7. Bring it to the table whole, and have guests help themselves by picking into the duck with chopsticks.

Meats

ALTHOUGH THE CHINESE eat much less meat than they do poultry and fish, it's not because they dislike it. Scarce grazing land and a lack of surplus grain for feed has kept beef from becoming a staple in China. For the same reason, no dairy products appear in the Chinese diet.

Pork, however, requires little grain to produce, is rich in vitamins and minerals, and is by far the favorite meat in Chinese cuisine. Chinese cooks apply a variety of techniques to the preparation of pork, including a unique process, twice-cooking (page 203), that makes even fatty side pork edible and delicious. Another technique, used for Roast Suckling Pig (page 214), makes a delicious and highly prized dish which the Chinese cook offers to honor a cherished guest.

The Chinese invented the original process for curing ham; in fact, American country hams are cured by almost the same process. Smithfield ham, because its taste is so close to its Chinese counterpart, is sold in many Chinese shops and certainly can be used whenever ham is called for. In the Chinese kitchen, however, ham is more a flavoring than a main ingredient, though it is sometimes used as such.

Beef may be substituted in equal amounts for pork in the demonstrated techniques that follow. Flank steak and top round are economical for use in stir-frying. For braising, brisket or chuck can be used. Don't forget that cattle in China are working creatures, not gastronomic delights. The little beef that is available is tough, stringy, and requires lengthy braising (see Chinese Beef Stew, page 217) to tenderize it. The Chinese are very clever at making tough cuts palatable.

Lamb is raised and served mostly in the northern regions of China, though lamb stew is occasional winter fare in other regions. Because Chinese lamb is usually mutton, with a strong, gamy taste, it is cooked with other strong flavors, such as scallions and garlic. In home kitchens, usually in the north of China, braised lamb is prepared much like braised beef (page 217).

Since the meat in most Chinese dishes is cut into small pieces, a little goes a long way. Compared with Americans' consumption of meat, the Chinese eat very little. In these days of high prices, this is especially economical. Try using smaller amounts of meat than you would prepare for an American meal, and you may find, as the Chinese have found, that the palate is sometimes better satisfied with less.

PORK

Barbecuing Pork

One of the great pleasures of barbecued meats is the crusty, tasty surface that results from direct exposure to the heat. The Chinese barbecue meats by hanging them in the oven. The fat drips off the meat into a pan of water at the bottom of the oven. The water serves two purposes: as a catchall for melting fat, and as a humidity-producing vehicle to prevent the meat from drying out.

Few Chinese homes have ovens, so barbecued pork is bought from stores that specialize in barbecuing, much as the French buy their pâtés and bread from *charcuteries* and *boulangeries*. Barbecued pork is a delicious appetizer and a common ingredient in soups, stir-fried dishes, and stuffings.

To maximize the amount of tasty surface area, we cut the pork into small strips and hang them in the oven so that air can circulate completely around them and brown them appetizingly. Barbecued Pork Strips can be made in advance; they also freeze well, so you can always have pork on hand when small amounts are called for in other recipes. Your own homemade pork strips needn't be made with monosodium glutamate and red dye, which are often used in restaurants. The pork is marinated for 3 hours or overnight, then roasted, basted occasionally with a sweet glaze. Spareribs can be barbecued in exactly the same way, with the same marinade and the same glaze. Have your butcher saw off the thick, bony top of the rack, leaving you with ribs approximately equal in size. Other meats can be barbecued in the same manner—slices of beef, whole pork roasts, pieces of chicken or turkey, even whole game birds (but not domesticated duck). Large birds or roasts should marinate overnight in the refrigerator and should be turned several times to baste evenly.

Barbecued Pork Strips

2 pounds boneless pork butt

MARINADE:
2 tablespoons thin soy sauce
2 tablespoons Shaoxing wine or dry sherry
2 tablespoons sugar
1 tablespoon minced garlic
1 tablespoon brown bean sauce
1 tablespoon hoisin sauce
1 tablespoon red bean curd
1 teaspoon five-spice powder

BASTING LIQUID:
3 tablespoons malt sugar or honey
3 tablespoons boiling water

METHOD: Barbecuing

SERVES 4 to 6 as a main course accompanied by vegetables, 8 to 10 as an appetizer.

MAY BE PREPARED in advance and frozen. Serve at room temperature or reheat when cooking vegetables.

SUGGESTED BEVERAGE: Rosé or light red wine, chilled

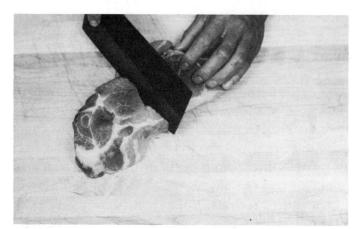

1. Cut the piece of pork butt in half.

2. Cut the two halves into ¾-inch strips.

3. Put the strips in a bowl with the marinade and mix well to coat them thoroughly. Marinate at room temperature for 3 hours, or overnight in the refrigerator.

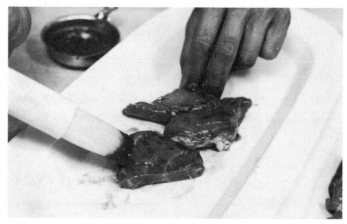

4. Remove the pork from the marinade and baste the strips with the malt-sugar mixture.

5. Use curved skewers (available in Chinese cookware shops and some restaurant-supply stores) to hang the meat from the top shelf of the oven over a large pan filled with water to a depth of ¼ inch. Roast the pork at 350 degrees for 45 minutes, basting occasionally with the malt sugar or honey. Increase the heat to 425 degrees and roast for 20 minutes more to finish the pork.

6. When the pork is cool enough to handle, cut it into ½-inch slices.

7. Arrange the pork slices on a platter.

Shredding Pork

Shredded pork is the base of countless quickly stir-fried entrées, as it combines well with almost any other ingredient. Shredded pork cooks very quickly, so take care not to overcook it.

Perhaps one of the most popular Chinese dishes in restaurants in this country is Mu Shu Pork, which is simply shredded pork quickly stir-fried with shredded vegetables and lightly scrambled eggs. Traditionally, the finished stir-fried mixture is spooned into the same pancakes used for Peking Duck (see page 294), although it makes a wonderful entrée even without them.

Mu Shu Pork

MARINADE:
1 tablespoon Shaoxing wine or dry sherry
1 tablespoon thin soy sauce
1 teaspoon cornstarch

½ pound boneless pork butt or shoulder, shredded
½ cup shredded lily stems
¼ cup tree ears, soaked, squeezed dry, and shredded
4 scallions, shredded
¼ cup shredded bamboo shoots
5 tablespoons peanut oil
4 eggs, lightly beaten
3 tablespoons chicken broth
½ teaspoon sugar
1 tablespoon Shaoxing wine or dry sherry
1 teaspoon thin soy sauce
2 teaspoons sesame oil
Salt to taste
12 pancakes (page 294)

METHOD: Stir-frying (page 52)
SERVES 2 to 4 as a main course.
MAY BE PREPARED in advance through step 4.
SUGGESTED BEVERAGE: Rosé or light red wine, chilled

Marinate the shredded pork for 20 to 30 minutes.

1. Prepare all the other shredded ingredients—tree ears, lily stems, scallions, and bamboo shoots.

2. In a separate steamer, heat the pancakes.

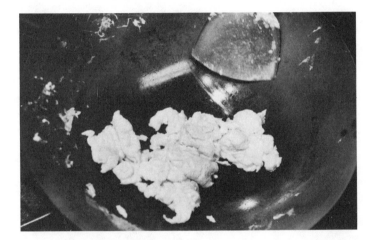

3. Heat 2 tablespoons of the oil in a wok over a moderate flame and pour in the beaten egg. As soon as the egg begins to cling to the wok, scoop it and fold it over to scramble it. Work fast because the egg solidifies quickly, and it can overcook. As soon as it solidifies, remove it from the wok and set it aside.

4. Stir-fry the pork over high heat in 1 tablespoon of the oil for 30 seconds, or until it no longer looks raw. Remove it from the wok and set it aside.

5. In the remaining 2 tablespoons of the oil, stir-fry the vegetables, more to combine them and heat them through than to cook them.

6. Add the pork and mix it well with the seasonings.

7. Finally, add the eggs, breaking them up to form bite-size lumps. Combine the ingredients well.

8. Arrange the heated pancakes, folded into quarters, around a small bowl of hoisin sauce. Serve the Mu Shu Pork on a separate platter.

1. Smear about a teaspoon of hoisin sauce with chopsticks (or a small spoon) over the middle of the unbrowned side of a pancake.

2. Spoon a couple of tablespoons of filling on the hoisin sauce.

3. Fold one end of the pancake over the filling.

4. Then fold the other half to wrap it like a crepe. The wrapped Mu Shu Pork is easiest to eat with the hands, but the proper way is to use chopsticks.

Cubing Pork

Cubed meats are frequently deep-fried because they provide the cook with an opportunity to enjoy a contrast of textures—the outside of the meat turns dark and crisp, yet the inside stays light and moist. Contrast—in texture, color, and flavor—is one of the most important attributes of a fine Chinese dish.

Sweet-and-Sour Pork, made from cubes of boneless pork butt, has the additional contrast of a sauce that balances sweet with sour flavors. Unfortunately, most restaurants overthicken their sweet-and-sour sauce, make it too sweet, and color it an unnatural red. This true homemade version is much more subtle, not unlike the sauce for French duck à l'orange.

Other meats, such as boned chicken or filleted fish, can be cubed, deep-fried, and served in this sweet-and-sour sauce if you adjust the cooking time.

Sweet-and-Sour Pork
[see photo in color section]

1 pound boneless pork butt, cut into ¾-inch cubes

MARINADE:
1 tablespoon thin soy sauce
1 tablespoon Shaoxing wine or dry sherry
½ teaspoon salt
1 teaspoon sesame oil
1 egg, beaten

½ fresh pineapple
½ cup water chestnut powder mixed with ½ cup unsweetened almond
*   powder, or ½ cup cornstarch mixed with ½ cup flour*
4 cups peanut oil for deep-frying

SWEET-AND-SOUR SAUCE:
1 tablespoon Shaoxing wine or dry sherry
1 tablespoon thin soy sauce
1 tablespoon minced garlic
1 tablespoon minced fresh ginger root
2 tablespoons tomato paste
½ cup Chinkiany vinegar, or ⅓ cup cider vinegar or red wine vinegar
¼ cup sugar or 3 Chinese sugar slabs
1 cup chicken broth
1 tablespoon cornstarch dissolved in 2 tablespoons cold chicken broth
1 tablespoon sesame oil

METHOD: Deep-frying (page 56)
SERVES 2 to 4 as a main course.
SUGGESTED BEVERAGE: Rosé wine or beer

1. Marinate the pork for at least 30 minutes.

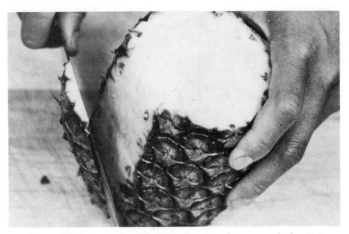

2. Cut off the ends of the pineapple, stand the pineapple on end, and shave off the skin with downward strokes of the cleaver.

3. Cut the pineapple into ¾-inch cubes.

4. Drain the marinade from the pork, blot it dry, and dust the cubes with the water chestnut–almond powder or cornstarch–flour mixture. Shake off any excess.

5. Heat the oil in a wok to 360 degrees (moderately hot). Fry the pork cubes a handful at a time for 3 minutes. (They are done when they feel springy instead of mushy.) Set them aside.

6. Empty the wok of the oil (or do these next steps in a large saucepan). Heat the Sweet-and-Sour Sauce ingredients (except for the cornstarch dissolved in broth) over a moderate flame with the pineapple.

201

7. When it comes to a boil, stir in the dissolved corn-starch, the sesame oil, and the fried pork cubes to heat them through.

8. Sweet-and-Sour Pork—the tart fruit balances the richness of the pork.

202

Twice-Cooking Pork

Most of the flavor of pork is concentrated in the fat, but the problem with fatty meat is its chewy, greasy texture. Twice-cooking (two cookings) is the Chinese solution. First the meat is simmered to render some of the fat, then it is stir-fried to rid it of the rest of the greasiness. The texture emerges firm and crisp, but not hard like cracklings. Twice-Cooked Pork also reheats well without losing its taste and texture. Fresh side pork is the preferred cut of meat for the proper texture, although a fatty piece of pork butt can be substituted. (Pork butt need not be simmered as long.) Fresh side pork is also known as uncured bacon. Do not confuse it with salt pork or cured or salted bacon.

Twice-cooking is an appealing technique for meats that would otherwise be tough or stringy. Beef that is twice-cooked is often called Sichuan Beef. It has a dried texture and is coated with a sauce like the one for Twice-Cooked Pork. Brisket or chuck roast, both of which need long cooking to make them tender, are delicious cooked in this manner. Game, such as venison, or goat meat would make unusual variations.

Twice-Cooked Pork

2 pounds fresh side pork (uncured bacon) or pork belly (if side pork is unavailable, boneless shoulder can be used)
2 slices fresh ginger root
6 scallions, cut into 3-inch sections, or 2 whole leeks
8 cloves garlic, minced

METHOD: Twice-cooking

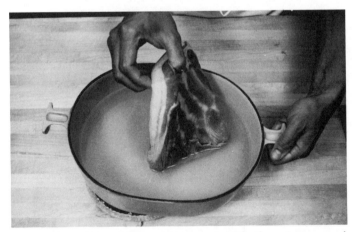

1. Put the piece of meat in a pot with the ginger and enough water to cover. Simmer 1 hour (30 minutes for pork shoulder).

2. Drain the pork, let it cool, and cut it lengthwise into 1½-inch pieces. Pat it dry.

3. Cut the pieces crosswise into thin slices.

4. Stir-fry the slices in their own fat. (You may want to start them off with a tablespoonful or so of oil.) Cook them until they are crisp and brown.

5. As the fat is rendered, pull the pork away from the middle of the wok and dip out the accumulated fat with a ladle.

6. When the pork is quite brown, add the scallions and garlic to stir-fry a few seconds.

7. Add the sauce mixture, and toss the pork well so that it is well coated.

8. This dish has little sauce. The well-coated slices of pork have plenty of flavor and a unique texture.

SAUCE:
2 tablespoons hoisin sauce
1 tablespoon chili paste with garlic
2 tablespoons Shaoxing wine or dry sherry
1 tablespoon dark soy sauce
1 teaspoon sugar

SERVES 4 to 6 as a main course.
MAY BE PREPARED in advance and kept refrigerated. Reheat in a little water or
     rice wine.
SUGGESTED BEVERAGE: Heavy Zinfandel or Barolo

Braising Pork

Heady with garlic and fermented black beans, the simmering sauce slowly braises the spareribs until they are tender, absorbing flavor from the bones in the process. Have the butcher cut the spareribs on the saw into three or four sections crosswise, since this is too difficult to do safely at home. Like most braised dishes, this one improves when reheated the next day, or even several days later. For a meatier dish, use the large "country-style" ribs, or even cubed pork butt.

The same technique can be used for tougher cuts of beef, including short ribs, or lamb as well. If you like oxtails, this is a perfect way to braise them; cut them up like ribs. For meats other than pork, substitute 5 tablespoons plum sauce for the fermented black beans and garlic.

Braised Spareribs

3 pounds spareribs, cut crosswise into 3 or 4 sections

SAUCE:
2½ tablespoons fermented black beans
2 cloves garlic, chopped
2 tablespoons thin soy sauce
2 tablespoons Shaoxing wine or dry sherry
1 teaspoon sugar
2½ cups chicken broth

GARNISH:
2 tablespoons coarsely chopped scallion tops

METHOD: Stir-frying (page 52), braising
SERVES 4 to 6 as a main course.
MAY BE PREPARED in advance and reheated in the sauce.
SUGGESTED BEVERAGE: Pinot Noir or Burgundy

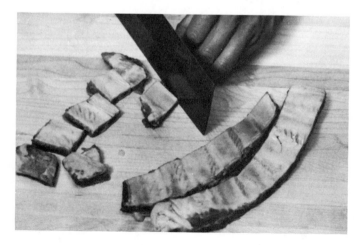

1. Cut the strips of ribs between the bones into riblets.

2. Stir-fry the spareribs in a wok over high heat to brown them in their own fat (about 4 minutes). (You may want to start them off with a tablespoonful of peanut oil.)

3. Drain off the fat, and add the sauce ingredients except the broth. Mix them well.

4. Add the broth and reduce the heat. Let the ribs simmer 60 minutes.

5. Remove the ribs to a serving plate and garnish them with the scallion tops. (The liquid in the wok can be skimmed of fat and thickened with cornstarch to make a sauce, if you like.)

Ground Pork for Meat Balls

Ground pork is a staple of the Chinese diet; it is as popular in China as ground beef in the West. As the basis of all sorts of meat balls and meat loaves, it can be poached, fried, or steamed. Its use reflects the Chinese knack of economical stretching of meat.

Although pork has more flavor and texture than beef, many of these same techniques can be used for beef, and for lamb as well. If you use ground beef, be sure to use the fatty type, which is also less expensive. Ground turkey mixed with a little ham fat may also be used.

The Basic Meat Ball recipe that follows is used to make deep-fried stuffed meat balls and steamed meat balls coated with glutinous rice. You can also deep-fry the Basic Meat Balls and top them with a tomato sauce, for example, for an unusual pasta sauce. Or simply deep-fry them and serve them with a plum sauce dip.

Basic Meat Balls

1 pound pork (pork butt), coarsely ground
1 tablespoon thin soy sauce
1 tablespoon Shaoxing wine or dry sherry
1 teaspoon minced fresh ginger root
2 tablespoons minced scallion
1 teaspoon salt
1 teaspoon sugar
1 egg, beaten
1 tablespoon sesame oil
½ teaspoon roasted and crushed Sichuan peppercorns
1 tablespoon cornstarch
4 fresh water chestnuts, peeled and minced

METHOD: Deep-frying (page 56)

Mix these ingredients together well. Rub vegetable oil over your hands to keep the meat from sticking to them. Roll about 2 tablespoons of meat mixture between the palms to form a ball. These can be deep-fried at 350 degrees for 8 to 10 minutes or prepared in either of the ways that follow.

Stuffed Meat Balls

[see photo in color section]

Instead of the spinach or cabbage filling, you could use sorrel, cooked zucchini, carrots, or other vegetable.

1 recipe Basic Meat Balls (see above)

FILLING:
1 cup cooked minced spinach or celery cabbage
1 teaspoon sesame oil
1 teaspoon thin soy sauce
¼ teaspoon sugar (for spinach)
Salt to taste

METHOD: Deep-frying (page 56)
MAKES ABOUT 14 meat balls, to serve 6 as an appetizer.
SUGGESTED BEVERAGE: Pinot Noir or Burgundy

1. Mix the stuffing ingredients together well. Pat the meat between oiled palms to make a flat patty.

2. Place a tablespoonful of the vegetable filling in the center of the patty.

3. Close the palm of the hand around it to begin forming a ball.

4. Finish forming the ball by rolling it between the palms.

5. Drop the meat balls one by one into the hot oil.
6. Fry them until they are done (about 8 to 10 minutes). Cut one open to be sure.

Steamed Pearl Balls

[see photo in color section]

For an unusual variation of Pearl Balls, roll the meat balls in spicy Rice Crumbs (page 287) and steam them as below.

1 recipe Basic Meat Balls (see above)
½ cup glutinous rice, soaked 30 minutes to soften

METHOD: Steaming (page 59)
MAKES ABOUT 14 meat balls, to serve 6 as an appetizer.
MAY BE PREPARED several hours in advance and reheated by steaming.
SUGGESTED BEVERAGE: Pinot Noir or Burgundy

1. Roll the meat balls in the presoaked glutinous rice.

2. Make sure they are thoroughly coated.

3. Put them in a bamboo steamer lined with cheese-cloth and steam them for 30 minutes. Cut one open to be sure they are done.

Steamed Pork Cake

This is essentially a Chinese meat loaf. Steaming cooks the pork gently and enhances its succulent flavor. This typical home-style dish can be made ahead and reheated. As in most meat loaf recipes, the ingredients are flexible. Preserved fish, here used as a seasoning, can be replaced with minced Smithfield ham or Sichuan preserved vegetables (for something spicier). Try it with ground beef for a change.

1 pound pork, coarsely ground
1 tablespoon chopped salted preserved fish
2 tablespoons coarsely chopped salted turnip bundle
6 fresh water chestnuts, peeled and minced
½ teaspoon salt
¼ teaspoon sugar
1 tablespoon thin soy sauce
2 tablespoons Shaoxing wine or dry sherry
2 teaspoons cornstarch
2 tablespoons minced scallion
¼ cup chicken broth

METHOD: Steaming (page 59)

SERVES 4 as a main course.

MAY BE PREPARED in advance and reheated by steaming.

SUGGESTED BEVERAGE: Beer

1. Mix together the pork, fish (or ham), turnip bundle, and water chestnuts. The hand is the best tool for this.

2. Mix in the remaining ingredients.

3. Pat the mixture into a flat cake on a platter.

4. Make a well in the center for liquid to collect.

5. Place the platter in a steamer. Steam it 20 to 30 minutes.

6. When the cake is cooked, serve it on the same plate. Pieces can be separated easily with chopsticks. Try spooning some of the pork juices over rice.

The Whole Pig

Suckling pig is sensational. It tastes sweeter and more delicate than mature pork, and in China it is reserved for such occasions as weddings or banquets. Though it is usually left to commercial establishments that specialize in roasting meat and poultry, as the French leave sausage making to the *charcuterie,* it is not hard to prepare at home if you have both a pan and an oven large enough to accommodate the whole pig. The best-tasting pigs are the smallest—around 10 pounds if you can find one. Most are closer to 20 pounds. The finished pig is cut up and served with pancakes and hoisin sauce, exactly like the first course of Peking Duck (see page 176). The remaining scraps of meat are delicious stir-fried with vegetables or stir-fried with deep-fried tofu (see page 89). Try this with a pig first, then with a kid, 10 to 20 pounds.

Preparing a Pig for Roasting

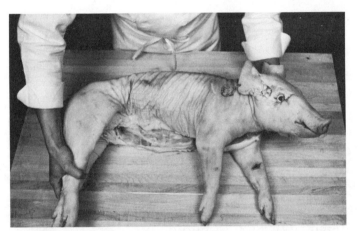

1. The pig comes from the butcher whole but eviscerated. The following steps, which essentially show how to butterfly the pig, can also be done by your butcher.

2. Start at the chin and split the pig down the middle, cutting through the chest and belly.

3. When you get to the bone, set the cleaver on the bone and hit it with a mallet to break through the bone.

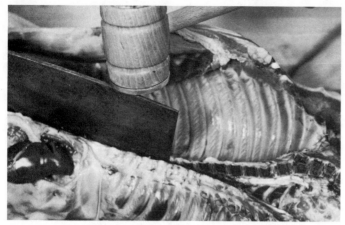 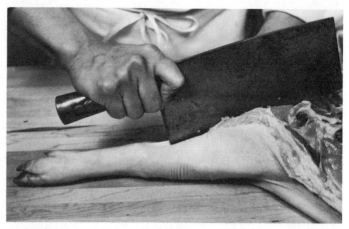

4. Split the spinal column the same way so that the pig will lie flat. It is not necessary to cut through the spine, but keep spreading the ribs apart so that the pig will lie flat.

5. Make a cut 1½ inches deep into the inside of the rear legs. This allows the thicker parts of the meat to cook evenly.

Roast Suckling Pig

[see photo in color section]

1 suckling pig, 10 lbs., prepared as above
½ cup coarse (kosher) salt
¼ cup five-spice powder
2 tablespoons roasted and crushed Sichuan peppercorns
2 tablespoons fennel seed

METHOD: Roasting
SERVES 20 as a main course.
SUGGESTED BEVERAGE: Zinfandel, Pinot Noir, or Burgundy

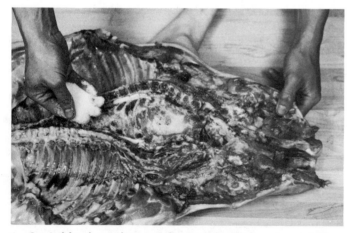 

1. Sprinkle the salt over the inside of the pig, rubbing it into the meat well so that it penetrates.

2. Mix the spices, sprinkle them over the inside of the pig, and rub them in well.

3. Hang the pig on a meat hook in a cool place. Direct a fan at the pig to dry it thoroughly. This can be done overnight.

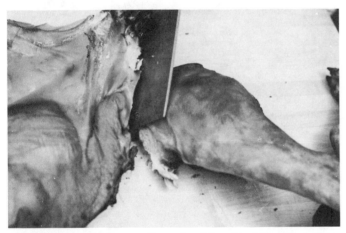

5. Cut the rear legs off at the hip. At this point they probably won't quite be cooked through and so are in need of further cooking.

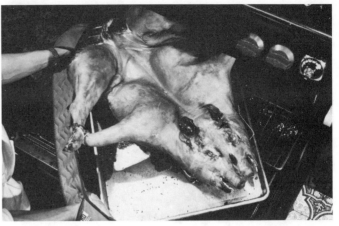

4. Set the pig on a rack in a large roasting pan, skin side up. Roast it at 450 degrees for 30 minutes, until the skin begins to brown. Then turn down the oven to 350 degrees for 1½ hours, or until a meat thermometer in the thickest part of the breast registers 170 degrees. For larger pigs, continue roasting at 350 degrees until the thermometer in the breast reaches 170 degrees.

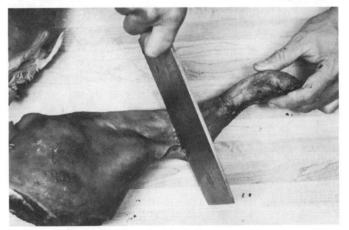

6. First cut the bottom half of the legs off and set them aside, as they will overcook. Return the thigh meat to the oven and continue to roast it while you cut up the rest of the pig.

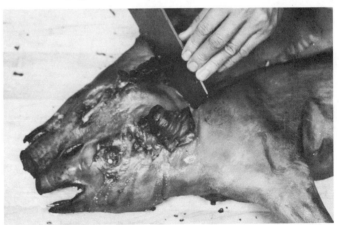

7. Cut off the head.

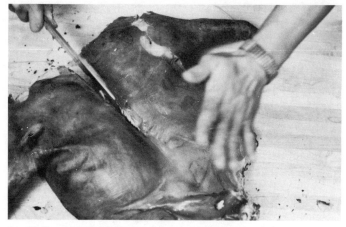

8. Split the body down the middle, along the spine.

9. Cut the body lengthwise into long strips about 2 inches wide.

10. Cut the strips crosswise into 1-inch segments. The skin and seasonings will crumble somewhat, but try to keep the skin attached to the meat.

11. Rearrange the pieces, including the thighs, which should now be done, to re-form the pig. Serve it with pancakes, scallions, and hoisin sauce, as for Peking Duck (page 176).

BEEF AND LAMB

Braising Beef

Tough beef is most flavorful, but you must simmer it gently for several hours to soften the sinewy muscle. Slow braising also encourages an exchange of flavors between the meat and the tangy sauce, enhancing both. Chinese radish adds just the right bite, much as turnips would in a Western stew. In effect, this is a Chinese beef stew.

Game meats or goat meat may be substituted for the beef for a delicious and unusual variation. Oxtails can also be braised in this manner, or even veal shanks. Almost any cut of meat or organ that requires extensive cooking does well if braised. The strong sauce keeps the meat flavorful throughout.

Turnips or carrots may be substituted for the Chinese radish, and chestnuts have a strong, sweet taste that holds up well to braising.

Chinese Beef Stew
[see photo in color section]

3 pounds brisket of beef or stew beef
4 tablespoons peanut oil

SAUCE:
2 cubes fermented red bean curd
3 tablespoons hoisin sauce
4 tablespoons Shaoxing wine or dry sherry
4 tablespoons thin soy sauce
1 tablespoon minced garlic
1 whole star anise
1 teaspoon roasted and crushed Sichuan peppercorns
1 teaspoon five-spice powder
2 teaspoons sugar
6 cups water

1 large (about 1½ to 2 pounds) Chinese (icicle) radish, roll-cut

METHOD: Stir-frying (page 52), braising
SERVES 6 as a main course.
MAY BE REFRIGERATED for several days or frozen. Reheating in the sauce improves the flavor.
SUGGESTED BEVERAGE: Generic dry red wine

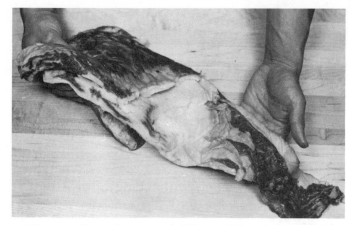

1. The preferred cut is brisket of beef, a boneless piece of tough meat from the underside of the steer, because of its rich, gelatinous texture when cooked. It is sold in Chinese meat markets as Chinese stew beef. Any tough beef cut can be used, such as boneless chuck and bottom round.

2. Trim away the outer layers of fat.

3. Cut the meat into 1½-inch strips.

4. Cut the strips into cubes.

5. Brown the meat on all sides in a wok over a high flame in 3 tablespoons of the oil. Set it aside.

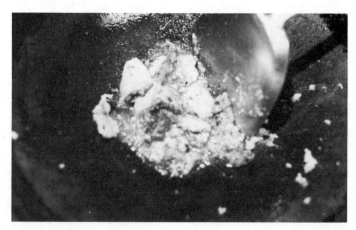

6. In the remaining 1 tablespoon of oil, over a high flame, break up the red bean curd with a spatula.

7. Add the remaining sauce ingredients. Bring them to a boil.

8. Add the beef to the sauce, reduce the heat to a simmer, cover the wok, and braise the beef for 2 hours. After 1½ hours, add the roll-cut radish. Cook 30 minutes more, until both beef and radish are tender.

9. Serve the stew immediately.

Stir-Frying Beef with Vegetables

This is the prototype for all meat-and-vegetable stir-fried dishes. The meat is stir-fried to brown, then set aside while the vegetable is stir-fried. Just before the vegetable is done, the meat rejoins it in the wok to heat through with any sauce. The variations and substitutions are endless—pork or lamb for beef, virtually any vegetable for asparagus. A good combination is beef with diagonally sliced bok choy or whole snow peas. Feel free to add seasonings to the marinade or additional flavors to the sauce; oyster sauce or chili paste with garlic are two possibilities. The cornstarch in the marinade lightly thickens the sauce.

Beef with Asparagus
[see photo in color section]

1 pound flank steak, membrane peeled, or boneless sirloin, thinly sliced against the grain into pieces 2 inches long

MARINADE:
2 teaspoons cornstarch
1½ tablespoons Shaoxing wine or dry sherry
2 tablespoons thin soy sauce

3 tablespoons peanut oil
½ pound fresh asparagus, sliced diagonally
Salt to taste
3 tablespoons chicken broth

METHOD: Stir-frying (page 52)
SERVES 3 or 4 as a main course.
SUGGESTED BEVERAGE: Pinot Noir, Burgundy, or Nebbiolo

1. Coat the beef thoroughly so that it will absorb the marinade, and let it stand in the marinade for 10 minutes.

2. Heat 1½ tablespoons of the peanut oil in a wok over a high flame and stir-fry the beef just long enough to brown it lightly. Remove it from the wok and let it drain.

3. In the remaining 1½ tablespoons of oil, stir-fry the asparagus for a few seconds to coat it. Add the salt and chicken broth and let it boil until the asparagus is tender-crisp (about 1 minute).

4. Add the beef and toss it with the asparagus to combine them.

5. Serve the beef immediately.

Stir-Frying Lamb

Lamb is used in Chinese cuisine in combination with other strong flavors because it is more strongly flavored than American lamb. Scallions and garlic are used here. The scallions are shredded to maximize their impact, and the garlic is sliced to extract the most flavor. If you want more lamb flavor, cut the scallions into 2-inch pieces and reduce the amount of garlic.

Scallion-Exploded Lamb

½ pound boneless tender lamb, loin or shoulder

MARINADE:
2 teaspoons thin soy sauce
1 tablespoon Shaoxing wine or dry sherry
½ teaspoon cornstarch
2 teaspoons sesame oil

12 scallions
3 tablespoons peanut oil
6 cloves garlic, sliced

SAUCE:
1 tablespoon hoisin sauce
1 tablespoon thin soy sauce
2 tablespoons Shaoxing wine or dry sherry
½ teaspoon sugar
2 teaspoons roasted and crushed Sichuan peppercorns

METHOD: Stir-frying (page 52)
SERVES 2 as a main course.
SUGGESTED BEVERAGE: Cabernet Sauvignon or young Bordeaux

1. Cut the lamb into thin slices, then cut the slices into shreds. Marinate the lamb at least 10 minutes.

2. Cut the scallions into 3-inch lengths and flatten them with the side of the cleaver to make them easier to cut.

3. Slice them lengthwise into shreds. This releases more of the flavor.

4. Stir-fry the lamb in the oil.

5. As soon as the red color is gone (only a few seconds), add the garlic and scallions. Toss them well, then add the sauce ingredients.

6. When the mixture boils, remove it to a serving dish.

Fish and Seafood

WITH THOUSANDS OF MILES of coastline and many more thousands of miles of rivers and lakes, China enjoys an abundance of fish and seafood. Chinese cuisine boasts a multitude of techniques to elevate the products of sea, lake, and river to the highest rank. A whole fish, steamed or braised, is the climactic dish of a multicourse banquet, served last with the head pointing toward the guest of honor.

Freshness is the most important consideration in selecting seafood. In Chinese fish markets, carp swim in aerated tanks, ready to be plucked from the water and rushed to a nearby kitchen to ensure the most delicate flavor. Crabs, kept alive until the last possible second before they are cooked, claw at each other in wooden bins. Young Chinese are taught to avoid eating crabs or lobsters that were not alive just before they were cooked. In Canton or Hong Kong, restaurant guests sometimes arrive with a catch of live shrimp for the chef to prepare to order.

Because fish deteriorates rapidly once caught, Chinese shoppers learn to be finicky about the freshness of the fish they buy. To select the freshest fish, follow these guidelines:

1. Buy whole fish, if at all possible. Telltale signs of freshness are detectable on whole fish: Does it feel firm when pressed lightly? Do the scales shimmer and glisten? Are the eyes clear and bulging? Are the gills bright red? If the answers are yes, the fish is sure to be fresh.

2. Smell the fish. It should have the aroma of the sea, the river, or the lake. That so-called fishy smell is really the odor of over-the-hill fish.

3. If the fish is already in fillets or steaks, look for pieces that are moist, not yellow or brown around the edges. Smell fillets for freshness, too.

The Chinese favor firm, white-fleshed ocean fish, such as sea bass, flounder, grouper, red snapper, rock cod (bass), and whitefish. Carp, a large freshwater fish, is also highly prized, as are freshwater trout and catfish. All these fish are low in fat and calories, and steamed or braised, they are perfect for today's lighter eating. There is almost no fresh or saltwater fish —or hard- or soft-shelled mollusk or crustacean—that doesn't make it to the Chinese table.

Because seafood is so delicate, the Chinese cook strives for minimum handling and simple preparation. Shrimp is stir-fried or deep-fried, or chopped into a paste and formed into shrimp balls to be deep-fried. Crab is stir-fried or steamed, and clams are simmered to extract their savory juice. With seafood, remember that all these techniques are interchangeable. Whatever technique applies to crab applies to lobster, shrimp, and crayfish as well. Any technique that works for shrimp also works for scallops, clams, and squid.

THE WHOLE FISH

Cleaning Whole Fish Chinese-Style

Though you can rely on your fish store to scale and gut fish for you (ask that the head and tail be left on), this quick and efficient Chinese technique is handy to know should you find yourself with a freshly caught uncleaned fish. It is also a good way to learn the anatomy of a fish.

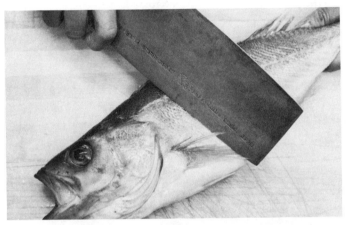

1. Using the back of a cleaver, scrape toward the head to scale the fish. The fresher the fish, the less the resistance to the cleaver.

2. Holding the fish belly up, free the head from the body with a partial cut under the mouth. Leave the head attached at the top so that the "neck" works as a hinge.

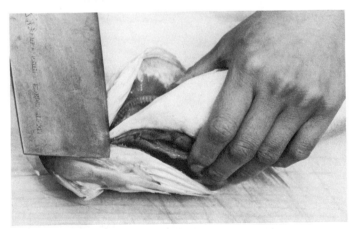

3. This exposes the gills, which can be cut out.

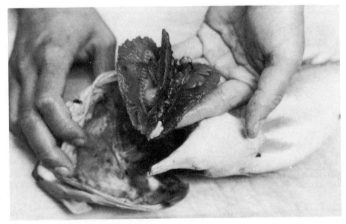

4. Discard the gills. They add a bitter taste.

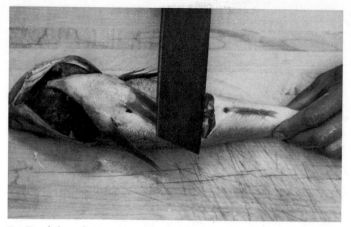

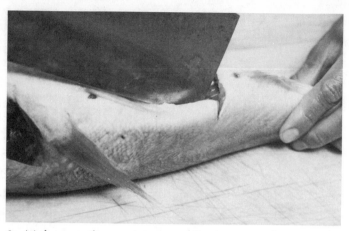

5. Feel for the point where the stomach sac ends and the bone structure of the tail begins. Make a cut 1 inch deep across the fish at that point.

6. Make another cut perpendicular to it through the stomach for about 2 inches toward the head.

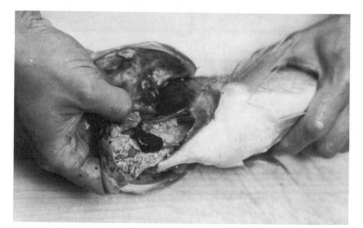

7. This exposes the entrails, which can now be pulled out easily. Rinse the cavity and the outside of the fish with cold water.

8. If the cavity of the fish is to be stuffed, the entrails can be pulled out instead through the gill cavity behind the head. In this case, do not make the V-shaped cut on the belly.

Steaming Whole Fish

Any type of firm white fish is suitable for steaming, a simple, quick cooking method that produces the most delicate finished dish. Oily fish, such as mackerel or sardine, are not suitable. The Chinese cook often uses ginger with fish, much as the Western cook uses lemon. Squeezing the ginger juice over the fish flavors it better than simply shredding the ginger and scattering the shreds on top. As an alternative to the Chinese seasonings of black beans, scallions, and soy sauce, try fresh herbs such as tarragon or fennel, and substitute hot butter for the final dousing with oil.

Steamed Fish with Black Beans

1 whole fish (sea bass, whitefish, pike, trout, rock cod), about 1½ to 2
  pounds, cleaned and scaled (see page 229)
1½ teaspoons salt
1 large chunk (1 inch) fresh ginger root, smashed
2 cloves garlic, roughly chopped
2 tablespoons fermented black beans
2 whole scallions, shredded
3 diagonal slices fresh ginger root, shredded
2 tablespoons thin soy sauce
2 tablespoons Shaoxing wine or dry sherry
Pinch of sugar
1½ tablespoons peanut oil
½ teaspoon sesame oil

METHOD: Steaming (see above)
SERVES 2 to 3 as a main course.
SUGGESTED BEVERAGE: Dry Sauvignon Blanc or Sancerre

1. Place the fish on a platter large enough to hold it, and sprinkle it with salt. Squeeze the chunk of ginger in your hand to extract the juice, letting it sprinkle over the fish. (The ginger must be fresh and you must have strong hands to do this; as an alternative, use a garlic press.)

2. Chop the garlic and fermented black beans together. Don't chop too fine or the mixture will become a paste and turn bitter.

231

3. Scatter the beans, garlic, shredded scallions, and shredded ginger over the fish.

4. Mix the soy sauce, Shaoxing wine, and sugar. Pour it over the fish.

5. If the plate is too long to fit in a bamboo steamer or a wok, improvise a steamer. In this case, a roasting pan serves the purpose. A trivet stands in the middle to hold the plate.

6. Set the plate on the trivet. Pour boiling water into the pan, but not enough to reach the plate.

7. Cover the pan with aluminum foil and crimp the edges to seal it. Put the pan over low heat to keep the water simmering. A fish 1 inch thick at its widest point will take 10 minutes in the steamer. (The covered pan can also be placed in a 400-degree oven to cook for the same length of time.)

8. When the fish is done, remove the plate from the steamer. A thin sauce will have formed on the plate. Heat the peanut oil and sesame oil in a small saucepan almost to the smoking point, and pour the mixture over the fish for the final touch to produce a sheen and add richness and flavor.

Braising Whole Fish

Before you braise a fish, dust it with water chestnut powder and deep-fry it quickly to brown it and give it a crusty exterior that protects the skin from falling apart during the remainder of the cooking. Then simmer the fish in a tasty braising liquid which keeps the fish moist and adds flavor. Here we use a spicy sauce, which is perfect for firmer-textured fish like rock cod or grouper. For a more delicate-textured fish, such as whitefish or sea bass, use a black bean sauce (see the one for clams, page 273) or even a sweet-and-sour sauce (see the one for pork, page 200).

Braised Sichuan Fish

1 whole fish, about 1½ to 2 pounds, cleaned and scaled (see page 229)
Water chestnut powder or cornstarch for dusting
4 cups peanut oil for deep-frying
4 dried chili peppers
4 cloves garlic, coarsely chopped
2 slices fresh ginger root, coarsely chopped

SAUCE:
1 tablespoon dark soy sauce
2 tablespoons Shaoxing wine or dry sherry
1 tablespoon chili paste
1 tablespoon bean sauce
1 tablespoon Chinese or red wine vinegar
1 teaspoon sugar
1 tablespoon cornstarch dissolved in ¾ cup cold chicken broth and 2 tablespoons sesame oil

GARNISH:
2 scallions, chopped

METHOD: Deep-frying (page 56), braising
SERVES 2 to 3 as a main course.
BEST SERVED immediately, but can be reheated slowly in braising liquid just before serving.
SUGGESTED BEVERAGE: Beer

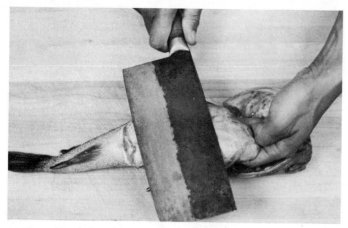

1. Set the fish on a cutting board belly up. With the blunt end of a cleaver, hit the fish a few times to crack the bones along the stomach. This makes it easier to serve the cooked fish right side up instead of on its side.

2. Score the sides of the fish deeply, right down to the bone, at 1½-inch intervals. This helps the fish cook more evenly and quickly.

4. Heat the 4 cups of oil in a wok until moderately hot (360 degrees). Slip the fish in head first. (The front end of the fish is the thickest part and needs the most cooking.)

3. Coat the fish evenly with cornstarch or water chestnut powder, making certain that the interior of the scoring cuts is coated as well. Shake the fish to remove any excess powder.

5. Scoop the hot oil over the fish to help it brown evenly.

6. As soon as it is lightly browned (after 5 to 8 minutes), remove the fish with a strainer, turn off the heat, and drain all but 2 tablespoons of the oil. (The excess oil may be strained and reserved for use with other fish preparations.)

7. Over high heat, stir-fry the peppers, garlic, and ginger to flavor the oil.

8. Add the sauce ingredients. As they come to a boil, the sauce will thicken.

9. Slide the fish into the sauce, reduce the heat to a simmer, and baste the fish with the sauce regularly while the fish is braising. Test for doneness by pushing one of the scored cuts with a chopstick to see if the fish is opaque all the way to the bone.

10. Transfer the fish and the sauce to a serving plate and sprinkle it with the chopped scallions.

Steeping Whole Fish

This is the Chinese equivalent of the popular French poached fish. The fish is lowered into boiling water, which is returned to a simmer; the heat then is turned off, and the fish finishes cooking in the gentle heat, leaving it especially succulent. A popular steeped fish dish known as West Lake Fish originated in Hangchow, which is famous for its fish-laden West Lake. The mildly sweet-and-sour sauce, typical of the region, is much more delicate than the usual sweet-and-sour sauce. A mild black bean sauce or a dipping sauce of soy sauce and vinegar could be used, too. Rock cod or carp is the favored fish for this dish, but if they are unavailable, try sea trout, red snapper, or mullet.

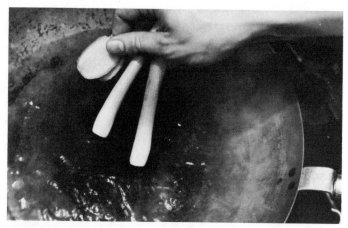

1. Fill the wok halfway with water. Add the salt, ginger, and scallions. Bring the water to a boil.

2. Lower the fish gently into the water. Add a little more water if necessary so that the fish is entirely covered. Bring it to a simmer.

3. Cover the top of the wok with foil and crimp the edge to seal it. Turn off the heat.

5. Remove the lid and the foil and check the fish for doneness. Place a bed of spinach on a hot platter, then gently lift the fish with a strainer and place it on top.

6. Pour over the sauce. Serve the fish immediately, surrounded with the stir-fried tree ears.

West Lake Fish

Salt to taste
2 slices fresh ginger root
2 scallions
1 whole rock cod or carp, about 2½ pounds, cleaned, scaled, and gutted (see page 229)

SAUCE:
½ cup chicken broth
¼ cup Chinese brown rock sugar or regular brown sugar
¼ cup Chinkiany vinegar, or ⅓ cup cider vinegar or British malt vinegar
1 tablespoon dark soy sauce
1 tablespoon Shaoxing wine or dry sherry
2 tablespoons minced fresh ginger root
3 tablespoons minced Smithfield ham

GARNISH:
1½ pounds spinach, stir-fried
¼ cup tree ears, soaked, rinsed, stems removed, shredded, and stir-fried
3 tablespoons peanut oil

METHOD: Steeping
SERVES 3 to 4 as a main course.
SUGGESTED BEVERAGE: Beer

FISH FILLETS

Filleting Fish

You can be extra sure your fish is fresh if you buy it whole and fillet it yourself. Not only does the fish taste fresher, but you can use the head and bones to make an excellent fish stock for soups and the like. Be certain that the blade of your cleaver is sharp, and always cut against the bone, following the skeleton of the fish. A light cleaver works best. Here we are filleting a rock cod, about 3 pounds in weight and no more than 8 hours out of the Pacific.

1. Gently cut to—not through—the backbone, behind the head and gill fins.

2. Make a long cut about ½ inch deep along the top of the backbone, connecting with the first cut behind the head.

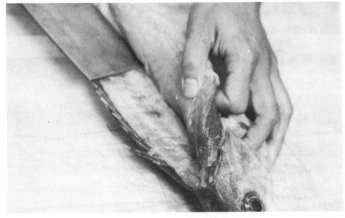

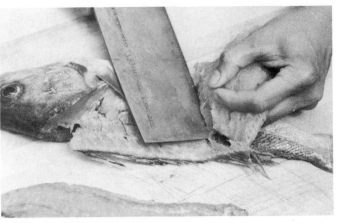

3. Keeping the cleaver angled slightly against the bones, and working from the head toward the tail, gently *pull* the fillet off the bone while freeing it from the bone with long, *gentle* strokes of the cleaver.

4. Do the same with the other side.

5. To skin the fillet, start from the narrow end, and scrape the end of the skin clean for about ½ inch.

6. Holding down the end of the skin with one hand, and holding the blade of the cleaver against the skin, pull the skin and run the cleaver along it, freeing the fillet.

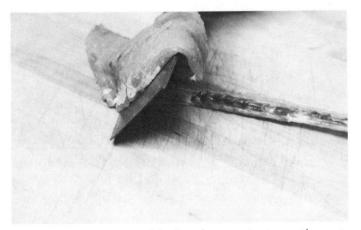

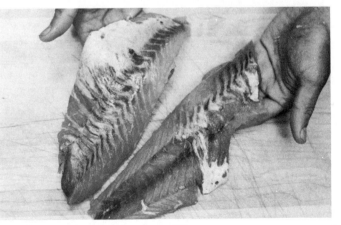

7. Do not try to *cut* with the cleaver. Just use the cutting edge as a guide.

8. This produces two clean fillets.

Frying Fish Fillets

A coating will protect delicate fish fillets from the fierce heat of deep-frying. It can be cornstarch, water chestnut powder, or a light batter such as the one for Spun Apples (page 334). A sesame-seed coating like the one used here is particularly good. It's not as heavy as a batter and is especially attractive. A first frying sets the coating; the second finishes the cooking. Everything but the final frying can be done hours in advance.

Fried Sesame Seed Fish

1 pound fish fillets, preferably thin small fillets

MARINADE:
3 slices fresh ginger root
3 scallions
2 tablespoons Shaoxing wine or dry sherry
Salt to taste

1 egg, beaten
½ cup white sesame seeds
½ cup dark sesame seeds

METHOD: Deep-frying (page 56)
SERVES 2 as a main course, 4 as a first course.
FILLETS can be marinated ahead of time and deep-fried at the last minute.
SUGGESTED BEVERAGE: Sauvignon Blanc or Graves

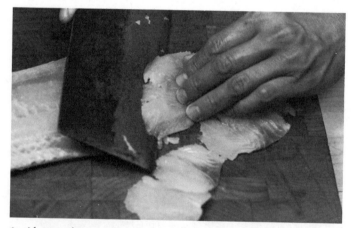

1. If you do not have thin fillets, cut thin scallop slices from a big fillet, and slice them at a 45-degree angle into ½-inch pieces.

2. Puree the marinade ingredients in a blender or food processor. Strain the marinade over the fish, brushing to coat the fillets. Marinate them for at least 20 minutes.

3. Drain the fillets and pat them dry. Dip each piece into the beaten egg.

4. Coat one side of each fillet with the white seeds.

5. Coat the other side with the dark seeds.

6. Heat the oil in a wok until it is moderately hot (about 350 degrees). Holding the pieces with long chopsticks, dip them into the oil one at a time for a few seconds, just long enough for the coating to set and the surface of the fish to turn opaque.

7. Just before serving, fry them all together for about 2 minutes. Arrange them to show off the contrast of light and dark seeds.

Filleting Whole Fish, Tail Intact

The Chinese, who are enchanted by surprises and things that aren't really as they appear, love this technique for preparing what looks like a whole fish (bones and all) but is really a pair of fillets left attached at the tail. Once it is fried, it curls up like a squirrel's bushy tail; hence the name of the dish most often associated with the technique, Squirrel Fish.

Select a fish that is not too bony, such as a small rock cod, snapper, or sea bass.

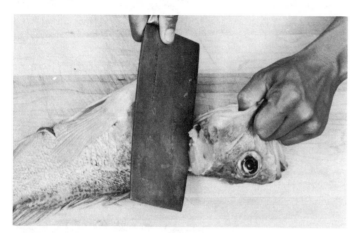

1. Cut off the head, chopping straight through the fish behind the gills. Reserve the head.

2. Starting at the cut end, cut about ½ inch deep along the backbone, stopping just short of the tail. Return again to the cut end and start to lift the fillet from the bone, freeing it with the cleaver.

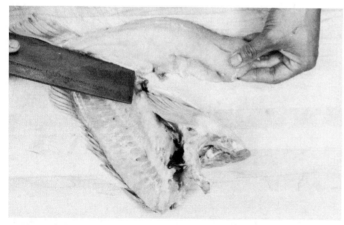

3. Work toward the tail, lifting the fillet and using the cleaver to cut against the bone to free the fillet. Lift the fillet away except for the tail.

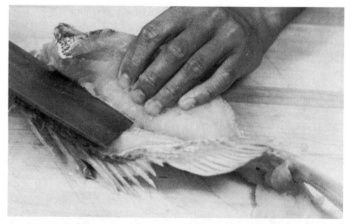

4. Repeat the procedure on the other side.

5. This separates the fillets from the bones, but leaves them attached at the tail.

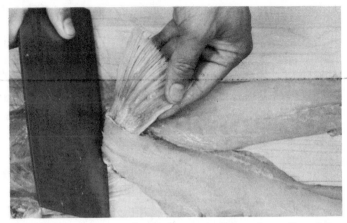

6. Cut the bones where they attach to the tail, taking care not to cut through the fillets. (Use the bones to make fish broth.)

7. To help ensure that the fish will fry evenly and quickly, score the flesh side (not the skin side, because the skin holds the fillet together). First make diagonal cuts ½ inch deep in one direction. Be careful not to cut through to the skin.

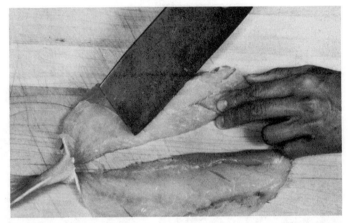

8. Then crisscross with slashes in the other direction.

9. Just before cooking, dust the fish evenly with cornstarch or water chestnut powder. Shake off any excess.

10. When the fish is dusted, the scoring is clearly visible. Dust the head well. Fry and serve it with the fish so that it looks complete.

Squirrel Fish

If you fillet the fish ahead of time, do it no more than a few hours before serving, and do not dust it with cornstarch or water chestnut powder until you are ready to fry it; otherwise the coating gets soggy. The sauce can be made ahead. Sweet-and-sour sauce is traditional, but a hot spicy one (such as the sauce for Braised Sichuan Fish, page 233) or a black bean sauce (like the Lobster Sauce on page 261) is excellent, too.

5 cups oil for deep-frying
1 white-fleshed fish, 2 to 2½ pounds, filleted with the tail attached (see
*   page 242)*
Water chestnut powder or cornstarch for dusting
1 recipe (2 cups) Sweet-and-Sour Sauce (page 200)
1 cup mixed pickled vegetables and rinds

METHOD: Deep-frying (page 56)

SERVES 2 as a main course.

SUGGESTED BEVERAGE: Beer

1. Heat the oil in a wok until it is moderately hot (about 350 degrees). Dust the fish with water chestnut powder or cornstarch, and put the fish into the oil.

2. Fry it for 5 to 7 minutes, or just long enough to brown it lightly.

3. Remove the fish with a strainer. Set it on paper towels to drain.

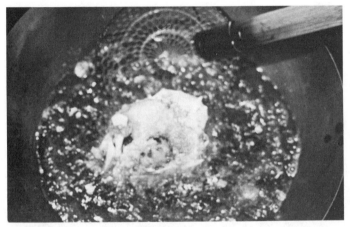

4. Fry the head the same way.

5. Remove all of the oil from the wok to make Sweet-and-Sour Sauce, or heat the sauce in a separate pan.

6. Arrange the fried fish and its head on a platter. Coat it with the sauce. Garnish with the pickled vegetables.

7. A good sweet-and-sour sauce has a good balance of tartness from the vinegar and sweetness from the sugar, neither dominating. Added flavor comes from the pickled vegetables.

Fish Paste

Fish paste is at the base of innumerable classic dishes—Fish Balls, Fish Cakes, Fish Roll, even substituting for shrimp paste in Shrimp Toast (page 256). Some Chinese fish stores sell it ready-made, but it tends to be salty and contains monosodium glutamate. We use a small amount of fat in the paste, which makes an enormous difference in richness and flavor. You'll find that a food processor is a tremendous help.

Basic Fish Paste

¾ pound fish fillets (rock cod, sea bass, or any white-fleshed fish), finely chopped to a paste
2 tablespoons Shaoxing wine or dry sherry
2 tablespoons minced scallion
2 teaspoons sesame oil
3 tablespoons minced Smithfield ham fat or chicken fat
½ teaspoon fresh ginger juice
Salt to taste
1 egg white
2 teaspoons cornstarch dissolved in 1 tablespoon cold chicken broth

1. Put the finely chopped fish through a food mill to remove any filaments. (This step is unnecessary if the chopping is done in a food processor.)

2. Mix the fish with the remaining ingredients to form a smooth paste. Use it to make any of the following recipes. Yields 1 to 1½ cups.

Fish Balls
[see photo in color section]

These light dumplings are like a Chinese gefilte fish. They cook quickly, so remove them from the water as soon as they float. If you are reheating them, say, in a soup, put them in just long enough to heat through. They can be made several hours ahead and kept refrigerated until you are ready to use them. The Chinese form balls by squeezing the mixture through the fist, then scooping it with a spoon to ensure equal-sized balls.

Bowl of ice water
1 recipe Basic Fish Paste

METHOD: Poaching
MAKES 15 to 20 balls, enough for 4 bowls of soup.
THE FISH BALLS can be prepared ahead and reheated in broth just before
    serving.
SUGGESTED BEVERAGE: Light, dry generic white wine

1. Prepare a pot of simmering water and a bowl of ice water. Set them side by side near the bowl of fish paste.

2. With wet hands, form a handful (3 tablespoons) of the paste into a fat cylinder. Plunge your hands into the ice water after forming each cylinder. If your hands are cool, the paste will be easier to manage.

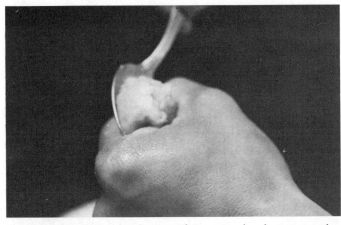

3. Squeeze the cylinder until it extrudes between the thumb and first finger to form a ball. You can use a spoon to help form the ball and scoop it off. This makes the fish balls lighter in texture than they would be if you rolled them between the palms. Repeat the process until enough fish balls are formed.

4. Drop the fish balls into the simmering water. When they float to the surface, remove them with a skimmer or a strainer. Do a dozen or so at a time as you form more.

Fish Cakes

[see photo in color section]

The same fish paste is very good formed into patties and deep-fried. Serve as an appetizer with a dipping sauce of soy, or soy sauce mixed with chili paste, or even tartar sauce; or stir-fry them with vegetables and serve as an entrée. Always slice the cakes so that they can be eaten with chopsticks.

1 recipe Basic Fish Paste (page 246)
3 cups peanut oil for deep-frying

ENTRÉE SAUCE:
2 slices fresh ginger root, shredded
2 tablespoons peanut oil
1½ pounds Chinese or American broccoli, sliced or cut into 2-inch pieces
2 tablespoons Shaoxing wine or dry sherry
1 scallion, shredded
1 cup chicken broth
3 tablespoons oyster sauce

METHOD: Deep-frying (page 56), stir-frying (page 52)
SERVES 3 to 4 as a main course, 6 as an appetizer.
CAN BE PREPARED ahead and served at room temperature as an appetizer, or prepared ahead up to step 4 as a main dish, then stir-fried just before serving.
SUGGESTED BEVERAGE: Chardonnay or Macon Blanc

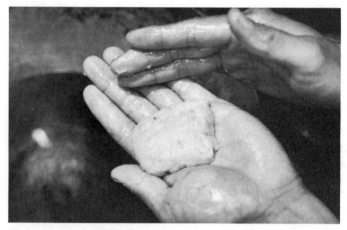

1. Moisten the hands with peanut oil to keep the paste from sticking. Form the paste into patties ¾ inch thick and 3 inches across.

2. Deep-fry the cakes in hot oil (375 degrees).

3. When they are brown, remove them from the oil with long chopsticks or a strainer.

4. When the cakes are cool enough to handle, slice them into ½-inch pieces. This reveals the contrast between the browned surface and the white interior. Serve them as an hors d'oeuvre with a dipping sauce, or combine them with vegetables to make an entrée, as follows:

5. Stir-fry the ginger shreds in the oil to flavor it.

6. Add the vegetables, Shaoxing wine or sherry, scallion, chicken broth, and oyster sauce. Cook the vegetables until they are tender-crisp.

7. Mix in the sliced fish cake. Serve the dish immediately.

8. The sauce may be thickened with 1 tablespoon cornstarch dissolved in 2 tablespoons chicken broth.

Fish Roll

[see photo in color section]

These resemble a fish *boudin,* or sausage. Slices of fish roll make a highly unusual and delicate appetizer served with lemon wedges and roasted salt and pepper. The fish paste is rolled up in sheets of caul fat, which form a light, crisp coating that protects the filling and keeps it moist. The rolls can be made ahead and refrigerated, but wait to fry them until the last minute.

4 pieces fresh caul fat, about 12 by 18 inches
1 recipe Basic Fish Paste (page 246)
Water chestnut powder or cornstarch for dusting
3 cups peanut oil for deep-frying

METHOD: Deep-frying (page 56)
SERVES 4 to 6 as an appetizer.
SUGGESTED BEVERAGE: Chardonnay or white Burgundy

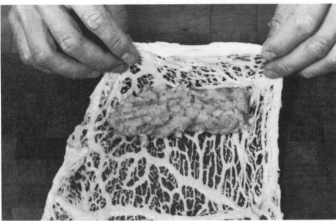

1. Spread out one of the pieces of caul fat. Form a cylinder of fish paste about 10 inches long, using about a quarter of the fish paste. Place it near one end of the piece of caul.

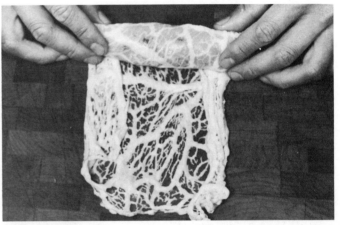

2. Roll it up in the caul, enclosing the ends by turning up the sides as you roll. Repeat to make 3 more rolls.

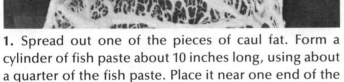

3. Caul fat is sticky enough to seal itself. It need not be sealed with egg.

4. Dust the surface of the rolls with water chestnut powder or cornstarch.

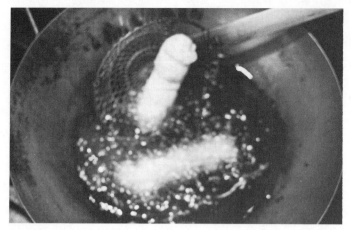

5. Heat 3 cups oil in a wok to 360 degrees and slide in the rolls one at a time.

6. Fry them until they are brown (about 5 minutes). The caul fat turns crisp and delicate when fried. (The oil may be strained and used again for deep-frying fish.)

7. Drain and slice the rolls at an angle into 1-inch pieces. Arrange the slices on a platter with lemon wedges and roasted salt and pepper (page 70) for dipping.

SHELLFISH AND MOLLUSKS

Cleaning and Preparing Shrimp in the Shell

The Chinese often cook shrimp with the shells intact because the shells contribute much of the flavor. Stir-fried or deep-fried, the shells offer a crunchy texture not unlike that of soft-shell crab. In addition, the good flavors of a sauce are captured between the flesh and the shell. The black vein running the length of the shrimp should be removed, however.

Use medium-sized shrimp, about 3 inches long.

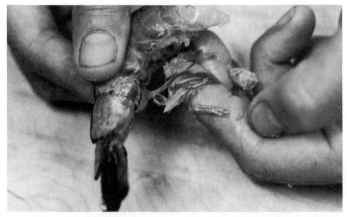

1. First, pull off the little legs.

2. Holding the shrimp flat, parallel-cut with a cleaver (or a paring knife) through the shell and about ½ inch into the shrimp along the back.

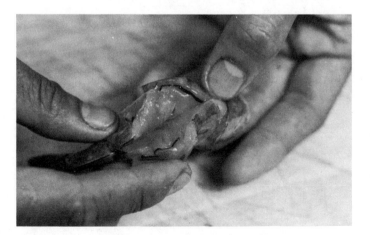

3. This cut exposes the black vein.

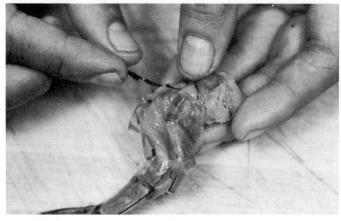

4. Pull the vein away.

5. Dry the shrimp thoroughly by blotting them between layers of paper towel.

Salt-Leeching Shrimp

Salt-leeching cuts through the sticky film on the outside of shelled shrimp, makes the shrimp crunchy, and gives them a glossy cast. It does not wash away flavor, but rather gives the shrimp what can only be described as a cleaner taste.

1. Toss the shrimp in salt (use 2 teaspoons coarse—kosher—salt per pound for each toss) to coat them well. Let stand about 1 minute.

2. Rinse and drain the shrimp.

3. Repeat the salting and draining procedure twice more. Then pat the shrimp dry with paper towels.

Crystal Shrimp

1 pound shrimp, salt-leeched (see above)
2 tablespoons peanut oil
3 cloves garlic, minced
1 slice fresh ginger root, minced
4 scallions, minced
1 tablespoon thin soy sauce
1 tablespoon Shaoxing wine or dry sherry

METHOD: Salt-leeching, stir-frying (page 52)

SERVES 2 to 3 as a main dish, 4 to 6 as an appetizer.

SERVE IMMEDIATELY, or prepare several hours ahead and serve at room temperature as a salad course.

SUGGESTED BEVERAGE: Chardonnay or white Burgundy

1. Heat the oil in a wok. Stir-fry the shrimp quickly to coat them.

2. Add the garlic, ginger, and scallions, and stir-fry for a moment. Then add the soy sauce and rice wine or sherry. Continue stirring until the shrimp are cooked (about 2 minutes).

3. Serve the shrimp immediately.

255

Shrimp Paste

This shrimp version of the fish paste described on page 246 is rich in flavor and somewhat firmer in texture. It makes an ideal stuffing for vegetables such as bitter melon (page 83) and can also be used to stuff bean curd (page 91) or to make Shrimp Toast. Here we form it into balls and deep-fry them for a superb and simple appetizer.

Basic Shrimp Paste
1 pound large or medium shrimp, shelled and finely chopped to a paste by hand or in a food processor
2 tablespoons ham fat, or chicken fat with 1 teaspoon salt
4 fresh water chestnuts, peeled and minced
1 tablespoon fresh ginger juice
Salt to taste
2 tablespoons minced scallion
1 egg white
1 tablespoon Shaoxing wine or dry sherry
Sesame oil for rolling

Mix these ingredients thoroughly to form a smooth paste. Yields 1 to 1¼ cups.

Shrimp Balls
[see photo in color section]

1 recipe Basic Shrimp Paste (see above)
2 cups peanut oil for deep-frying

METHOD: Deep-frying (page 56)
MAKES 15 to 20 shrimp balls, to serve 4 as an appetizer.
SUGGESTED BEVERAGE: Chardonnay or white Burgundy

1. With hands moistened with sesame oil, form the paste into large balls between the palms.

2. Slip the shrimp balls one by one into the 2 cups of oil at 360 degrees. When they brown (about 3 minutes), remove them with long chopsticks or a strainer.

3. If you have the shrimp heads, fry them in the oil until they turn red (about 30 seconds) for use as a garnish.

4. Arrange the shrimp balls and the heads on a platter.

Shrimp Toast

Shrimp Toast makes an irresistible finger-food appetizer to accompany cocktails and to serve as part of a buffet, or as an East-meets-West sandwich lunch. It is made from leftover bread that has dried out, or fresh bread sliced and dried in the oven, so it won't absorb the oil. It is also excellent made with fish paste (page 246), which has its own unique texture and taste and can be made at less cost.

1 recipe Basic Shrimp Paste (page 256)
10 slices stale white bread (use 2-day-old bread, or dry fresh bread in the
*   oven with the pilot light on)*
4 cups peanut oil for deep-frying

METHOD: Deep-frying (page 56)
MAKES 20 pieces, to serve 5 as an appetizer, 3 as a luncheon main course.
SUGGESTED BEVERAGE: Dry Chenin Blanc or Macon Blanc

1. Prepare the shrimp paste. Cut the bread slices in half, into triangles or rectangles. Spread them with shrimp paste.

2. Mound the paste so that it is thickest in the middle.

3. Deep-fry the shrimp-spread bread slices in the hot oil (375 degrees) to brown them.

4. Serve them while they are hot and crisp.

258

Deep-Frying Shrimp

When we deep-fry shrimp, we leave the tails on and partially butterfly the shrimp so that they cook fast and evenly. With the tails intact, the fried shrimp resemble the colorful tail of the phoenix, the Chinese symbol of rebirth, auspiciousness, and the feminine qualities of yin-yang. One popular name for shrimp prepared this way is Phoenix-Tailed Shrimp. It is also known as Butterflied Shrimp because the shrimp fan out like butterfly wings when fried. Although it is usually an appetizer, deep-fried shrimp makes a fine entrée served on top of Stir-Fried Bok Choy in Garlic Oil (page 77).

Phoenix Shrimp

[see photo in color section]

1 pound shrimp, medium or large

MARINADE:
1 tablespoon Shaoxing wine or dry sherry
1 tablespoon thin soy sauce

4 cups peanut oil for deep-frying

BATTER:
1 cup water chestnut powder or flour
1 tablespoon baking powder
¾ cup cold water

METHOD: Deep-frying (page 56)
SERVES 2 as a main course, 4 as an appetizer.
SUGGESTED BEVERAGE: Chardonnay or white Burgundy

1. Peel the shrimp, breaking the shell away at the tail.

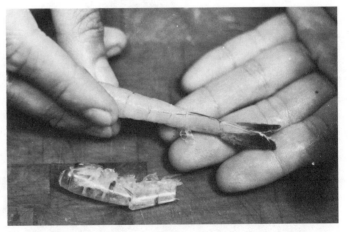

2. The tail remains attached to the shelled shrimp.

3. Holding the shrimp flat on a cutting board, parallel-cut ½ inch deep to expose the vein and partially butterfly the shrimp. Remove the vein. Marinate the shrimp 10 minutes or more. Mix the batter.

4. Heat the oil in a wok to moderate (350 degrees). Dip the shrimp into the batter. With long chopsticks, lift them out one by one, letting the excess batter drip away. Slide them into the oil one at a time to keep them from sticking together.

5. When the shrimp are crisp and lightly browned (large shrimp take about 3 minutes, smaller ones 2 minutes), lift them from the oil with a strainer. (The oil may be cooled, strained, and stored for reuse to deep-fry seafood.)

6. An attractive and simple presentation is to fry a handful of shrimp chips (see page 39) to serve as a bed for the shrimp. A whole shrimp, head and tail on, makes a dramatic garnish.

Lobster Sauce

Lobster sauce contains no lobster; it is made from egg and pork. The name comes from its use on the popular restaurant and banquet dish, Lobster Cantonese. The eggs are incorporated into the sauce in slow motion to produce strands of egg and a beautiful flower pattern, which are critical to the texture and appearance of the dish. This is entirely unlike the Western way of smoothly mixing in eggs to thicken sauces. Here we use the sauce on shrimp, because it is slightly less expensive than lobster, but it is equally good cooked with beef and tomatoes, crayfish, clams, or crabs.

Shrimp in Lobster Sauce
[see photo in color section]

*1 pound medium shrimp, completely shelled, tails removed, cleaned
    (see page 253), and blotted dry*

MARINADE:
1 egg white, lightly beaten
1 teaspoon cornstarch
1½ cups peanut oil for deep-frying

SAUCE:
½ pound pork, coarsely ground
2 tablespoons peanut oil
1½ tablespoons fermented black beans
2 tablespoons coarsely chopped garlic
1 teaspoon finely chopped fresh ginger root
2 scallions, finely chopped
1½ tablespoons thin soy sauce
2 tablespoons Shaoxing wine or dry sherry
¼ teaspoon sugar
Pinch of salt
½ cup chicken broth

1 tablespoon cornstarch dissolved in 2 tablespoons cold chicken broth
1 egg beaten with 2 teaspoons sesame oil

METHOD: Velveting (page 143), stir-frying (page 52)
SERVES 2 to 3 as a main course.
SUGGESTED BEVERAGE: Chardonnay or light, chilled red wine

Marinate the shrimp for 20 minutes in the refrigerator.

1. Velvet the shrimp (see Velveting Chicken, page 143) in 1½ cups oil at a moderate temperature (325 degrees). Or, to simplify, stir-fry them in 3 tablespoons of oil just until they turn opaque. Remove them from the wok.

2. Brown the ground pork in 2 tablespoons of oil.

3. Add the rest of the sauce ingredients. Bring them to a boil and add the cornstarch to thicken the sauce lightly.

4. Turn off the heat. Stir in the beaten egg, pulling the clumps of egg into thin strands with chopsticks as they cook.

5. Stir in the cooked shrimp to coat them with the sauce.

Cooking Live Shellfish

This technique stands as a statement of the Chinese philosophy of seafood: for seafood to be truly fresh, it should still be alive when it hits the wok. When it comes to shellfish, the crustaceans are dry-fried, which means they are cooked without a sauce. The tender and sweet meat is presented nearly unadorned. A sauce, such as Lobster Sauce (page 261), would help extend the dish, but it would mask the delicate flavor of the shellfish. If you are lucky enough to obtain some live shrimp, try them this way.

Dry-Fried Crayfish
[see photo in color section]

4 tablespoons peanut oil
2 pounds live, rinsed crayfish or cleaned, unshelled shrimp (see page 253)
2 tablespoons minced garlic
1 teaspoon minced fresh ginger root
4 tablespoons coarsely chopped scallion
2 tablespoons Shaoxing wine or dry sherry
2 tablespoons thin soy sauce
½ teaspoon sugar
Pinch of salt
¼ cup chicken broth

METHOD: Stir-frying (page 52)
SERVES 4 as an appetizer.
SERVE HOT or at room temperature with salad for a summer lunch.
SUGGESTED BEVERAGE: Chardonnay or white Burgundy

1. Heat a wok over a high flame. Add the oil, and when it is hot, stir-fry the crayfish or shrimp quickly until they turn red.

2. Add the remaining ingredients. Continue stirring until the crayfish or shrimp are cooked (about 3 minutes).

3. Arrange the crayfish or shrimp attractively on a platter. They are eaten with chopsticks (if you are adept), or with the fingers.

Cracking and Cleaning Live Crab

As soon as a crab (or any shellfish) is killed, it starts to lose flavor. To preserve the full freshness and taste, crab must be cut up just before cooking. Once you eat crab prepared this way, you will never want to go back to precooked crab. The texture and flavor are worlds apart. West Coast Dungeness crab, used here, is meatier and sweeter than the blue crabs caught in eastern waters. Their structures are identical, however, so the technique is the same for both. To keep from getting pinched, hold the crab from the back, or wear thick gloves. The cracked and cleaned crab pieces can be stir-fried or steamed. If you can't imagine yourself cutting up a live crab, steam it for 5 minutes first, then cut it up as described here.

1. Always hold the crab at the back to avoid the large pincers.

2. Twist off the large pincers. Then break off the rest of the smaller legs. Scrub the shells clean under running water.

3. Pull the large top shell off the crab in one piece. Set it aside.

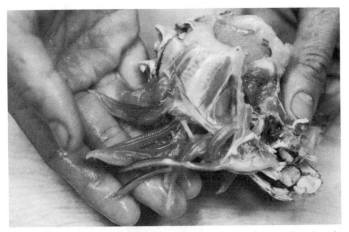

4. Pull off the feathery lungs and rinse the crab's body clean under running water.

5. On the bottom of the crab, find the "tail," a piece of shell that is folded against the crab's bottom. Pull this tail away from the body.

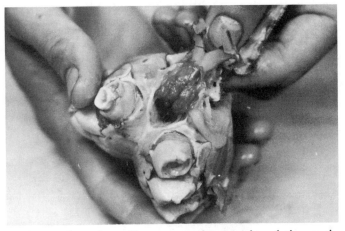

6. Removing the tail exposes the inside of the crab. Rinse it out.

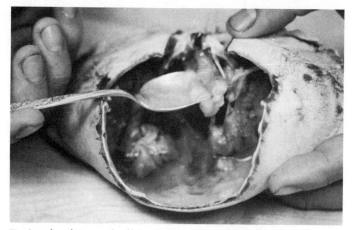

7. In the large shell, near the mouth, there is a small dark sac. Remove it with a spoon, being careful not to break it. Don't remove the yellowish-brown "crab butter" from the shell, which has a rich flavor.

8. Cut the body into quarters.

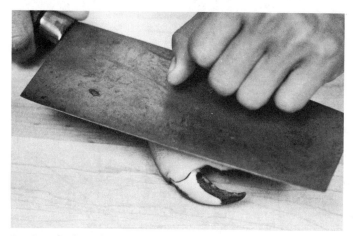

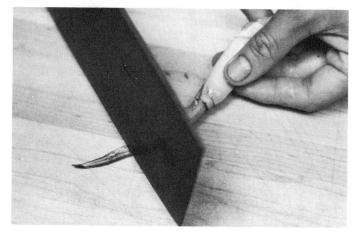

9. Crack the claws by tapping them with a cleaver, or by placing a cleaver on top of the claw and hitting the back of the cleaver with the heel of the hand.

10. Cut the tops off the legs.

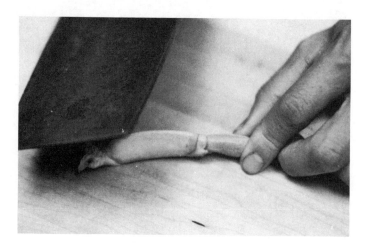

11. Crack the legs one by one. Turn each leg so that the edge is up, enabling you to tap the shell with the side of a cleaver just hard enough to crack the shell, but not so hard as to crush the fragile meat.

Steamed Crab with Custard

Steaming is a gentle, moist method of cooking that minimizes the possibility of overcooking and drying out the crab. Here the crab is steamed with an unusual custard that provides a counterpoint to the crab with its salty flavor and its soft texture. The custard cooks on the same plate as the crab for an exquisite banquet presentation. It is equally good made with clams or lobster. The custard is delicious by itself, too. Without the custard, the cut-up crab may be steamed with the same seasonings as steamed whole fish (page 231) or in black bean sauce (page 273).

1 live crab, about 1¼ to 1½ pounds, cut up just before cooking (see above)
2 preserved salted duck eggs (optional)

CUSTARD:
4 large chicken eggs (use 2 if using the duck eggs)
1 tablespoon Shaoxing wine or dry sherry
Pinch of salt, or more if duck eggs are not being used
2 tablespoons finely chopped Chinese chives
¼ cup chicken broth

GARNISH:
4 scallions, white part only, shredded
2 tablespoons peanut oil

METHOD: Steaming (page 59)
SERVES 2 as a main course.
SUGGESTED BEVERAGE: Chardonnay or white Burgundy

1. Reassemble the raw crab on a serving plate, tucking the meat back inside the body and the legs underneath.

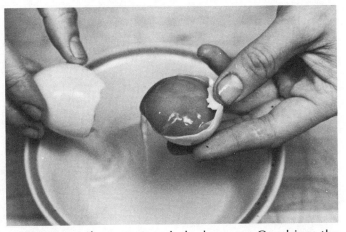

2. Separate the preserved duck eggs. Combine the whites with the rest of the custard ingredients. Set the yolks aside.

3. Set the yolks at either side of the crab, then pour the custard mixture over all.

4. Set the platter in a steamer. (If it won't fit in a wok, improvise a steamer like the one used for fish on page 00.) Cover and steam for 20 to 25 minutes, until the crab is cooked through.

5. Garnish the crab with shredded scallions. Just before serving, heat 2 tablespoons oil to the smoking point and drizzle it over the crab.

Cleaning and Preparing Squid

Cleaning squid is not difficult, but it takes time. Fortunately, it can be done hours ahead. Properly cooked, squid has a firm texture, not unlike lobster, and a mild flavor. The Chinese often call it "poor man's lobster," as it is one of the least expensive seafoods available.

1. Place the squid flat on a cutting board. With one hand hold the body, and with the other pull out the tentacles. The inner matter of the squid will come with them.

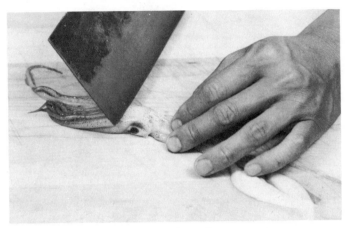

2. Cut the tentacles just below the eye.

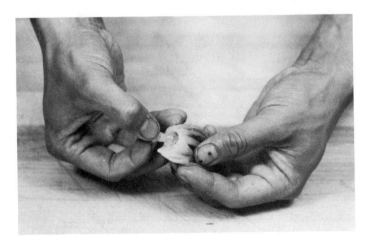

3. With your finger, remove the beak.

4. Split the body lengthwise, but don't cut all the way through.

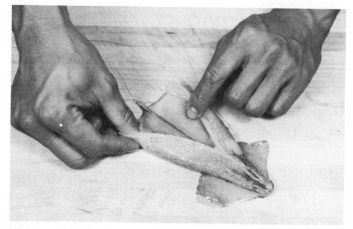

5. You should just cut through one layer so that the squid can be opened up.

6. Lift out the semitransparent "quill" and any remaining jellylike inner matter.

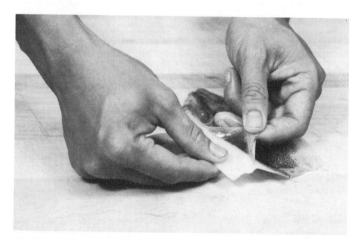

7. Starting at one end, remove the purple-spotted skin with your fingers.

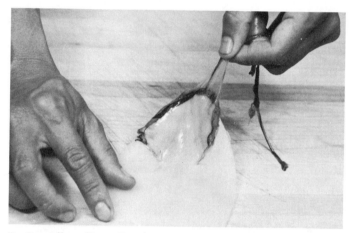

8. It pulls off easily, but it may not come off in one piece.

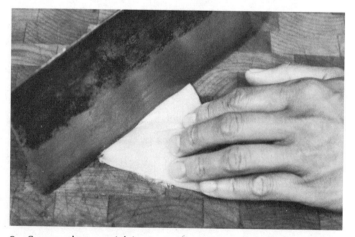

9. Score the squid in two directions lightly (see page 50).

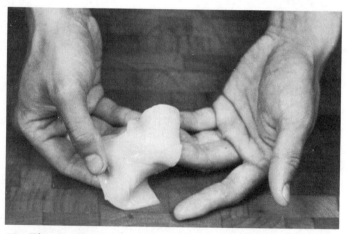

10. The crisscross pattern of scoring tenderizes the squid and makes it look more attractive when it is cooked.

Stir-Fried Squid with Mustard Greens

We are certain that people who dislike squid have only eaten it overcooked. Here it is quickly stir-fried so that it stays tender, delicate, and juicy. The squid curl into attractive shells. The mustard greens act like lemon, a sharp contrast to the mild squid.

4 tablespoons peanut oil
2 pounds squid, cleaned and scored (see above)
1 cup cut-up Pickled Chinese Mustard Greens (page 88)
1 teaspoon minced fresh ginger root
Pinch of salt
1 tablespoon Shaoxing wine or dry sherry
1 tablespoon sugar
½ cup chicken broth
1 teaspoon cornstarch dissolved in 1 tablespoon cold chicken broth

METHOD: Stir-frying (page 52)
SERVES 6 as an appetizer, 4 as a main course.
SERVE HOT as an entrée or cold as a cold salad or appetizer.
SUGGESTED BEVERAGE: Sauvignon Blanc or Sancerre

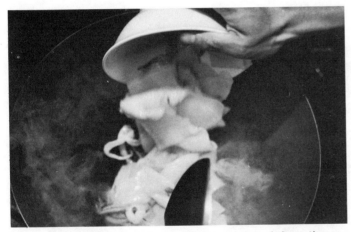

1. Heat a wok containing 2 tablespoons of the oil over a high flame. Add the squid.

2. Stir-fry it just until it curls up and turns opaque (about 30 seconds). Remove it and drain it.

3. Heat the remaining 2 tablespoons of the oil in the wok and stir-fry the mustard greens with the minced ginger for 30 seconds. Then add the remaining ingredients.

4. When the mixture thickens, add the squid and stir-fry quickly to mix them in well.

5. Immediately transfer the mixture to a serving dish.

Cleaning and Preparing Clams

Clams are as popular in China as they are in the West, but the Chinese rarely eat them raw. Instead, techniques for cooking clams strive to make the best of the clam's flavorful juices. Often the clams are simply steamed and dipped into a sauce that incorporates the juices. Stir-fried and simmered with black beans, the juices become the foundation of the sauce. The Chinese prefer smaller clams because they are more tender.

1. Scrub the grit from the clam shells under running water. Feel the weight of each clam. If it feels especially light, discard it; the clam is dead.

2. Put the clams in a large bowl and cover them with water. Put a clean cleaver in the water with the clams. The iron in the cleaver causes the clams to spew out any sand and grit that may be inside the shells (this takes about two hours). Drain the clams. (Note the sand at the bottom of the bowl.)

Clams with Black Beans

5 pounds small clams in their shells
2 tablespoons peanut oil
1 clove garlic, finely chopped
1 small shallot, finely chopped
2 tablespoons fermented black beans, coarsely chopped
1 tablespoon thin soy sauce
2 tablespoons Shaoxing wine or dry sherry
½ cup chicken broth
1 tablespoon cornstarch dissolved in 1 tablespoon cold chicken broth, if
  necessary

GARNISH:
2 tablespoons chopped scallion tops

METHOD: Stir-frying (page 52), simmering
SERVES 6 as an appetizer, 4 as a main course.
SUGGESTED BEVERAGE: Dry Chenin Blanc or Muscadet

1. Heat a wok and add the oil. When it is very hot, add the clams and stir-fry them for about 30 seconds.

2. Add the remaining ingredients. Let them simmer about 5 minutes.

3. As the clams open wide, remove them one by one to a serving platter with long chopsticks. As you remove them, tip them to drain all the juices into the wok.

4. Any clams that fail to open should be discarded. They were dead before they were cooked. (If the beans and juice from the clams don't thicken the sauce sufficiently, add the cornstarch dissolved in water.) Taste the sauce. During the long simmering, it can be reduced and become excessively salty. If it is too salty, thin it with water or more chicken broth. Pour the sauce over the clams and sprinkle the dish with chopped scallion.

Cleaning and Preparing Conch

The conch is actually a large sea snail with a texture like that of abalone. It must be cut into thin slices and quickly cooked to be tender. A spicy sauce helps balance the flavor. Conch must be absolutely fresh or its scent can be overwhelming. It has a strong flavor of the sea and is an acquired taste.

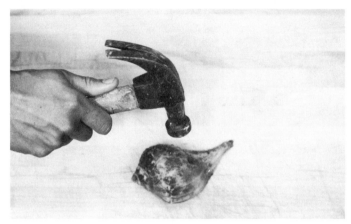

1. Tap a hole in the shell with a hammer.

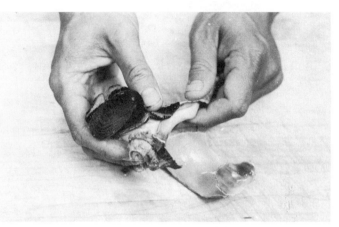

2. Pull the shell away from the flesh.

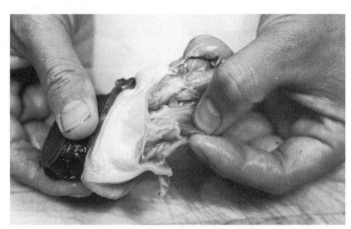

3. Only the white part of the flesh is edible.

4. Cut away the hard, dark part.

5. Trim away any other material attached to the white part.

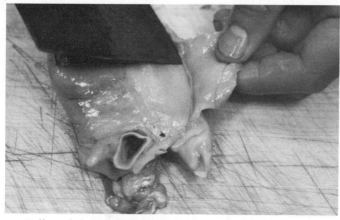

6. Pull and cut the white part away from the "legs."

7. Slice it as thin as possible.

Stir-Fried Conch with Vegetables

3 tablespoons peanut oil
2 to 4 live conch in shells, about 2 pounds, sliced thin (about 1 cup)
2 teaspoons minced fresh ginger root
2 tablespoons minced scallion
1 pound bok choy stems, cut into 1½-inch sections

SAUCE:
2 tablespoons thin soy sauce
1 tablespoon Shaoxing wine or dry sherry
1 tablespoon chili paste

1 teaspoon sesame oil

METHOD: Stir-frying (page 52)
SERVES 4 as an appetizer, 2 as a main course.
SUGGESTED BEVERAGE: Dry generic white wine

Heat the peanut oil, and when it is hot, add the conch slices and stir-fry for 1 minute. Add the ginger and scallions. Continue to stir-fry for a few more seconds. Add the cut-up bok choy and the sauce ingredients. Continue to cook for another 4 to 5 minutes, until the bok choy is tender-crisp. Taste and adjust the seasoning according to your personal preference. To finish, add the sesame oil. Serve immediately.

Rice, Doughs, and Noodles

RICE IS TO MOST OF CHINA what bread is to the Western world, and more. A familiar Chinese greeting is "Have you eaten rice yet?" It is more than a staple; it is an integral part of every meal, eaten with main dishes to extend them and to act as a foil for sauces. The only time rice is not served with a meal is at banquets, where it is served at the end to help cleanse the palate.

Although many types of rice are used in China, the two main types are long-grain white rice (Carolina brand is fine) and short-grain glutinous rice, which is more like an Italian arborio rice (at a Chinese market, ask for sweet rice). The Chinese prefer not to eat brown rice.

Long-grain rice is simply boiled and eaten with meals. Leftover boiled rice makes a nutritious porridge (page 282), further simmered to make it very soft. Fried Rice (page 280) is leftover cooked rice tossed in a hot wok with bits of cooked meat and vegetables. Even the crust that forms on the bottom of the pot when the rice boils can be used to make something delicious—Rice Crust (page 285).

Glutinous rice, as the name implies, is stickier than long-grain white rice. This makes it ideal for stuffings, because it holds together so well. Sometimes flavored glutinous rice is wrapped in bamboo leaves or lotus leaves and eaten as a pastry. Glutinous rice, sometimes called sweet rice, is used to make Fermented Wine Rice (page 289).

In the northern provinces of China, which are too cool and dry to grow rice, wheat replaces rice as the staple, usually in the form of steamed breads or noodles. Flat pancakes made from wheat flour are not so common as bread, but they are traditional with Peking Duck, Mu Shu Pork, and Roast Suckling Pig. The pancakes also are used to make Onion Cakes (page 299).

The myth that Marco Polo discovered pasta on his visits to China and brought the idea back to Italy probably began when Western food lovers discovered the variety of Chinese noodles (some of which look exactly like spaghetti) and wonton wrappings (which resemble tortellini). Actually, the Romans were making noodles centuries before Marco Polo. But so were the Chinese.

There are Chinese pastas made of flour with egg, flour and water, or all three. In northern China, breakfast often consists of noodles in broth. Throughout China, pasta dough is used to wrap all manner of dumplings and wontons. These are popular choices for Chinese luncheons.

RICE

Preparing Boiled Rice

Boiled rice is a basic staple and for the majority of Chinese a part of every meal. It absorbs the flavors of sauces and acts as a contrast to the spiciness of many entrées. The Chinese like to cook their rice *al dente* ("with a bite"): that is, not too soft, but with a slight bite to it. It's much more filling that way, and you can better taste its flavor. Although in China there are many varieties of rice, here the rice to use is long-grain white rice or extra-long-grain white rice. The type found in the supermarket need not be rinsed, though some rice purchased in Chinatown should be (unless instructions indicate otherwise). The rice should not be sticky, but it should be sufficiently starchy that the grains hold together and can be eaten with chopsticks. Don't use converted rice, which cooks up into individual grains.

The Chinese cook brings rice and water to a boil, then lets the rice simmer over medium heat until the water level sinks below the surface of the rice. The pot is then covered and the rice gently cooked until all the water has been absorbed. The simple method that follows for determining how much water to use with any quantity of rice needs no measuring cups. (Glutinous rice must be measured, though.)

Rice may be prepared in advance; to reheat it, steam it in a heavy, closed saucepan.

1. Put the rice in a heavy pot. Use one-third as much raw rice as you want to have when cooked.

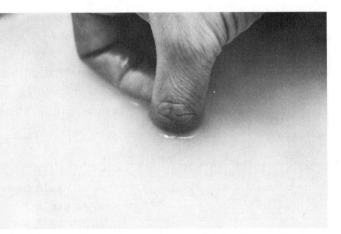

2. Add enough water to come 1 inch above the level of the rice (about the distance from the tip of the thumb to the first knuckle).

3. Bring the water and the rice to a boil, then reduce the heat to medium and let the water be absorbed until it sinks just below the level of the rice. It has reached the right stage when the surface of the rice appears to be pockmarked.

4. Cover the pot and reduce the heat to the lowest possible setting. Let the rice cook 15 minutes, or until all the water has been absorbed.

Fried Rice
[see photo in color section]

The trick to making perfect fried rice is to be certain the rice is absolutely dry. If it is too moist, it tends to clump and absorb too much oil. Fried rice is a great way to use leftover rice, and the possible variations are endless. Bits of ham, chicken, roast pork, vegetables, and eggs contrast visually and flavor the rice. Unlike boiled rice, this is served as a separate course. At a banquet, it would come at the very end. For a variation, try making it with shredded chicken. Cool and serve as a cold rice salad.

2 tablespoons peanut oil
1 cup assorted cooked meat and/or shrimp
3 cups cooked rice, cooled
3 eggs, scrambled in oil and broken up
1 cup bean sprouts, plucked at both ends
½ cup shredded lettuce
2 scallions, chopped

METHOD: Stir-frying (page 52)
SERVES 4 as a side dish or separate course.
RICE MAY BE COOKED ahead of time and the dish assembled at the last minute; or it may be prepared entirely in advance and served cold as a salad.

1. Heat the oil in a wok and stir-fry the cooked meat and shrimp. (Here we use ½ cup diced cooked shrimp and ½ cup diced Smithfield ham.)

2. Add the rice, and continue stir-frying until it is lightly browned (2 to 3 minutes). Mix in the eggs, sprouts, lettuce, and scallions to heat through.

3. Serve the rice simply.

Rice Porridge (Jook)

This dish is one of those childhood favorites that lingers fondly in one's memory. It is eaten as often at breakfast as it is for a midnight snack, rather like a Chinese "cream of wheat." A variety of ingredients can be added (such as fish, meats, vegetables, thousand-year-old eggs), depending on one's mood. The starch from the rice gradually thickens the porridge as it slowly simmers. It is a great way to use up leftovers and also reheats well.

4 cups water
1 cup rice

METHOD: Simmering, steaming (page 59)
SERVES 2 as a breakfast or snack.
MAY BE PREPARED in advance and reheated in a heavy, closed saucepan.

1. Bring the water to a boil. Add the rice, let it return to a boil, stir periodically for 2 minutes, cover the pot, and turn down the heat. Let it simmer 30 minutes.

2. Stir in seasonings, such as soy sauce or salt, and shredded leftovers, if desired.

Preparing Flavored Glutinous Rice

Glutinous rice (often called sweet rice) is a sticky, short-grain rice often used in desserts, such as rice pudding, or in stuffings (see Whole Stuffed Chicken Skin, page 120, or Eight-Jewel Duck, page 187). It absorbs flavor like bread crumbs and can be cooked longer than long-grain rice without falling apart. It is rich and heavy, which is why a little goes a long way.

Cooked with flavorful meats, vegetables, or spices, glutinous rice produces a delicious, simple, home-style dish, rather like an Italian risotto. Here we simply and delicately flavor it with Chinese sausage. The rice is soaked a couple of hours in cold water to cover, to soften it and make it more absorbent. This can be done up to 6 hours in advance. The finished dish reheats beautifully and can be prepared ahead of time. Instead of Chinese sausages, pickled vegetables or preserved fish may be substituted.

1 cup glutinous rice, soaked and drained
4 Chinese sausages, cut into ¼-inch slices

1. Line a bamboo steamer with cheesecloth. Spread the glutinous rice over it and scatter the sliced sausages on top.

2. Cover and steam over simmering water in a wok for 30 minutes.

Glutinous Rice Stuffing

Glutinous rice is the base for this ideal stuffing made with four different kinds of pork. Be sure to use enough liquid (in this case chicken broth) that the rice softens properly, and keep stirring it so that it doesn't stick to the bottom of the pot. For a regional Chinese variation, try substituting rough chopped Sichuan mustard greens and tree ears for the ground pork. For a non-Chinese variation, try just vegetables and ricotta cheese. This stuffing can be used for chicken and Whole Stuffed Chicken Skin (page 120), turkey, Cornish game hens, and squabs, or it can be served as a meal in itself (wrap in lotus leaves and steam 25 minutes).

1 pound pork, coarsely ground

MARINADE:
1 tablespoon thin soy sauce
1½ tablespoons Shaoxing wine or dry sherry
1 tablespoon minced scallion
2 teaspoons minced fresh ginger root

2 tablespoons peanut oil
6 large Chinese black mushrooms, soaked, squeezed dry, and chopped
4 Chinese pork sausages, chopped
4 scallions, chopped
4 tablespoons chopped Smithfield ham
½ cup chopped Barbecued Pork Strips (page 193)
1½ cups glutinous rice, soaked overnight and drained
2 cups chicken broth
Few grindings of fresh pepper
2 tablespoons Shaoxing wine or dry sherry
1 tablespoon thin soy sauce

METHOD: Stir-frying (page 52)
MAKES ENOUGH to stuff a 4½-pound chicken.
MAY BE PREPARED a day in advance.

Marinate the pork for at least 15 minutes.

1. In the peanut oil over a high flame, stir-fry the pork with the chopped ingredients until the pork loses its raw color.

2. Add the glutinous rice and mix well.

3. Add the chicken broth, pepper, wine, and soy sauce.

4. Cover the wok and reduce the heat to a simmer. Let the ingredients cook 15 minutes, until the rice absorbs all the broth. Let it cool.

Rice Crust

A rice crust is a great way to enjoy the true tastiness of rice. It is delicious just by itself as a crunchy finish to a meal. (Drizzle with a tablespoon or so of peanut oil and cook over very low heat until hot. Salt lightly and serve.) Deep-fried, it puffs dramatically and makes a great show when you add it to a soup or any dish with a sauce. It absorbs the flavors of the soup or sauce without getting soggy. The trick to sizzling rice is to transfer the deep-fried rice crust straight from the oil to the soup or sauce. If you let it cool, you will lose the sizzle.

You can make a crust any time you prepare rice, or make it specifically for the purpose. It can be made with water or chicken stock, and because it freezes well, it can be made ahead of time and stacked away. Some people let it sit until completely dry and then store it in jars.

l. Prepare rice as you normally would, but cook it in a heavy wide pot at least 15 minutes after the rice is soft so that a crust forms on the bottom of the pot. Spoon off the top layer of loose rice; set this rice aside for Fried Rice (page 280), or freeze it for future use.

2. If left to stand overnight at room temperature, the crust will be easier to remove from the pot. To use the rice right away, keep the pot on low heat and dribble peanut oil around the edge.

3. Heat for a few minutes, then loosen the crust with a spatula. It should come out in one whole piece.

4. Invert the crust onto a plate. It can now be frozen for future use or used while still hot. To deep-fry for Sizzling Rice Soup, see page 327. To use after freezing, thaw and dry for 5 minutes in a 250-degree oven, then proceed.

Rice Crumbs

Rice crumbs are the Chinese counterpart of bread crumbs. They are seasoned and mixed into ground meats to improve texture and flavor, and they are used as a light, flavorful coating for steamed foods. Rice crumbs, always used crushed, go particularly well with pork, which takes slow cooking and allows the flavor of the crumbs to develop fully, but they may be used with beef, fish, and chicken as well. The crumbs can be made ahead and stored in a tightly covered jar at room temperature indefinitely, ready to be used at any time.

Our favorite rice crumbs are made with citrus peel, five-spice powder, and peppercorns, combined and browned to release their flavor, then pulverized to a texture like that of coarse cornmeal.

1 cup raw long-grain white rice
2 pieces dried citrus peel
1 tablespoon five-spice powder
1 teaspoon whole Sichuan peppercorns

1. Combine the ingredients in a dry wok.

2. Over moderate heat, toast and stir the rice until it browns.

3. Wrap the rice and seasonings in a towel.

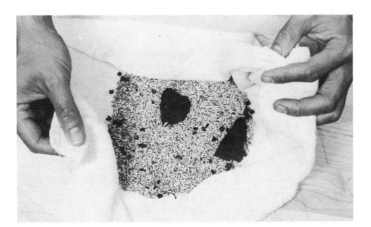

4. Crush the rice with a mallet. This can also be done in a blender or a food processor, but take care not to overprocess the rice to a powder. The mixture should resemble coarse cornmeal.

5. Store the aromatic mixture in a covered jar.

Steamed Pork in Rice Crumbs
[see photo in color section]

The rice crumbs adhere to the meat, absorb its flavor as it steams, and provide a spicy flavor that contrasts with the texture of the cooked meat.

1 pound boned pork shoulder, sliced

MARINADE:
2 tablespoons thin soy sauce
1½ tablespoons Shaoxing wine or dry sherry
1 tablespoon minced garlic
1 teaspoon minced fresh ginger root
2 teaspoons salt
1 tablespoon sesame oil
1 tablespoon minced scallion

½ cup Rice Crumbs (see above)

GARNISH:
Scallion shreds

METHOD: Steaming (page 59)
SERVES 2 to 4 as a main course.
MAY BE PREPARED up to a day in advance and reheated by steaming.

Marinate the pork for about 30 minutes.

1. Coat the pork slices with rice crumbs.

2. Toss the mixture with the hands to coat each piece well.

3. Arrange the coated pork on a plate. Position the plate on a trivet in a wok and steam over simmering water for 45 minutes. Garnish with a few shreds of scallion.

Fermented Wine Rice

Homemade fermented wine rice adds an intoxicating richness to spicy foods that's both sweet and winy at the same time. Made ahead, it keeps refrigerated for months, ready to be added to finish a dish, much as a French chef might add a splash of Cognac. We use it in the following recipe with shrimp, but it is also delicious with stir-fried crabs. It can also be served by itself as a sweet, porridgelike dessert, perhaps with poached pears.

It is made from wine balls, which are available in Chinese groceries. The balls are crushed with flour and combined with glutinous rice that has been previously soaked and steamed. Make sure the rice is not too hot, or the mixture will ferment too fast—but not too cold, or the wine balls won't react. Allow at least 24 hours to make fermented wine rice. Add some already made fermented wine rice to a new batch to give it an extra kick. This recipe makes about 1 quart.

1 pound glutinous rice
2 wine balls (see page 42)
Flour

1. Soak the glutinous rice overnight in enough water to cover it. Drain the rice. Line a bamboo steamer with wet cheesecloth and fill it with the drained rice. Steam it for 1 hour.

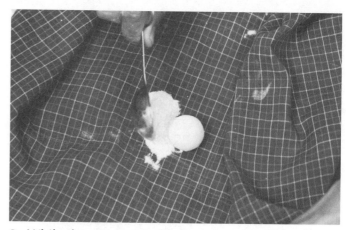

2. While the rice is steaming, put a wine ball in a towel with a pinch of flour.

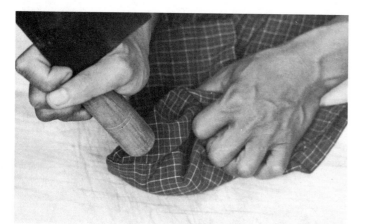

3. Wrap them tightly and crush the ball with the base of a cleaver to make a powder. (If you use a blender, use about 1 teaspoon flour. Food processors do not work as well.)

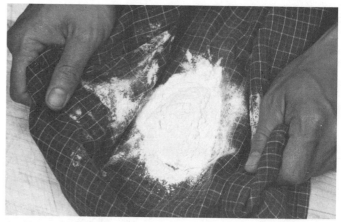

4. Repeat with the other wine ball.

5. When the rice is cooked, turn it out into a bowl of warm, not hot, water. This helps keep the rice from clumping.

6. Strain it through a colander and put it in a mixing bowl with the crushed wine balls.

7. Mix the rice thoroughly with your hands.

8. Make a well in the center of the rice and cover the bowl with a wet cloth. Set it in a turned-off oven or another warm place that's between 95 and 105 degrees in temperature.

9. After 24 hours, liquid will begin to fill the well in the center of the rice. This indicates that the rice has begun to ferment. The liquid and rice can then be transferred to a jar and stored in the refrigerator for several months.

Spicy Shrimp with Wine Rice
[see photo in color section]

This is one of the most delicious ways of using fermented wine rice. The combination of wine rice with minced garlic and ginger, and the richness of the pork, makes this a perfect example of a Sichuan dish. Its unique taste is quite unexpected. The shells are left on the shrimp because they add flavor and hold the sauce. The key to this dish is to warm the wine rice barely and not to overcook it, making it too mushy. The unshelled shrimp are deep-fried so that their shells split open, both cooking them and making them attractive.

Much of the preliminary mincing and chopping can be done ahead of time and the dish put together at the last minute.

½ pound pork, ground

MARINADE:
1½ tablespoons Shaoxing wine or dry sherry
1 tablespoon thin soy sauce

1 pound large, unshelled shrimp, cleaned and prepared (see page 253)
2 cups peanut oil for deep-frying
2 tablespoons minced fresh ginger root
2 tablespoons minced garlic
6 dried hot red peppers

SAUCE:
1 tablespoon dark soy sauce
1 tablespoon Shaoxing wine or dry sherry
1 teaspoon sugar
2 tablespoons chili paste
½ cup chicken broth

1½ cups Fermented Wine Rice (see above)
1 tablespoon sesame oil

GARNISH:
½ cup minced scallion

METHOD: Deep-frying (page 56), stir-frying (page 52)
SERVES 4 as a main course.
INDIVIDUAL INGREDIENTS may be prepared in advance, and the dish assembled and stir-fried just before serving.

Marinate the pork for 15 minutes or more.

1. Deep-fry the unshelled shrimp in hot oil until they turn opaque (about 1 minute). (Alternatively, they may be stir-fried in 3 tablespoons oil for the same length of time.) Remove the shrimp, drain them, and set them aside. Drain the oil except for 2 tablespoons, or drain it completely and add 2 tablespoons fresh oil. (The oil may be cooled, strained, stored, and reused later to deep-fry other seafood dishes.)

2. Flavor the oil with ginger, garlic, and hot peppers.

4. Add the sauce ingredients and the wine rice. Stir the mixture thoroughly as it boils for a few seconds.

3. Add the marinated ground pork and stir-fry until it loses its raw appearance.

5. Stir in the shrimp to heat them through. Add the sesame oil.

293

6. This dish can be served garnished with minced scallion or with boiled or fried crayfish.

DOUGHS AND NOODLES

Pancakes

An ingenious process transforms flour and water into the light wrappings used for such dishes as Peking Duck (page 176), Mu Shu Pork (page 196), or Roast Suckling Pig (page 214). Stuffed with scallions and fried, they make Onion Cakes (page 299), which are positively addictive. The process breaks down into three simple parts: making the dough; flattening chunks of dough into patties and rolling pairs of patties into pancakes; then baking the pancakes in a dry skillet. The pancakes freeze well, so they can be made in advance and used any time. Five minutes in a steamer warms them from room temperature, 10 minutes from a frozen state. Rolling out two pancakes at a time keeps the pancakes thin and moist.

As with other doughs, making pancakes is easy once you acquire the feel. This comes from experience. To get the proper consistency—light but chewy, not as thin as a crepe but not as heavy as a tortilla; thick enough to separate after cooking but not so thick that the pancake overpowers the food it accompanies—practice before the actual meal preparation. You will find your pancakes far superior to store-bought ones. The quantities used here will make twenty to thirty pancakes.

Preparing Pancake Dough

¾ to 1 cup boiling water
2 cups all-purpose unbleached flour

1. Stir the boiling water into the flour a little at a time. Some types of flour require more water than others; add just enough to make a lumpy dough.

2. The dough should just hold together when pressed into a ball.

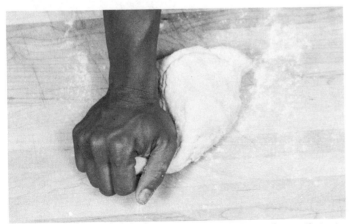

3. Knead the dough on a floured board until it is smooth (about 3 to 5 minutes).

4. Put the ball of dough in a bowl and cover it with a damp cloth. Let it rest at least 30 minutes.

1. Knead the dough again for 20 to 30 seconds, just to make sure it is smooth.

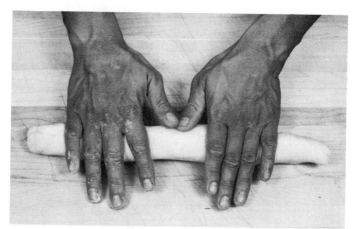

2. With your hands, roll the dough into a log 1½ inches thick.

3. Cut the dough into 1½-inch chunks.

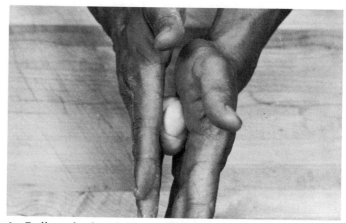

4. Roll each chunk into a ball between your palms.

5. Flatten it into a patty. Repeat with the remaining balls of dough.

6. Brush one side of a patty with sesame oil.

7. Align the oiled side with another patty and press them together.

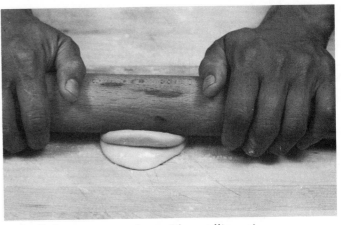

8. Roll the two pancakes with a rolling pin.

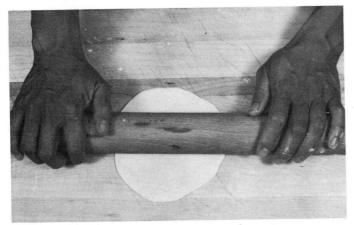

9. Roll until they are about 5 or 6 inches across.

10. Alternatively, a tortilla press may be used. Place the unrolled but slightly flattened pair of pancakes in the middle of the lightly floured press.

11. Flatten the press.

12. Remove the flattened pancakes. (These are not quite as fine as the hand-rolled type, but they are easier to make perfectly round.

Baking Pancakes

1. Heat a dry iron skillet (do not grease it) over a moderate flame. When the skillet is hot, put the flattened pair of pancakes in it.

2. When brown specks begin to appear on the side exposed to the heat, turn over the pancakes, still together. When both sides are lightly specked with brown, remove the pancakes from the heat. Repeat with the remaining pancakes.

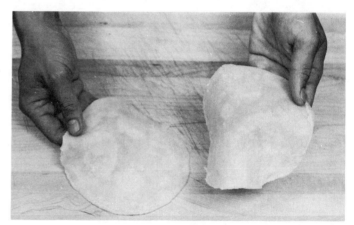

3. When the pancakes are cool enough to handle but still warm, carefully separate them, peeling them apart gently.

4. Only one side of each pancake is browned. The unbrowned side is still quite tender. Chinese pancakes have a tender and soft texture that's moist and chewy. To freeze, stack one on top of another, wrap well in plastic wrap, and place in the freezer. They can be steamed from their frozen state, but should be thawed if you plan to deep-fry them.

Onion Cakes
[see photos in color section]

Here we sandwich chopped scallions between layers of pancake, then deep-fry them to make a light, flaky pastry. The process is remarkably simple, and the results are super. You can make Onion Cakes flat or rolled. Both make a fine appetizer or can be served as an accompaniment to soup.

Pancakes (see above)
1 egg, beaten
Pinch of salt
Chopped scallions and Chinese chives or shallots, or scallions only
4 cups peanut oil for deep-frying

METHOD: Deep-frying (page 56)
EACH CAKE SERVES 2 as an appetizer or as an accompaniment to soup.
THE PANCAKES CAN BE PREPARED up to an hour ahead through step 3 and stored in tightly wrapped plastic so that they don't dry out.

FLAT ONION CAKES

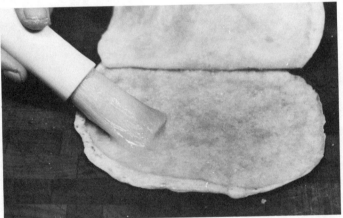

1. Separate a double pancake. Paint the inside surface with beaten egg. Sprinkle it with a pinch of salt. Then sprinkle with chopped scallion and chopped Chinese chives or shallots (or use all scallions).

2. Paint the inside of the other pancake with beaten egg and position it on top of the first.

3. Press them together to seal.

299

4. Heat the oil in a wok or a deep skillet. Using chopsticks or tongs to hold the halves together, slip each pancake into the hot oil to brown well. Turn it over to brown the other side. With chopsticks or tongs, hold the finished cake on end over the oil to let it drain well. (The oil may be put aside and reused for Onion Cakes, but it should not be used with other foods. Strain it before reusing.)

5. Place the cake on a cutting board and chop it into 8 pie-shaped wedges. Arrange them on a plate.

ROLLED ONION CAKES

These Onion Cakes are rolled into a cylinder, as you would a Mexican *flauta,* and cut on the diagonal to reveal an attractive spiral pattern inside. Begin by separating a double pancake.

EACH CAKE SERVES 1 as an appetizer.
MAY BE PREPARED several hours in advance and served at room temperature.

1. Paint the inside surface of one pancake with beaten egg; sprinkle it with salt, scallions, and chives; then roll it up like a jelly roll into a long cylinder. Repeat with the other pancake.

2. Heat 4 cups oil in a wok and deep-fry the rolled-up pancakes until they are brown. (As many as 4 rolled pancakes can be fried at once.) Hold them on end with long chopsticks to drain over the wok. (Again, the oil may be reused to make Onion Cakes.)

3. Cut the roll with 3 diagonal slices into 4 pieces. Arrange the pieces on a plate.

Egg Wrappers

Egg wrappers are made from a batter, like crepes. They can be filled and shaped into dumplings that are steamed or braised for a hearty, home-style meal-in-a-dish (Braised Egg Dumplings, page 304, for example), or wrapped in a spiral with a tasty filling, then deep-fried to make a crunchy, light appetizer that is as pretty as it is delicious (Fried Egg Wrappers, page 302). The wrappers are fragile, soft, and less chewy than the eggless flour-and-water pancakes (page 295). The egg adds flavor as well. They are best made no more than a day or two in advance. The quantities here make seven to ten wrappers.

Preparing Egg Wrappers
3 eggs, beaten
3 tablespoons flour
1 tablespoon sesame oil
Pinch of salt

1. Combine the batter ingredients and mix until smooth with chopsticks or in a blender. There should be no lumps; the flour must be totally incorporated into a smooth batter. Heat a heavy skillet lightly greased with peanut oil over a low to moderate flame. Put a couple of tablespoons of the batter in the pan.

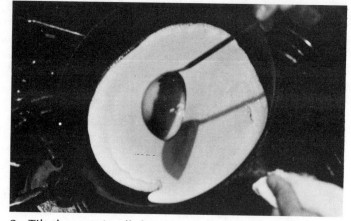

2. Tilt the pan in all directions to coat the bottom.

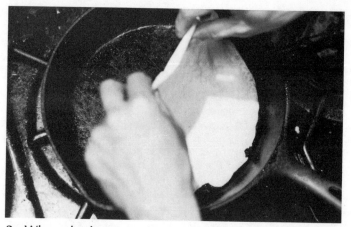

3. When the batter is set, peel it off and flip it over. (If getting your fingers that close to the pan makes you nervous, use a thin spatula to lift the edge.) Let the wrappers dry a little and stack them on top of each other, with a layer of parchment paper or aluminum foil between them. Then store in a plastic bag, closely fastened so that they won't dry out, and use them as soon as you can. Egg wrappers should not be frozen.

Fried Egg Wrappers

Fried egg wrappers are a little drier than spring rolls. They hold up a lot better than spring rolls and can be made ahead and served cold, whereas spring rolls must be eaten immediately. Fried egg wrappers are easier and quicker to do, and so are preferable for a large gathering.

Here, a thin layer of marinated ground pork is used for the stuffing.

FILLING:
½ pound pork, ground
1 tablespoon thin soy sauce
1 tablespoon Shaoxing wine or dry sherry
2 fresh water chestnuts, peeled and minced
3 tablespoons minced scallion
Pinch of salt
1 teaspoon cornstarch
½ teaspoon roasted and crushed Sichuan peppercorns

7 to 10 egg wrappers (see above)
1 egg, beaten

METHOD: Deep-frying (page 56)
SERVES 5 as an appetizer.
MAY BE PREPARED in advance and served cold, or prepared ahead through step 3, wrapped and refrigerated, then deep-fried just before serving.

302

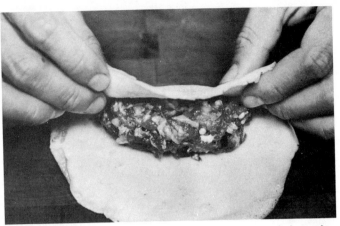

1. Prepare the pork filling, mixing well, and spread some over the surface of each pancake, leaving a margin of 1 inch around the edge.

2. Roll each pancake like a jelly roll, and seal the edge with a little beaten egg.

3. Slice the rolls diagonally into 4 pieces, to reveal the spiral pattern within.

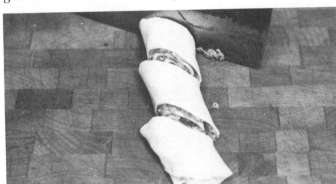

4. Deep-fry the spirals in hot oil (375 degrees), and serve them with roasted salt and pepper (page 70) or plum sauce for dipping.

Braised Egg Dumplings

[see photo in color section]

Braised dumplings make a hearty winter dish that is warm and filling. The egg wrappers absorb the juice from the filling and the sauce, lose their fragility, and become resilient. The dish reheats well and can be made ahead of time.

FILLING:
½ pound pork, ground
1 teaspoon minced fresh ginger root
3 scallions, minced
1 tablespoon thin soy sauce
1½ tablespoons Shaoxing wine or dry sherry
1 teaspoon sesame oil
1 egg white
2 teaspoons cornstarch
Pinch of salt

7 to 10 egg wrappers (page 301)
1 egg, beaten

SAUCE:
2 tablespoons peanut oil
4 scallions, shredded
6 tree ears, soaked, squeezed dry, and shredded
¼ cup lily stems, soaked, squeezed dry, and shredded
2 tablespoons Shaoxing wine or dry sherry
2 tablespoons thin soy sauce
2 teaspoons sugar
½ teaspoon roasted and crushed Sichuan peppercorns
1 tablespoon sesame oil
Pinch of salt
½ cup chicken broth

1 teaspoon cornstarch dissolved in 2 teaspoons cold chicken broth

METHOD: Simmering

SERVES 4 as a main course.

MAY BE PREPARED in advance, stored in plastic wrap in the refrigerator, then reheated gently in a wok or heavy pan.

SUGGESTED BEVERAGE: Gamay or Beaujolais

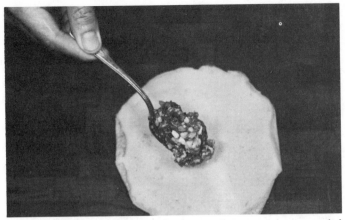

1. Prepare the filling, and place a large tablespoonful in the middle of an egg wrapper.

2. Moisten the edge all the way around with beaten egg, and fold over the wrapper to make a semicircle.

3. Crimp the edges to seal the package.

4. Heat a wok, add the 2 tablespoons of oil, and stir-fry the scallions, tree ears, and lily stems until they have softened. Add the remaining ingredients, except the cornstarch. Bring the mixture to a simmer and reduce the heat.

5. Put the dumplings into the sauce.

6. Stir some of the vegetables over the dumplings, cover the wok, and let the dumplings simmer for about 20 minutes, or until they feel firm when pressed.

305

7. Serve the dumplings with the vegetables in their sauce, thickened with the cornstarch dissolved in broth.

Wontons

Wonton dough is easy to make, but the commercial wontons available from Chinese groceries are so inexpensive and so thin, fresh, and well made, it doesn't really pay to make them yourself. The wonton skins sold in supermarkets, however, tend to be too thick. If you want to make your own wonton skins, a pasta machine saves time and elbow grease. The finished skins freeze well, but wrap them tightly so that they don't dry out.

Wontons can be filled, folded, and cooked in a variety of ways for entirely different effects. Home-filled wontons are far superior to most you've eaten at a restaurant.

2 cups flour
½ teaspoon salt
1 egg
1 teaspoon peanut oil
½ cup cold water
Cornstarch for dusting

1. Form the flour into a mound and make a well in the center. Mix the remaining ingredients and pour them into the well.

2. Mix them with the flour.

3. Continue to mix until they form a dough.

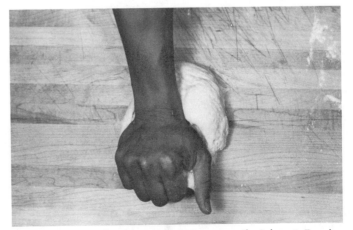

4. Knead the dough until it is smooth (about 5 minutes).

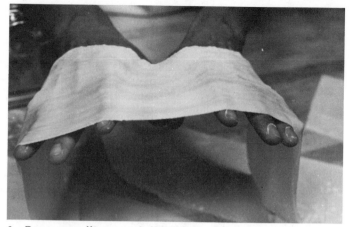

6. Repeat rolling and folding to make thin sheets of dough. (Alternatively, you may roll the dough out very thin by hand.)

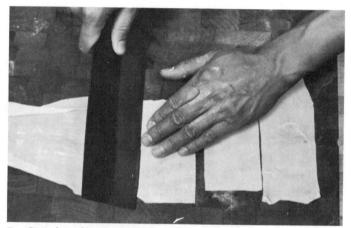

7. Cut the sheets into 3-inch rectangles.

8. Cut the rectangles into squares. Dust each one with cornstarch so that you can stack them without their sticking to each other. Refrigerate until ready to use (use within 4 days), or freeze. Makes 75 to 100 skins.

5. Work the dough through a pasta machine. Roll it through the different levels, making it thinner and thinner. Cut it into smaller lengths when they become too long to be manageable.

Wontons for Soup
[see photo in color section]

To truly enjoy wontons, you should fill them yourself. A good filling combines contrasting flavors and textures. In this recipe the soy sauce, rice wine, and sesame oil flavor the pork, and the sweetness of the water chestnuts, the smoky mushrooms, the sharp scallions and ginger, and the salty ham provide contrast. The filled wontons are blanched briefly to rid them of their cornstarch coating so that they won't cloud the soup. Once blanched, the wontons can be kept refrigerated for a day or two until they are used.

FILLING:
1 pound pork butt or shoulder, coarsely ground
2 tablespoons thin soy sauce
2 tablespoons Shaoxing wine or dry sherry
1 tablespoon sesame oil
8 fresh water chestnuts, peeled and minced
8 Chinese black mushrooms, soaked, squeezed dry, and minced
¼ cup minced scallion
1 teaspoon minced fresh ginger root
4 tablespoons minced Smithfield ham
1 egg, beaten
1 teaspoon salt
Pepper to taste

25 wonton skins (page 307)

METHOD: Blanching
MAKES ABOUT 25 wontons.
MAY BE PREPARED in advance and refrigerated until ready for use.

Mix all the filling ingredients in a large bowl by hand until they are thoroughly combined.

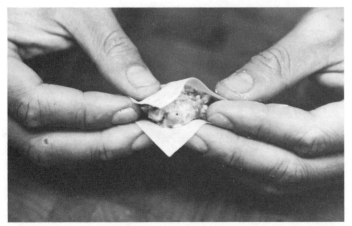

1. Place a teaspoonful of the filling in the center of a wonton square. Fold it in half.

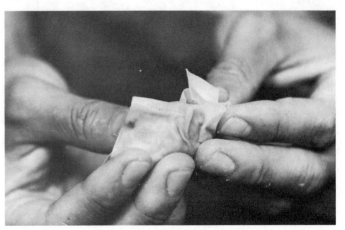

2. Gather up the loose corners.

309

3. Pinch the edges to form the filling into a ball.

4. The wonton looks like a sack or package.

5. Plunge the stuffed wontons into boiling salted water until they float to the surface (about 30 seconds). This rids them of their starchy dusting.

6. Drain them and set them aside. They can be cooled, then refrigerated for up to 2 days.

7. To make soup, simply simmer the wontons in chicken broth for 5 minutes. The soup can be served as is or garnished with shredded vegetables.

Wonton Dumplings

[see photo in color section]

The same filling can be wrapped differently (pleated) and cooked differently (steamed) to produce an entirely new dish. Instead of completely enclosing the filling, as for wontons made for soup, the dough is gathered around the filling and pleated to form a cylinder. The cylinder is flattened on the bottom so that it can stand up. Steamed dumplings have a distinct texture. Steaming highlights the flavor and retains the identity of the ingredients and the wrapper instead of dispersing them into the broth in which they are cooked. Similarly, the flavor of the wrapper is more pronounced. These dumplings make an attractive appetizer. They reheat well and can be made ahead of time. Serve on a bamboo steamer.

1 recipe pork filling (page 309)
25 to 30 wonton skins (page 307)

METHOD: Steaming (page 59)
MAKES ABOUT 25 dumplings, to serve 5 as an appetizer.
MAY BE PREPARED in advance and reheated by steaming.
SUGGESTED BEVERAGE: Dry rosé or blanc de noir

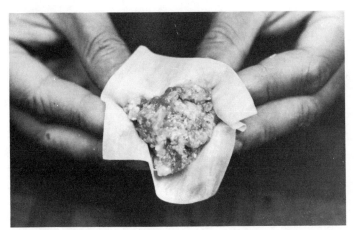

1. Place a teaspoonful of filling in the center of the wonton square, pressing in at the sides to pleat the edge.

2. Flatten the pleats around the edge to form a cylinder—the top is left uncovered. Stand it up and tap it on a flat surface to flatten the bottom.

311

3. The finished dumpling is basically a cylinder open at the top and pleated around the side.

4. Arrange layers of dumplings in baskets lined with cheesecloth. Stack the baskets and steam them over water in a wok for 15 minutes.

5. The cooked dumplings can be served in the bamboo steamer itself. (Remove the cheesecloth.) Have some thin soy sauce available for dipping.

Fried Wontons

[see photo in color section]

This crisp, delightful hors d'oeuvre takes the same pork filling. The dough, which is shaped into triangles, curls up, and the surface bubbles and puckers as it browns and deep-fries. Because deep-frying is a quicker method of cooking than steaming, use a little less of the filling so that it cooks through without overcooking the dough.

1 recipe pork filling (page 309)
25 to 30 wonton skins (page 307)
3 to 4 cups peanut oil for deep-frying

METHOD: Deep-frying (page 56)
MAKES 25 to 30 wontons, to serve 5 to 6 as an appetizer.

1. Place a teaspoonful of filling in the center of the wonton square and fold it in half to form a lumpy triangle. Pinch the edges together to flatten.

2. Pinch up the corners.

3. Heat the oil in a wok to about 365 degrees. Add the wontons and deep-fry them until they are crisp and lightly browned (about 5 minutes). Drain them well and serve them alone with plum sauce or your favorite jams, or on a platter with fried shrimp chips (page 68) and fried transparent noodles (page 69).

313

Spring Roll Wrappers

Spring roll wrappers are not widely available outside Chinese markets. The egg roll wrappers available in supermarkets can be used instead, as can the basic egg wrapper (page 301), but they make a thicker skin. Handmade Filipino lumpia skins found in Asian communities are the closest substitute. Spring roll wrappers are so thin (like a crepe) that when they are deep-fried they become crisp, brittle, and translucent, like a piece of fine parchment paper.

The flour-and-water batter is painted onto a crepe pan to get the thinnest possible wrapper. It is then cooked over low heat until it turns translucent, then slowly peeled from the pan. Make sure the pan is cool before making the next wrapper so that it doesn't brown and start to cook unevenly.

The following quantities make about ten to twelve wrappers. They may be prepared in advance and frozen; reheat by steaming.

¾ cup water
1 cup flour
½ teaspoon salt

1. Mix the water, flour, and salt to form a thick batter.

2. Paint the batter on the inside surface of a cold crepe pan.

3. Put it over low heat until the batter begins to turn translucent.

4. Loosen the edge with a thin spatula, and peel the wrapper from the pan. Stack the wrappers between layers of waxed paper and seal in plastic wrap because they dry out very easily.

5. Let the pan cool between wrappers; dip it in water to hasten the process. (If you try to paint the batter on while the pan is hot, it cooks unevenly.)

Spring Rolls
[see photo in color section]

Spring rolls are not simply refined egg rolls. Egg rolls are made from an egg-based pasta and are rolled out; spring rolls are made with water and are prepared in a pan. A good filling for spring rolls (as well as egg rolls) should provide a balance of textures, with dense meats offset by light, crisp vegetables such as bean sprouts, water chestnuts, bamboo shoots, or zucchini. Here we use ham, snow peas, chicken, and bean sprouts. Do not overload the wrapper. It's better to have too little filling than too much, or it will burst open when fried.

The filling can be made up to a day in advance, but the spring rolls shouldn't be filled until the last moment for best results. The skins tend to get soggy if they sit around filled and won't crisp properly when fried.

You can make egg roll skins using the basic pasta recipe, or you can purchase them. The techniques for rolling and sealing are the same as for spring rolls.

MARINADE:
2 tablespoons Shaoxing wine or dry sherry
3 slices fresh ginger root
4 scallions, white parts only
1 tablespoon oyster sauce

½ pound chicken breast, boned (see page 134) and shredded

FILLING:
¼ cup shredded Smithfield ham
8 black Chinese mushrooms, soaked, squeezed dry, and shredded
½ cup shredded snow peas
2 cups bean sprouts, plucked at both ends
2 tablespoons peanut oil

3 scallions, shredded
1 tablespoon thin soy sauce
2 tablespoons Shaoxing wine or dry sherry
12 spring roll wrappers (see above)
1 egg, beaten

METHOD: Deep-frying (page 56)
MAKES 12 spring rolls, to serve 4 to 6 as an appetizer.

Crush the rice wine, ginger, and scallions in a blender; strain the mixture, and mix it with the oyster sauce. Marinate the chicken in this mixture at least 10 minutes.

1. Stir-fry the ham, mushrooms, snow peas, and bean sprouts in the oil until the vegetables begin to wilt. Put them in a large bowl and let cool.

2. Add the marinated chicken and the remaining ingredients to the vegetables. Mix well.

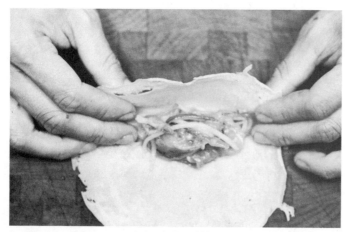

3. Put a tablespoonful of the filling in the middle of a wrapper. Fold the bottom third up and over it.

4. Fold in the sides, and continue rolling up the wrapper.

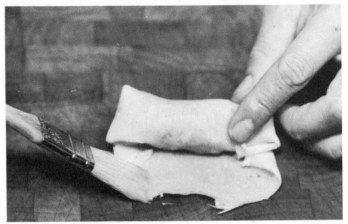

5. Seal the edge with a little beaten egg. Put the rolls on a plate and cover well with plastic wrap to keep them from drying out until you are ready to fry them.

6. Heat the oil in a wok to about 350 degrees. Slide the rolls into the oil one by one to keep them from sticking to each other. Fry them until they are browned and crisp (about 5 minutes).

7. Remove them from the oil with chopsticks or with a strainer.

8. If you wish to slice them (optional), cut them in two at a 30-degree angle. Serve them with plum sauce and hot mustard.

Wheat-Flour Noodles

Many types of Chinese pasta are available, both fresh and dried, in a great range of sizes and thicknesses. Their variety is comparable to that of Italian pasta.

There are also a multiple of noodles made from rice flour. Rice sticks which come dry are treated in the same manner as transparent noodles (page 40) and fresh rice noodles which are often found in Chinese markets and in tea houses. Rice flour is also commonly used to make desserts; it is flour ground from raw rice.

Cooked noodles can be used simply as a garnish for broth. Boiled or crisped by pan-frying, they serve as a bed for other dishes or sauces. They can also be stir-fried with poultry, meat, seafood, and/or vegetables to become part of a main dish themselves.

All wheat-flour noodles should be tossed in hot water first to remove their starchy coating.

Stir-Fried Noodles

You may know this classic Chinese pasta dish by its common Cantonese name, Lo Mein. It's a favorite luncheon dish, often served at the end of a meal of dim sum. It's very simple and can be served as is or with shredded vegetables and meat. Use fresh Chinese noodles (called lo mein in Chinese markets) or fresh or dried spaghetti. Leftover stir-fried noodles make a wonderful cold salad.

1 pound fresh lo mein–type (thick) noodles
2 tablespoons peanut oil
Salt to taste
½ cup shredded Barbecued Pork Strips (page 193) or cooked chicken
½ cup bean sprouts
1 tablespoon Shaoxing wine or dry sherry
1 tablespoon dark soy sauce
½ tablespoon thin soy sauce
1 teaspoon sesame oil

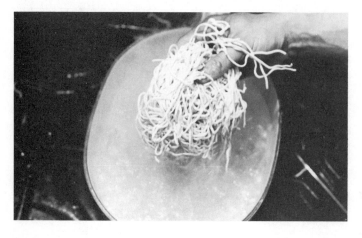

1. Blanch the noodles in boiling water for 10 seconds to rinse off the flour that remains attached to them. If you are using dried noodles, cook them in boiling water according to the package directions, but for only about half the time called for. Drain the noodles and spread them out on a flat pan to cool before you proceed to the next step. The cooling dries them a little, so that they become less starchy and therefore don't stick.

METHOD: Stir-frying (page 52)
SERVES 2 as a main course or cold luncheon dish.
SERVE HOT OR PREPARE IN ADVANCE, refrigerate, and serve cold.

2. Heat the oil in a wok with a pinch of salt. Toss the noodles rapidly to coat them with the oil.

3. Add the pork or chicken and bean sprouts. Toss the mixture well and season it with the rice wine or sherry, soy sauces, and sesame oil. Toss to mix thoroughly.

4. Serve immediately.

Crisp Noodle Cake

[see photo in color section]

Crisp Noodle Cake is made like a potato pancake. The two sides are brown and crisp, while the inside stays moist and soft.

Use very thin egg noodles. In Chinese markets they are called "Hong Kong–style" or "extra-thin chow mein." Fresh or dried vermicelli can be used, too. If you use dried noodles, boil them first for half the time you'd normally cook them; drain and proceed with step 2.

This dish is often called Hong Kong Fried Noodles or in restaurants, Pan-Fried Noodles.

1 pound fresh thin noodles
3–4 tablespoons peanut oil
⅔ cup chicken broth

METHOD: Pan-frying

1. Blanch 1 pound fresh egg noodles in boiling water to wash away the starch and to loosen them up (about 2 minutes). Drain them well.

2. Scatter the noodles in a baking pan. Use a pair of chopsticks and your hands to untangle them as much as possible.

3. Put a layer of the noodles 1 inch deep in each of two large heavy skillets. Pour 2 tablespoons of oil and ⅓ cup chicken broth in each. Cook over a low flame until the broth boils away and the bottom becomes brown and crisp. From time to time add a little oil and broth to keep the noodles moist and allow the crust to develop slowly. This should take about 10 to 12 minutes.

4. To flip the cake, first shake the pan to make sure the cake is not stuck to the bottom. (If it is, dribble some oil around the edge to loosen it.) Cover the pan with a wide lid.

5. Flip the skillet over, holding the lid firmly.

6. The cake will drop onto the lid.

7. Slide the cake back into the pan to brown it on the other side. Add more oil around the edge if it seems to be sticking. To serve it, slide it out onto a plate and use it as a base for any dish with sauce, such as Beef with Asparagus (page 220) or Braised Spareribs (page 206) served with vegetables. Or serve with the following topping:

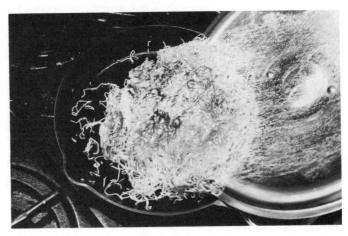

Barbecued Pork with Vegetables

2 tablespoons peanut oil
1 pound bok choy, cut into 2-inch sections
½ pound Barbecued Pork Strips (page 193)
½ cup chicken broth
1 tablespoon thin soy sauce
1 tablespoon Shaoxing wine or dry sherry
1 tablespoon oyster sauce
1 tablespoon cornstarch dissolved in 2 tablespoons cold chicken broth

Heat the peanut oil in a wok. When it is hot, add the bok choy and stir-fry to coat with oil. Add the pieces of pork and stir-fry to heat through. Add the broth. Stir in the soy sauce, rice wine or sherry, and oyster sauce. When the sauce is hot, thicken it with the dissolved cornstarch and serve.

SERVES 2 to 4 as an accompaniment or base for any sauced dish.

Soups

MOST CHINESE SOUPS are made from a plain, rich, flavorful broth garnished with one or more compatible ingredients—combinations of vegetables, wontons, fish or meat balls, noodles, or bits of roast pork—the variations are endless. They are all easy to assemble, once you make the broth, and the broth becomes the demure backdrop for the flavors you put into it.

In China, soup is sipped throughout the meal and is better light than hearty. The closest we come to a hearty soup might be Steamed Chicken in a Yunnan Pot (page 132), which begins with a broth but has chunks of chicken in it.

The Chinese do not clarify stock with egg white like the French; instead, they simmer or sometimes steam the stock for a long time.

Fish Ball and Watercress Soup (page 326) is a delicate offering, and rice crust highlights another favorite, Sizzling Rice Soup (page 327). Elaborate soups such as Winter Melon Soup in a Whole Winter Melon (page 330) are for banquets. But generally, soups tend to be uncomplicated, uncluttered with many ingredients, more like a refreshment or beverage than a hearty soup. At large dinners and banquets soup is served several times during the meal. Recipes for wonton soup and duck soup appear on pages 309 and 177.

Chicken Broth

This is the foundation of nearly every soup in Chinese cuisine. It is also used in small quantities to flavor many dishes and as the basis of countless made-in-the-wok sauces. We dissolve cornstarch in a little cool chicken broth instead of water when we want to thicken sauces so that the taste of the sauce is not diluted. Unlike Western stocks, which are flavored with vegetables and seasonings, Chinese broth aims for pure chicken seasoned only with a little ginger and scallion. Making your own stock requires very little effort; once the initial skimming is complete, the broth simmers unattended for hours. Freeze the finished broth in small containers to be heated in a saucepan or wok whenever you need it. Canned broth may be substituted in a pinch, but the flavor of homemade broth is much superior.

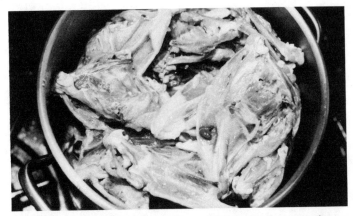

1. Use one or two whole chickens, bones from chicken carcasses, or backs and wings purchased from the poultry market. Use a pot large enough to accommodate them all without being more than three-fourths full.

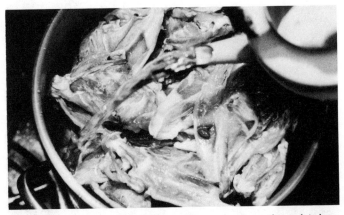

2. Pour in enough cold water to cover the chicken bones completely. Bring the liquid to a simmer.

3. As the broth heats, a scum rises to the surface. Skim it off periodically. From time to time add a little cold water to stop it from boiling and to bring more scum to the surface. Boiling binds the scum to the liquid and makes the broth cloudy.

4. After about 15 minutes, the scum stops appearing and white foam begins to appear. Now add 3 or 4 slices of unpeeled fresh ginger root and 3 or 4 scallions, cut into thirds. Salt to taste. Let the broth continue to simmer, partially covered, for at least 2 hours, preferably for 4 to 5 hours. Strain it through a sieve lined with cheesecloth. When it has cooled sufficiently, the fat rises to the surface and can be skimmed off. To make a richer broth, reduce the degreased broth slowly by half the amount.

Fish Ball and Watercress Soup

Fish balls can be made from any finely chopped white-fleshed fish. They are seasoned with Shaoxing wine, scallions, and ginger and enriched with ham or chicken fat. Light and delectable, they are a pleasure to encounter in a clear soup. The blanched greens add contrast in color.

1 recipe Fish Balls (page 246)
4 cups Chicken Broth (page 325)
Salt and freshly ground black pepper
1 cup loosely packed watercress leaves or spinach, blanched

METHOD: Garnishing broth
SERVES 4.

1. If the fish balls are still warm from their boiling, add them to hot chicken broth and season the soup to taste with salt and pepper. Or reheat the fish balls in the broth for 2 minutes, and season to taste.

2. Spoon the broth over the blanched watercress in a serving bowl.

Sizzling Rice Soup

[see photo in color section]

Few ingredients bring out the natural flavor of a rich chicken broth more than the toastiness of rice crust. Unfortunately, restaurants tend to clutter the soup with too many ingredients. This version contains only a little ham for salty flavor, mushrooms for smokiness, and bean curd for a contrasting texture. When hot rice crust meets hot soup, it sizzles and steams dramatically. Some people think it tastes a little like fresh popcorn.

6 cups Chicken Broth (page 325)
2 tablespoons shredded Smithfield ham
4 small cakes Chinese bean curd, cubed, rinsed in cold water
6 large Chinese black mushrooms, soaked, squeezed dry, and shredded
4 cups peanut oil for deep-frying
1 Rice Crust (page 285)

GARNISH:
Chopped scallions
Sesame oil

METHOD: Deep-frying (page 56), garnishing broth
SERVES 6.

1. Bring the broth to a simmer in a pot and add the ham, bean curd, and mushrooms. Let it simmer 5 minutes.

2. Heat the oil in a wok to very hot (about 380 degrees). Test the oil by dropping a small piece of rice crust into it. It should float immediately.

3. Slip the whole rice crust into the oil.

4. As it begins to puff up like popcorn, break it up into large chunks with long chopsticks. Turn it to brown on all sides (about 1 minute). Remove the rice and drain it.

5. At the table, add the rice to the serving bowl of soup. It will sizzle as the steam rises and provide quite a show.

6. Add the scallions and sesame oil just before serving. (The oil used for deep-frying can be cooled, strained through a fine sieve, and stored in a jar for future use.)

Egg-Flower Soup

[see photo in color section]

Gossamer strands of egg floating ethereally in a clear broth form delicate flower patterns. The technique is to pull the egg into long threads with chopsticks as you stream it into the hot broth. Do not try to blend the egg with the soup or let the egg form clumps. It's easy once you get the hang of it. As a variation, make a dessert soup by substituting water for broth, adding a teaspoonful of almond extract and sugar to taste.

4 to 6 cups Chicken Broth (page 325)
Salt to taste
1 large egg or 2 small eggs, lightly beaten with 1 teaspoon sesame oil

GARNISH:
3 tablespoons chopped scallions
Sesame oil

METHOD: Egg-threading
SERVES 4 to 6.

1. Bring the broth to a simmer and turn off the heat. Add salt to taste. Very slowly stream in the egg. Use the chopsticks to *pull* the strands of egg. Do not stir vigorously.

2. Using slow, circular motions, pull any clumps of egg into long strands with chopsticks, while adding the rest of the egg.

3. Garnish the soup with a little chopped scallion and a few drops of sesame oil.

Winter Melon Soup in a Whole Winter Melon

This soup actually steams in the melon while the melon itself steams, producing a light, delicate broth. Most winter melons are too enormous to be manageable in a home kitchen, though a 4-pound melon fits neatly in an 8-quart pot. If you can't find a 4-pounder, cut a 3-pound piece of winter melon into 1-inch cubes, add it to the broth with the other ingredients, and steam or simmer the soup for 40 minutes. For an unusual variation, substitute watermelon for winter melon.

1 4-pound winter melon, or a 3-pound piece of winter melon
6 cups Chicken Broth (page 325)
8 fresh water chestnuts, peeled and sliced
6 Chinese black mushrooms, soaked, squeezed dry, and shredded
Salt and white pepper to taste
4 tablespoons minced Smithfield ham

METHOD: Steaming (page 59)
SERVES 6 as a first course.

1. Shave a thin slice from the bottom of the melon so that it will stand upright in a bowl.

2. With a pencil trace a circle around the melon about a third of the way down from the top. With a sharp paring knife cut a zigzag along the line all the way around the melon. Gently pull to separate lid from base.

3. Scoop out the seeds and pulp from the base and top. The interior is rather like a pumpkin in texture but a little softer. Set the base on a bowl.

4. Heat the broth with the chestnuts and mushrooms. Ladle it into the melon. Season lightly and replace the lid.

5. Place a trivet or inverted heatproof bowl in the bottom of a pot large enough to hold the entire melon.

6. Drape cheesecloth inside the pot but over the trivet. It should be long enough to extend over the lip of the pot on either side so that it can be used as a sling to lift the fragile cooked melon from the pot. Set the bowl containing the melon on the cheesecloth on the trivet.

7. Add enough boiling water to the pot to come up almost to the base of the bowl. Cover the pot and let the melon steam over moderate or low heat for 1 hour, until the melon is tender.

8. Lift the melon from the pot. Open the lid and add ¼ cup chopped Smithfield ham. Close the lid and bring the melon whole to the table.

9. Scrape some of the melon into the broth as you serve it.

Chicken Velvet for Soup

This is a fluffy chicken mixture made from tiny bits of breast meat that disperses through the soup, imparting its fine, light texture and taste. It can be used in any light broth or delicate soup, such as Winter Melon Soup (page 330). You may make it up to 4 hours in advance and keep it refrigerated until you are ready to use it.

1 whole chicken breast, boned and skinned (see page 134)
1 to 2 teaspoons water
1 egg white
2 teaspoons to 1 tablespoon cornstarch

1. Place the breast on the cutting board inside up. (The outside surface has a thin membrane that makes it impossible to scrape.) Scrape the cleaver against the meat.

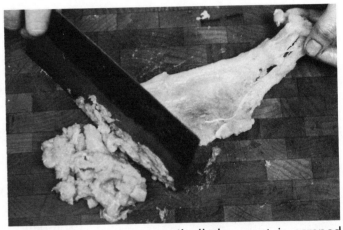

2. Continue to scrape until all the meat is scraped away from the membrane into a mound.

3. Start mincing the chicken, adding a splash of water, a dash of cornstarch, and a bit of the egg white.

4. As the mixture spreads, scoop it back into a smaller mound with the cleaver.

5. Continue to mince, scooping and adding water, cornstarch, and egg white until it forms a thick paste. The fluffed chicken can be made ahead to this stage and kept refrigerated up to 4 hours. Add the chicken velvet to hot broth just before serving.

Spun Apples

[see photo in color section]

We are not offering a chapter on desserts because we find most Chinese desserts heavy or overly sweet and prefer to end our meals with fresh fruit, especially citrus fruits. But here is one Chinese dessert that we particularly like. It combines the sweetness of caramel and the tartness of apples, and if you lift the apples from the caramel just right, the caramel forms long, thin strands, which harden as you dip the apples into ice water—hence the name. The apples can be prepared ahead, including the first frying. Then, at the last minute, give the apples a quick frying to crisp the coating, then dip them into the caramel. Slightly unripe pears that are still firm make a pleasant variation. A Chinese version of this dish is made with whole, peeled, fresh water chestnuts.

2 large, firm apples, cored and cut into eighths

BATTER:
⅓ cup water chestnut powder or plain flour
1 egg, lightly beaten
3 cups peanut oil for deep frying

CARAMEL COATING:
1 cup sugar
2 tablespoons peanut oil
1 tablespoon dark sesame seeds
2 teaspoons white sesame seeds

Large bowl of ice water

METHOD: Deep-frying (page 56), caramelizing
SERVES 4 to 6 as a dessert.
FIRST DEEP-FRYING (step 1) may be done in advance.

1. First frying (can be done hours in advance): Dip the apple pieces into the batter, let the excess batter drip away, and deep-fry a few pieces at a time to crisp the batter. Set them aside.

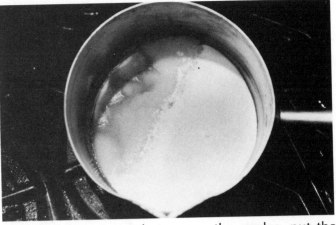

2. When you are ready to serve the apples, put the sugar and the oil for the caramel coating into a heavy saucepan. Prepare the large bowl of ice water. At the same time, heat the oil for deep-frying in a wok. After the deep-frying oil is hot, adjust the heat under it to keep it constant and put the sugar pan over a separate fire at moderately high heat.

3. Within a couple of minutes, the sugar will dissolve and begin to caramelize. Add the sesame seeds to the caramel. Turn off the heat under it. When the caramel is ready, refry the apple pieces until they are crisp (about 1½ minutes). One by one, dip them into the caramel to coat them thoroughly.

4. Then dip them immediately into the ice water to harden the caramel.

5. Serve the caramelized apples immediately.

335

CREDITS

The author is also particularly indebted to the following for their support in the production of this book:

Man Sung Market / Peter Chi / San Francisco, CA
Norton Pearl Photography / Burlingame, CA
Sang Sang Market / San Francisco, CA
Williams-Sonoma / Chuck Williams, Anne Kupper / San Francisco, CA
Charles Gautreaux, San Francisco, CA
Wo Soon Produce / San Francisco, CA
La Cuisine / Tom Williams / San Francisco, CA
Barbara's Bakery / Murray Jaffe /Novato, CA
Caravansary / Ortrun Neisat / San Francisco, CA
Monterey Fish Market / Paul Johnson / Berkeley, CA
The Kitchen / Gene Opton / Berkeley, CA
The Coffee Roaster / Murray Jaffe / San Francisco, CA
John A. Brown / Bill Hughes / Oakland, CA
The California Culinary Academy / Ron Batori / Danielle Carlisle, Silvio Plaz / San
        Francisco, CA
Corti Brothers Market / Darrell Corti / Sacramento, CA
Top Quality Meat Co. / San Francisco, CA
Metro Food Co. / James Chung / San Francisco, CA
Ver Brugge Meats / Jerry Ver Brugge / Oakland, CA
Andersen Travel Orinda / Harry Andersen, Susan Maurer / Orinda, CA
Simon & Schuster / Kim Honig, Eve Metz / New York, NY
C. Steele & Co. / Carol Steele / Scottsdale, AZ

INDEX

ABOUT THE AUTHORS

KEN HOM, according to Craig Claiborne of *The New York Times,* is "one of the best-known Chinese cooking school teachers on the West Coast." He is a highly respected instructor with an international following. Besides teaching in his own school, he is also a member of the faculty of the California Culinary Academy (a school for professional chefs) and will be teaching cooking classes in Hong Kong. Mr. Hom has frequently been a radio and television guest and gives demonstrations throughout the country. Born in 1949 in Tucson, Arizona, Mr. Hom, who speaks several languages, studied medieval art history and was formerly a professional photographer and free-lance television producer. He has traveled extensively and lived in Europe, where he studied film. A documentary he produced on modern Chinese history was nominated for an Emmy in 1976.

HARVEY STEIMAN is a respected food and wine writer who writes a column for the *San Francisco Examiner.* He is the author of *Great Recipes from San Francisco* and *Guide to Restaurants of Greater Miami.* Mr. Steiman has been a writer and editor for newspapers in Los Angeles and Miami.

About the Photographer
WILLIE KEE is a newsreel cameraman with KTVU television in Oakland, California. He is a prize-winning photographer whose credits include seven Emmy Awards.